£32·00

The
Joy of
TEX

A
Gourmet Guide
to Typesetting
with the $\mathcal{A}_{\mathcal{M}}\mathcal{S}$-TEX
macro package

Illustrations by Duane Bibby

The Joy of TeX

A Gourmet Guide to Typesetting with the $\mathcal{AMS}$-TeX macro package

M. D. SPIVAK, Ph.D.

American Mathematical Society

Providence, Rhode Island

TEX and $\mathcal{A}_{\mathcal{M}}\mathcal{S}$-TEX are trademarks of the American Mathematical Society. This book was prepared in $\mathcal{A}_{\mathcal{M}}\mathcal{S}$-TEX by the author.

Library of Congress Cataloging-in-Publication Data

Spivak, Michael.
  The joy of TeX.

  Includes index.
   1. TeX (Computer system) 2. Mathematics printing.
3. Computerized typesetting. I. Title.
Z253.4.T47S673 1986   686.2'2544   85-7506
ISBN 0-8218-2999-8 (alk. paper)

$$\text{686.2254'4}$$
$$SPI$$

Printed in the United States of America.

Second printing with corrections 1986

For My Mother

CONTENTS

Acknowledgements

At about the time that I first started eyeing computers with anything less than malevolence, my friend Richard Palais was enthusiastically investigating a new computer typesetting program that he had heard about as a member of the AMS Committee on Composition Technology. He suggested that I learn something about this system and then describe it in a little manual, one that would be oriented toward the naïve user, of which I was so perfect a specimen. Accordingly, we repaired to Stanford, where we were joined by Barbara Beeton, Robert Morris and Rilla Thedford for a projected two-week project.

That was six years ago. Now that the official first edition of this manual is finally appearing, numerous other people may also be named as accomplices before the fact.

The initial stages of the project would have been impossible without the help of all the people at the AMS, including Barbara Beeton, Sam Whidden, and Ray Goucher. I am extremely grateful to David Fuchs, John Hobby, Arthur Keller and Joe Weening for allowing me to pester them about arcane matters during a five-week stay at Stanford in 1983, and to Leslie Lamport for discussions about LaTeX. Michael Harrison graciously helped me work on the project at U. C. Berkeley in the summer of 1984. In the end, all this shuffling from university to university began to take its toll, and it is doubtful whether the project would have been completed in its present form had I not been able to use a PC implementation of TeX on my own personal computer.

ABOVE ALL, HOWEVER, I CANNOT EXPRESS TOO MUCH GRATITUDE TO Donald E. Knuth, the author of TeX, for his interest in the AMS macro project, for the help that he has extended to me, and most especially for this wonderful gift that he has given the world.

Personal Pronoun Pronouncement

Which The Reader Skips At
His or Her Peril

Since TEX is a rather revolutionary approach to typesetting, I decided that a rather revolutionary approach to non-SEXist terminology would be appropriate in this manual. I myself am completely unprejudiced, of course. As Mark Twain said, or should have said: All I care to know is that a man or woman is a human being—that is enough for me; he or she can't be any worse. But I hate having to say "he or she" or "his or her" or using awkward circumlocutions. Numerous approaches to this problem have been suggested, but one strikes me as particularly simple and sensible. Just as 'I' is the first person singular pronoun, regardless of gender, so 'E' will be used in this book as the third person singular pronoun for both genders. Thus, 'E' is the singular of 'they'. Accordingly, 'Eir' (pronounced to rhyme with 'their') will be the possessive, and 'Em' (rhyming with 'them') will stand for either 'him' or 'her'. Here is an example that illustrates all three forms:

E loves Em only for Eir body.

•Exercise PPP.1[1]
How many possible meanings does this sentence have?

---

[1] Answers to all the Exercises will be found in Appendix A.

Introduction
On Advanced Typesetting

The title of this book is a little deceptive. It might give you wrong ideas about the pronunciation of TeX, which actually stands for the Greek letters TAU EPSILON CHI; according to its creator, Donald E. Knuth, insiders pronounce TeX so that it rhymes with blecchhh. TeX is thus an upper-case, or capital letter, form of $\tau\epsilon\chi$, the beginning of the Greek word that means art, a word that is also the root of English terms like technology. This name emphasizes two basic features of TeX: it is a computer system for typesetting *technical* text, especially text containing a lot of mathematics; and it is a system for producing *beautiful* text, comparable to the work of the finest printers.

TeX's official name implicitly advertises another of its advantages: traditional typesetters would have to cast a special piece of type to get the "TeX" logo, but TeX can print its own name simply by moving letters down a little and backing up a bit. On your computer terminal, where such shenanigans aren't possible, the standard way of referring to TeX is by typing 'TeX'. This helps to distinguish TeX from various other computer programs that are named TEX (and prosaically pronounced that way).

In addition to all of TeX's capabilities, one other feature of the system needs to be emphasized: TeX allows you to do all of these things *easily*. In fact, this is a manual for someone who knows nothing about computers, written *by* someone who knows nothing about computers.

Actually, that last statement isn't quite true: the one thing we assume is that you already know how to use a "text editor" to create a file on your computer. Nothing about typesetting itself is assumed, although a few printers' terms will be introduced along the way. You can remain blissfully ignorant of the complicated rules that typesetters have developed for the proper setting of mathematics formulas—TeX knows them all. Nor is any knowledge of mathematics required. But you will still need to have a general idea of what printed mathematics ought to look like. Mathematicians and experienced technical typists—who already know this—will find that TeX allows them to specify mathematics formulas with less effort than before, yet with greater control over the finished product. Novice technical typists have a dual task: learning what mathematicians want, and learning how to get TeX to produce it. This manual will tell you all about the second, and give you as much help as possible with the first.

In order to get some idea just how TeX works, we will examine a recent paper from a well-known journal that was typeset by TeX.

BULLETIN OF THE
ADVANCED MATHEMATICAL SOCIETY
Volume 23, Number 6, November 2001

WHAT EVERY YOUNG MATHEMATICIAN SHOULD KNOW

BY LORD K. ELVIN

ABSTRACT. We evaluate an interesting definite integral.

The purpose of this paper is to call attention to a result of which many mathematicians seem to be ignorant.

THEOREM. *The value of $\int_{-\infty}^{\infty} e^{-x^2}\,dx$ is*

$$\int_{-\infty}^{\infty} e^{-x^2}\,dx = \sqrt{\pi}.$$

PROOF: We have

$$
\begin{aligned}
\left(\int_{-\infty}^{\infty} e^{-x^2}\,dx \right)^2 &= \left(\int_{-\infty}^{\infty} e^{-x^2}\,dx \right) \left(\int_{-\infty}^{\infty} e^{-y^2}\,dy \right) \\
&= \int_{-\infty}^{\infty} \int_{-\infty}^{\infty} e^{-x^2} e^{-y^2}\,dx\,dy \quad \text{by Fubini} \\
&= \int_{-\infty}^{\infty} \int_{-\infty}^{\infty} e^{-(x^2+y^2)}\,dx\,dy \\
&= \int_{0}^{2\pi} \int_{0}^{\infty} e^{-r^2} r\,dr\,d\theta \quad \text{using polar coordinates} \\
&= \int_{0}^{2\pi} \left[\int_{0}^{\infty} e^{-r^2} r\,dr \right] d\theta \\
&= \int_{0}^{2\pi} \left[-\frac{e^{-r^2}}{2} \Big|_{r=0}^{r=\infty} \right] d\theta \\
&= \int_{0}^{2\pi} \left[\frac{1}{2} \right] d\theta \\
&= \pi.
\end{aligned}
$$

Remark: A mathematician is one to whom *that* is as obvious as that twice two makes four is to you.

INSTITUTE FOR HAUGHTY ATTITUDES

Received by the editors April 1, 2001
Research supported in part by the National Foundation.

The author first wrote this paper by hand, and then, being a lazy fellow himself, gave it to a technical typist to produce a computer file. Parts of this file are shown below, in a style of type that will always be used to indicate input typed on a terminal, as opposed to the output TEX will produce, or the contents of this manual itself. Don't worry if your keyboard lacks some of these symbols—TEX has a way of getting around this.

. . .

```
\title What Every Young Mathematician Should Know\endtitle
\author Lord K. Elvin\endauthor
```

. . .

```
The purpose of this paper is to call attention to a result
of which many mathematicians seem to be ignorant.
\proclaim{Theorem} The value of
$\int_{-\infty}^\infty e^{-x^2}\,dx$ is
$$\int_{-\infty}^\infty e^{-x^2}\,dx=
\sqrt\pi.$$
```

. . .

```
We have
$$\align
  \left( \int_{-\infty}^\infty e^{-x^2}\,dx \right)^2
  &=\left( \int_{-\infty}^\infty e^{-x^2}\,dx \right)
    \left( \int_{-\infty}^\infty e^{-y^2}\,dy \right) \\
  &=\int_{-\infty}^\infty \int_{-\infty}^\infty
    e^{-x^2}e^{-y^2}\,dx\,dy
```

. . .

Even a cursory examination of this file gives some idea how TEX is used. For example, all of the English words that appear in the article are embedded somewhere in the file, while specifications for formulas are set off either by **$** signs (when the formula is set within text), or by **$$** signs (when it is displayed). In addition to the English words and the letters in formulas, there are lots of cryptic combinations, called *control sequences*, which begin with the "backslash" \. Some control sequences are the names of special symbols; for example, \int stands for the "integral sign" $\int$ in the expression $\int_{-\infty}^\infty$, while \pi stands for the Greek letter π (pi). Other control sequences, like \title, \author and \proclaim, are more complicated, and tell TEX how to process the input that follows.

Once this file was produced, a few simple instructions told TEX to set the paper in a style suitable for preprints, on a printer that quickly and cheaply produces output suitable for proofreading, though a little blurry:

What Every Young Mathematician Should Know

LORD K. ELVIN

Institute for Haughty Attitudes

April 1, 2001

ABSTRACT. We evaluate an interesting definite integral.

The purpose of this paper is to call attention to a result of which many mathematicians seem to be ignorant.

THEOREM. *The value of $\int_{-\infty}^{\infty} e^{-x^2}\,dx$ is*

$$\int_{-\infty}^{\infty} e^{-x^2}\,dx = \sqrt{\pi}.$$

PROOF: We have

$$\left(\int_{-\infty}^{\infty} e^{-x^2}\,dx \right)^2 = \left(\int_{-\infty}^{\infty} e^{-x^2}\,dx \right) \left(\int_{-\infty}^{\infty} e^{-y^2}\,dy \right)$$

$$= \int_{-\infty}^{\infty} \int_{-\infty}^{\infty} e^{-x^2} e^{-y^2}\,dx\,dy \qquad \text{by Fubini}$$

$$= \int_{-\infty}^{\infty} \int_{-\infty}^{\infty} e^{-(x^2+y^2)}\,dx\,dy$$

$$= \int_{0}^{2\pi} \int_{0}^{\infty} e^{-r^2} r\,dr\,d\theta \qquad \text{using polar coordinates}$$

$$= \int_{0}^{2\pi} \left[\int_{0}^{\infty} e^{-r^2} r\,dr \right] d\theta$$

$$= \int_{0}^{2\pi} \left[-\frac{e^{-r^2}}{2} \Big|_{r=0}^{r=\infty} \right] d\theta$$

$$= \int_{0}^{2\pi} \left[\frac{1}{2} \right] d\theta$$

$$= \pi.$$

Remark: A mathematician is one to whom *that* is as obvious as that twice two makes four is to you.

Research supported in part by the National Foundation.

Typeset by $\mathcal{A}_{\mathcal{M}}\mathcal{S}$-TEX

Once satisfied with the reactions to his preprint, the author submitted the paper to the journal (all he had to do was send them the original computer file). The journal made a single change in the file that caused TEX to typeset the paper in the journal's style, this time on a high-resolution printing device that produces "camera copy" suitable for printing.[1] Had the journal rejected the paper, the author could have sent it (that is, the computer file) to another journal, which could typeset it in *their* style, again by changing just one line.

As you can see, TEX appears to be awfully knowledgeable! Actually, the system we have been describing is a specialized version of TEX, known as $\mathcal{A}_{\mathcal{M}}\mathcal{S}$-TEX. It has been developed by the American Mathematical Society as a particularly simple system for printing papers in a preprint style, or in the style of any journal (with a little extra work it can also be used to typeset entire books). The present manual is devoted entirely to the specialized system $\mathcal{A}_{\mathcal{M}}\mathcal{S}$-TEX, although we will often refer to it familiarly as TEX, and adopt the more formal name only when we want to mention a feature of TEX that is peculiar to $\mathcal{A}_{\mathcal{M}}\mathcal{S}$-TEX.

Despite its specialized nature, $\mathcal{A}_{\mathcal{M}}\mathcal{S}$-TEX will do almost anything that a mathematician will ever need. Parts 1 and 2 of this manual explain how to typeset almost all the mathematics you will normally encounter; Part 3, which you can peruse at your leisure, describes $\mathcal{A}_{\mathcal{M}}\mathcal{S}$-TEX's abilities to handle more exotic typesetting problems. Parts 1 and 2 also contain occasional digressions into more specialized material; these side-trips are set in separate paragraphs that begin with the road-sign

Parts 1 and 2 of this manual occupy over 100 pages, but you needn't fear that $\mathcal{A}_{\mathcal{M}}\mathcal{S}$-TEX is particularly complicated, or difficult to learn. In order to make this new experience with typesetting more pleasurable, the introduction has purposely been made easy-going rather than concise. Moreover, the exposition—such as it is—has been supplemented by numerous Exercises, interspersed with many examples of what the author seems to think are jokes, along with puns, innuendos, and other fossil evidence of literary low-life. You can skip any jokes you are unfortunate enough to notice, but *please* don't skip the Exercises! Answers to all the Exercises are given in Appendix A, and they often mention little details that didn't seem to fit in comfortably anywhere else, but it is strongly

---

[1] Nowadays nearly all printing is done by photo-offset—the ink adheres to a thin piece of metal that has been chemically treated by a photographic process. Until the advent of computer-run photo-typesetting processes, these plates were made by first setting metal type and printing one copy, which was used for the photographic process—and then destroying the original type!

recommended that you first try all the Exercises yourself—that way you'll learn far more effectively than by reading passively.

When you have finished all the Exercises, you may consider yourself an accomplished $\mathcal{A}_{\mathcal{M}}\mathcal{S}$-TEX user. Then you might be interested in learning more about TEX itself.[1] $\mathcal{A}_{\mathcal{M}}\mathcal{S}$-TEX is just a specialized version of TEX, but once you have mastered it you will have joined the TEXnical revolution.

---

[1]Everything about TEX is explained in *The TEXbook*, by Donald E. Knuth, published jointly by the American Mathematical Society and Addison-Wesley Publishing Company.

Part 1

Starters
the basic ingredients

Chapter 0. Getting Acquainted; A Key Chapter

Before we start learning about TeX's approach to typesetting, it's a good idea to take a look at the keyboard of your terminal, to see which symbols are already available there. Many terminals have additional special keys, but at least the following symbols should all appear—exceptions are discussed below.

First we have the upper- and lower-case letters, and the numerals:

```
ABCDEFGHIJKLMNOPQRSTUVWXYZ
abcdefghijklmnopqrstuvwxyz
0123456789
```

You're probably already aware of the fact that the numeral 1 has to be distinguished from the lower-case letter l, and that the numeral 0 has to be distinguished from the upper-case letter O. On the screen O and 0 may look almost the same, but on the keyboard the numeral 0 will be close to the other numerals.

Next we have the symbols

```
    ,   .   ;   :   ?   !
    ' (apostrophe or single right quote)   ' (single left quote)
    (   )   [   ]
    / (slash)  - (hyphen)  * (asterisk)
```

which are used for punctuation, for writing numbers like 1,376.0003, for hyphenation and/or word-building, and for parenthetical remarks [possibly in brackets instead of parentheses]; on most fonts the asterisk prints high* to serve as an indicator for footnotes. On your keyboard and screen, the quote marks ' and ' might appear in the less aesthetically pleasing forms ` and ´. Don't feel deprived—TeX will still set them the right way. All terminals also have a double quote mark " (or "), but it hasn't been listed in this group because TeX has its own method for producing double quote marks. Notice that the hyphen - shouldn't be confused with another key that appears on most keyboards, _ (underscore or underline).

---

*Like this.

Next come the few standard keyboard characters that will be used in mathe-matical formulas:

$$+ \quad = \quad < \quad > \quad |$$

The symbol | may appear broken, as ¦, but TEX will always set it solid. TEX has control sequences to name all the other mathematical symbols, including letters from foreign alphabets. Of course, English letters and numerals are also used in mathematics formulas, and most of the punctuation symbols are used as well. For example, / is used in fractions like a/b, and the hyphen will be used for the minus sign in formulas like $x - y$. However, TEX will use different spacing rules in mathematics, and the minus sign prints differently than a hyphen. Moreover, letters are normally italicized in formulas.

The fourth group of symbols that normally appear on every keyboard includes the following:

$$\backslash \quad \{ \quad \} \quad \$ \quad \& \quad \# \quad \% \quad @ \quad \sim \quad \hat{} \quad \_ \quad ''$$

Each of these symbols has a special usage in $\mathcal{A_MS}$-TEX; for example, as we mentioned in the Introduction, all control sequences begin with the "backslash" character \, while $ signs or $$ signs are used to set off mathematics formulas.

There is one further symbol that most users tend to overlook: pressing the space bar produces a symbol that appears blank on the screen. We will use the symbol

⊔

whenever it is necessary to emphasize that the *blank space* has been entered.

There are two other keys that we should also mention explicitly. The first is the ⟨carriage-return⟩ key, which moves the cursor down to the beginning of the next line. Pressing ⟨carriage-return⟩ twice in succession produces a blank line on the screen. The other is the key labelled TAB. This key moves the cursor over a certain number of spaces on the screen, although it actually enters a single specific character into the file. TEX usually treats the TAB key exactly like a space, although Part 3 discusses one circumstance in which its specialized nature is put to good use.

Exceptions. Some of these symbols may be difficult, or even impossible, to obtain on your terminal, so TEX has control sequences that can be used instead. For example, the left quote ' often doesn't make it onto the keyboard, but you can use \lq for ' (and \rq for '). There are also control sequences that can replace the symbols |, [,], ^, _ and ~. They will be introduced as needed, and a complete survey is presented in Appendix D.

Of course, none of these substitutions will do you much good if you are also missing the \ key! And TEX relies heavily on the curly braces { and }, which have a special role, and can't be replaced by control sequences either. Actually, even if \, { and } are missing from your keyboard, all is not lost, because TEX can be changed so that some other keys will serve instead. But such modifications require a little TEXpertise, and should be done in some consistent way by everyone who encounters these problems, to minimize confusion when TEX files are moved from one machine to another.

If you have such problems—or even if you don't—you will probably want to join TUG, the TEX Users Group, to get acquainted with other people who are using TEX. Information about joining the TEX Users Group will be found in Appendix G.

Chapter 1. Learning TₑX's Lingo

Although TₑX is especially well suited for typesetting books and papers that contain lots of mathematics, it also does a superior job of typesetting ordinary text. In Part 1 we will be concentrating almost exclusively on text that does not involve the peculiarities of mathematical formulas. This will give us a leisurely opportunity to become acquainted with TₑX's special language, and to learn how it handles the numerous peculiarities with which our literary friends like to deal.

When you want to use TₑX to set ordinary text you basically just type in what you want to come out, and let TₑX worry about all the details. For example, suppose that you enter the following in your file:

```
This    is the   first paragraph of
a  1,000  word document
that has been set by TeX.  The lines are
automatically justified, i.e., they are
all set to the same length.
      To do this, TeX
inserts extra space between words,
and/or hyphenates words that are
too long to fit on the line. ( But it
can't correct your errors.)


Now let's get down to the nitty-gritty: how
did TeX  know  that it  was supposed
to begin a new paragraph here?  Come, come,
you really should be able to figure that
out for yourself!
```

Using this input file, TₑX will produce output like the following:

> This is the first paragraph of a 1,000 word document that has been set by TeX. The lines are automatically justified, i.e., they are all set to the same length. To do this, TeX inserts extra space between words, and/or hyphenates words that are too long to fit on the line. (But it can't correct your errors.)
>
> Now let's get down to the nitty-gritty: how did TeX know that it was supposed to begin a new paragraph here? Come, come, you really should be able to figure that out for yourself!

Notice that the input lines can be of any convenient size; TEX automatically arranges them in paragraphs, with all lines made equally long. Similarly, extra spaces between words have no particular significance for TEX; when a sequence of spaces appears in the input file, TEX simply ignores all the spaces after the first one. The ⟨carriage-return⟩ at the end of a line also tells TEX to insert a space, and TEX then ignores any extra spaces that occur at the beginning of the next line—so the five spaces at the beginning of the line

     ⌞⌞⌞⌞⌞To do this, TeX

were completely ignored. (That would be true even if the spaces had been inserted by the TAB key, since TEX normally treats TAB exactly like a space.)

To the virtuoso typist, some of these features might seem unnecessary, or even downright perverse. But once you start getting serious with a text editor, and begin using it to make corrections—to insert and delete words, and to move whole sentences around—you'll appreciate the fact that you don't have to worry about any extra spaces that might creep in.

The number of spaces after punctuation marks is likewise irrelevant. Typists usually leave two spaces after the punctuation marks ., :, ? and !, but such niceties are irrelevant to TEX, which uses its own judgment for the spacing after punctuation. However, if you leave no space at all, then TEX also leaves no space, so that you can get expressions like "1,000" and "i.e.," in the output. On the other hand, the space between (and But was a bad mistake, which caused an unwanted space in the output. TEX essentially set "(" as a one-letter word, and since this "word" happened to come at the end of a line, it was torn apart from the word "But", which came at the beginning of the next line.

• **Exercise 1.1:**
The input file for this book contains the lines

```
First we have the upper- and
lower-case letters, and the numerals:
```

What would have happened if the following had been typed instead?

```
First we have the upper-
and lower-
case letters, and the numerals:
```

And what if the following had been typed?

```
First we have the upper- and lower-case let-
ters, and the numerals:
```

Since multiple spaces at the beginning of a line won't begin a new paragraph, TEX has a simple alternate device to indicate paragraphing, which you have probably already figured out: TEX ends a paragraph when it encounters a blank line—and starts a new paragraph as soon as it sees the next thing to be printed. Of course, a blank line on the screen might really be a line like

⎵⎵⎵

consisting of three blank spaces; in fact, it is easy to end up with such lines when you use a text editor to delete all the visible portions of a line. Fortunately, TEX will interpret such a line as a "blank line" also. You can also leave several blank lines in a row at the end of a paragraph—TEX will simply count them all as one blank line.

TEX also has a simple device to get all 4 varieties of quotation marks that you will need for ordinary text. To get single-quote marks you just type single-quote marks: the input ' produces ' and the input ' produces '. And to produce double-quote marks, you simply type two single-quote marks of the appropriate kind immediately in succession. The input

```
''Oh, so that's how the letter 'A'  is produced!''
```

produces

"Oh, so that's how the letter 'A' is produced!"

Remember that you can use `\lq` for ' and `\rq` for ' if you are missing these keys; and `\lq\lq` and `\rq\rq` give the desired double-quotes.

In addition to single- and double-quote marks, text often contains dashes—as in sentences like this one. A dash is not the same as a hyphen or a minus sign. In fact, carefully printed mathematics books have hyphens, minus signs, and *two* kinds of dashes,

an en-dash –   and   an em-dash —

(traditionally, an em-dash was the width of a capital M, while an en-dash was half that width). En-dashes are used for number ranges, like "pages 13–34", and also in contexts like "Fig. A–12". Em-dashes are used for punctuation in sentences—they are the kinds of dashes to which the author of this manual has apparently become addicted. These different symbols can be produced as follows:

for a hyphen, type a hyphen (-);
for an en-dash, type two hyphens (--);
for an em-dash, type three hyphens (---).

Dashes, like hyphens, usually have no spaces on either side of them, so don't inadvertently put any into the input file. As we have already mentioned, a hyphen will automatically be turned into a minus sign when it is used between the $ signs that indicate mathematics formulas; in this case you won't have to worry about spaces, because TEX's own mathematics spacing conventions will take over.

• **Exercise 1.2:**
Explain how the following should be typed in a TEX file:

> E said, "I still type two spaces after a period—I just can't break the habit—but I'm always careful to use an en-dash rather than a hyphen for number ranges like '480–491' in a bibliography."

• **Exercise 1.3:**
What happens if you mistype `-- -` instead of `---`? What do you think happens if you type `----`?

In addition to quote marks and dashes, in all their variety, occasionally you may need some special symbol, like '¶', which is sometimes used to signal a paragraph. For example, we might like to number the paragraphs of our sample text as ¶a, ¶b, and so forth:

> ¶a. This is the first paragraph of a 1,000 word document that has been set by ...

> ¶b. Now let's get down to the nitty-gritty: how did TeX know that it was ...

We can do this by typing

```
\P a. This is the first paragraph of
   . . .

\P b. Now let's get down to the nitty-gritty: how
   . . .
```

`\P` is one of TEX's many "control words". A control word is a combination consisting of the "backslash" character `\` followed by any number of letters. The backslash `\` tells TEX that what follows is not some text to be set, but the name of a symbol, or some other special command.

Notice that the input `\P a` has a space after the `\P`. This space is essential, because if we omitted it TEX would think that we were trying to use a control word named \Pa. But the space doesn't show up in the output '¶a'; TEX always regards the spaces after a control word simply as an indication of where the name of the control word ends, not as a space to be typeset. Actually, the name of a control word doesn't always have to end with a space; it can also be terminated by any other non-letter. For example, if we wanted to number our paragraphs ¶1, ¶2, etc., we could type \P1, \P2, etc. (Since spaces after control words never appear in the output, you can also type \P 1, \P 2, with the same output '¶1', '¶2'; so you can *always* put a space at the end of a control word, if you don't want to bother anticipating what sort of symbol comes next.)

Although we didn't mention it before, TEX also has a control word to indicate the end of a paragraph. If we typed

```
    . . .
too long. ( But it can't correct errors.) \par Now let's
get down . . .
```

then the words "Now let's ... " would have begun a new paragraph, just as if Now let's ... were preceded by a blank line. In fact, a blank line has exactly the same significance in TEX's mind as the control sequence \par—when TEX sees a blank line, it simply pretends that \par had been typed.

The blank line convention is basically an added convenience for the typist—it's a lot easier to hit ⟨carriage-return⟩ twice than to type \par. But the blank lines also make your input file a lot more readable. Remember that after the document has been printed the first time, there are sure to be some changes, so you're going to be searching through that file again. Then you'll appreciate the fact that the file has been divided into convenient chunks. **ALWAYS PLAN AHEAD!**

- **Exercise 1.4:**
What happens if you type \Par instead of \par?

- **Exercise 1.5:**
What happens if your file has the following?

```
    . . . end of first paragraph.\par
⊔⊔⊔
The second paragraph begins here . . .
```

The control word \par isn't used very often, because of the blank line convention, and \P isn't used very often either, since ¶ signs are rather unusual. But there's one special symbol that you will need if the author is so crass as to mention money (actual dollars and cents). Suppose that we want to end our little document, a bit shy of its advertised 1,000 words, with a final paragraph:

$1.95 (cheap!) is the price of this document.

Typing

```
$2.00 (cheap!) is the price of this document.
```

would be a big marketing mistake, but it would be an even worse TEX error, because the **$** sign tells TEX to start setting a math formula. TEX would start setting the weird formula 2.00(*cheap!*)*isthepriceofthisdocument.* and then complain that it never found the second **$** sign to tell it where the math formula ends! Since the **$** sign has the special role of indicating math formulas, we need a different way of naming a printed $ sign. One possibility would be a control word like **\dollar**, but TEX has a shorter, and much more obvious, name—the combination **\$**. Using **\$** we can type our final paragraph as

```
\$1.95 (cheap!) is the price of this document.
```

Note that **\$** is not a control word—control words must contain only *letters* after the \ —but is instead what is called a "control symbol". A control symbol consists of \ followed by a *single non-letter* (so there is never any ambiguity about where the name of the control symbol ends). Examples of other possible control symbols are **\1**, **\:**, **\+** and even ****.

Control words and control symbols are known collectively as "control sequences", and this is the term we will normally use, since there will seldom be any need to distinguish between the two. There is, however, one important way that control symbols differ from control words. We've seen that TEX always ignores spaces after control words, since a space is usually needed just to indicate the end of the control word. But a space after a control symbol is *not* ignored (this arrangement seems to concur with the expectations of most typists). So if you typed

```
\$ 1.00
```

you would get '$ 1.00', with a space after the $ sign.

Which brings up an interesting point. What happens if you *want* a space after a control word—how do you get output like '¶ 1'? It won't help to type **\P␣␣1**, with two spaces after the control word **\P**, since TEX always treats a whole sequence of spaces as just a single space. What we actually need is *a new control sequence to stand for a space!* A reasonable candidate might be the control sequence **\space**, but again TEX has a much shorter and (once you think of it) more obvious solution. When you need to tell TEX explicitly that you want a space, just use the combination **\␣** (that is, \ followed by a blank space). Thus we can type **\P\ 1** to get the output '¶ 1'.

● **Exercise 1.6:**
Explain how to type the following sentence:

> Most people can print '$$' passably, but it's harder to print U.S.
> $$ that are passable.

● **Exercise 1.7:**
$\mathcal{A}_{\mathcal{M}}\mathcal{S}$-TeX, unconstrained by false modesty, provides you with the control sequences \TeX and \AmSTeX, to produce the 'TeX' and '$\mathcal{A}_{\mathcal{M}}\mathcal{S}$-TeX' logos. Explain how to type the following sentence:

> $\mathcal{A}_{\mathcal{M}}\mathcal{S}$-TeX is just a specialized version of TeX, but once you have
> mastered it you will have joined the TeXnical revolution.

● **Exercise 1.8:**
What output is produced by \$\␣\␣1.00 and by \$␣\␣1.00?

Notice that \␣ is a control *symbol*—it consists of \ followed by a non-letter. Having solved the previous three exercises, you should already be adept at using it, but if you try to figure out what happens when you type

> \␣␣

you might be a little disconcerted, because we actually have two conflicting rules. A space after a control *symbol* is not supposed to be ignored, so we should get \␣ followed by another space, and thus two spaces. But we also have the general rule that TeX treats a sequence of spaces as a single space, so our input should be equivalent to \␣, giving just one space. For this special case TeX goes along with the latter rule: \␣␣ is the same as \␣.

By now we've learned quite a lot about getting things into print:
(1) Multiple spaces count as a single space, as does a ⟨carriage-return⟩.
(2) Blank lines indicate the end of a paragraph.
(3) ' and ' give single quotes, `` and '' give double quotes, -- gives an en-dash and --- gives an em-dash.
(4) Special symbols and instructions are produced by control words (e.g., \P, \par) and control symbols (e.g., \$, \␣), known collectively as control sequences. Spaces are ignored after control words, but not after control symbols, except that \␣␣ is the same as \␣.

As every prominent person knows, however, sometimes the real problem is keeping things *out* of print. TeX uses % as a special device to help you do this— when TeX sees the character % on a line of input text it ignores that % together with everything else that comes after it on that line. This allows you to insert "comments" into your file—material that will be ommitted in print (even spaces, if you're not careful). For example, if you type

```
material that will be ommitted %Check spelling of ommitted
% it would be embarrasing to have it mispelled in the manual
in print (even spaces, if you're not careful).
```

you will get

    material that will be ommitted in print (even spaces, if you're not careful).

If you aren't careful, and type

```
material that will be ommitted% Check spelling of ommitted
% it would be embarrasing to have it mispelled in the manual
in print (even spaces, if you're not careful).
```

you will get something much worse than a spelling error:

    material that will be ommittedin print (even spaces, if you're not careful).

That's because the % causes TₑX to omit **everything** after it, *including* the ⟨carriage-return⟩.

    Although this feature of % necessitates some extra care, you can also use it to advantage, in order to split a long word into two lines on the input file *without* splitting it in the output: The input

```
the longest English word pneumonoultramicroscopic%
silicovolcanoconiosis
```

will give you the longest English word pneumonoultramicroscopicsilicovolcanoconiosis in the output (hyphenated, if necessary). And if you get to an em-dash near the end of an input line—which frequently happens—you can use % to avoid an unwanted space:

```
if you get to an em-dash near the end of an input line---%
which frequently happens---you ...
```

You can "comment out" a large amount of text by putting % in front of each line. But 𝒜ₘ𝒮-TₑX also provides a much more convenient mechanism for this, which is explained in Part 3.

When the control symbol \␣ occurs at the end of a line it looks a little strange, since you can't actually see the final space:

```
I don't like the idea of putting all those \P\
signs at the beginning of paragraphs.
```

I like to put an innocent % at the end to make the \␣ stand out:

```
I don't like the idea of putting all those \P\ %
signs at the beginning of paragraphs.
```

These final % characters can also prevent confusion when files are transferred between machines, since ␣ symbols at the end of a line are sometimes discarded during this process. The way TEX is set up, this really shouldn't matter, but with % at the end you don't even have to think about the possibility.

Chapter 2. Printers Do It With All Types

Our experiments with the control word \P and the control symbols \$ and \␣ were useful in teaching us the subtleties involved in the use of control sequences, but of course what we all *really* want to know about is italic print, though you've *surely* noticed that in this manual we tend to favor slanted print, a rather recent innovation (for **extra** emphasis we resort to boldface print). You can change to these fonts by using the control sequences \it, \sl and \bf; the control sequence \rm returns you to ordinary (roman) type. Thus, the input

```
Don't confuse \it emphasizing \rm something
with boldly \bf asserting \rm it.
```

produces the output

Don't confuse *emphasizing* something with boldly **asserting** it.

Simply by changing \it to \sl in the above example, we could get the word "*emphasizing*" to be set in slanted type, rather than in italics. And you'll be happy to learn that if $\mathcal{A}_{\mathcal{M}}\mathcal{S}$-TEX happens to be setting text in a different typesize, as in a footnote, it will automatically choose the proper size type for the italic, slanted, or bold font. Despite these amenities, you might resent having to include all the extra \rm instructions. They're certainly a nuisance to type, and an omission can be disastrous—you might end up with pages and pages of italicized words instead of just one! Actually, there's a way of switching fonts that doesn't require the extra \rm instructions and that is much better for most purposes. Use the input

```
Don't confuse {\it emphasizing} something
with boldly {\bf asserting} it.
```

The braces { and } tell TEX that {\it emphasizing} and {\bf asserting} are separate "groups" within the ordinary roman type. When TEX sees the left curly brace { that starts a group it makes a mental note of the type font that was being used, and it reverts to that same font once it sees the } that ends the group—the right curly brace } "turns off" the \it command.

Of course, if you forget the closing } that turns off the \it command, you'll still get pages and pages of italic type. And forgetting closing }'s can have even more dire consequences in some situations. You can avoid these problems if you have a computer terminal with extra keys that can be programmed to produce any sequence of input, or a text editor that can be customized so that a single key stroke (usually some control key) can have the same effect. You can arrange for a single key stroke to produce input like {\it } and also move the cursor back before the }; then you just have to type in the text you want to be italicized and skip past the } when you are finished. This saves a bit of typing, and virtually guarantees that you won't forget the closing }.

Because of the way braces turn off TEX's activities, grouping is also useful in many other situations. For example, when we wanted to get the output '¶ a', with a space after the ¶, we previously typed \P\␣a. But we could also have typed {\P} a. Now the control word \P is followed by } rather than a space, and the space that follows the } isn't ignored. In order to pull this trick we've put \P into a group all by itself, but that doesn't matter—this is simply a group in which nothing particularly interesting happens.

Actually, there's yet another way to use braces to get '¶ a', which might seem even trickier. You can type

    \P{} a

using an *empty group*: the {} combination is a group of no characters, so it produces no output, but it still intervenes between \P and the space, thereby aborting TEX's mission to search out and destroy extra blank spaces. The empty group {} may seem like a cheap trick, but it has lots of neat uses in math formulas, and is sometimes almost indispensable.

● **Exercise 2.1:**
Redo Exercise 1.7 in 2 different ways, both without using the control symbol \␣.

As a final grapple with grouping here are two rather technical exercises designed more to make you think about the issues than to illustrate problems that are very likely to come up.

● **Exercise 2.2:**
What output would be produced by {\P␣␣}␣␣{␣}{␣}a ?

● **Exercise 2.3:**
What can you type if you want the output to contain two hyphens in a row? (You can't type --, but there are many possible solutions.)

In our discussion of italic and slanted type we skipped over one detail that might have been more noticeable if we had looked at a *different* transition from italic to roman type. Notice that the space after "*different*" in the previous sentence seems to be too small, because the *t* slants over into that space. This wasn't as noticeable in our previous examples, because an italic *g* slants over much less than an italic *t*. The amount that a letter slants over is called its "italic correction", and TₑX allows you to insert this extra amount of space simply by typing the control symbol \/ after the letter. Thus the proper way to get a *different* transition from italic to roman type is to type

```
... a {\it different\/} transition from ...
```

As a general rule, use \/ after a group of words in a slanted font unless the next symbol is a *comma*, or a *period*.

- **Exercise 2.4:**
Explain how to type the following:

> *The Joy of TₑX* explains how to put things in the file that will be ommitted [*sic*] in print.

(If you don't have [and] you can use \lbrack and \rbrack instead.)

- **Exercise 2.5:**
What's the preferred way to type the following sentence to TₑX?

> Italicizing just *one* word or even the *pre*fix or *suf*fix of a word is fine, but don't go *overboard.*

- **Exercise 2.6:**
Explain how to typeset the following:

> Most grammarians say that punctuation after a word should be in the *same font:* but many writers prefer to *switch back*; this is especially true when the punctuation is a semi-colon.

- **Exercise 2.7:**
What nasty mistake could you make in typing the following sentence?

> Notice that the space after "*different*" seems to be too small here.

- **Exercise 2.8:**
Explain how to type the following bibliographic reference:

> W. Ambrose, *Higher order Grassmann bundles* **3** (1964), 199–238.

The answer to Exercise 2.8 might startle you at first, until you get used to the idea that within a group you can do the same sorts of things that you do outside the group. In fact, you can even put a group inside another group. When we start typesetting mathematics formulas we will be doing this with perhaps alarming frequency, but for now just bear the possibility in mind for the following.

● **Exercise 2.9:**
Explain how to typeset a roman *word in the midst of an italicized sentence.*

Even with all the possibilities afforded by *italic,* *slanted* and **boldface** type, there's always the enthusiast who wants to use underlined words. TEX doesn't provide you with a convenient method of underlining—you can't type something like {\ul ...} to underline a whole group of words. If a book designer wanted to use underlining extensively, E would have to design a special '\ul' font in which each letter has an underline as part of it; of course, the letters g, j, p, q and y would be one of Eir design problems. TEX does give you a way to underline individual words, however. If you type \underbar{problems} you will get problems, which shows one solution to these problems.

Barring unusual circumstances, \underbar'ing isn't very important. But it *is* important to observe the way that the curly braces are used in the input \underbar{problems}, because \underbar acts differently from the control sequences we have learned about so far. The control sequences \P, \$, \␣ and \/ indicate special symbols or certain amounts of space, and the control sequences \par, \it, \sl and \bf tell TEX to alter its activities (end a paragraph or change to a different font), but \underbar tells TEX to process a certain amount of input in a special way. In TEXnical jargon, \underbar is a "control sequence with an argument", the "argument" being the amount of input that receives special processing. If we were to type \underbar doesn't then we would get the output "doesn't" because TEX would think that the single character d was the argument of \underbar: when the argument of a control sequence consists of more than one character, you must enclose the argument in braces, to tell TEX that the whole group is the argument.

Most of the other control sequences that we will be learning about also tell TEX to do something special to some particular amount of input. In fact, so many of TEX's control sequences are control sequences with arguments that novice TEXnical typists sometimes forget that \it, \sl and \bf are different. A common error is to type

```
    ... italicize just \it {one} word in a sentence.
```

expecting to italicize just *one* word. What happens instead is quite different! The braces around {one} have no effect at all. The control sequence \it simply tells TEX to start using italic type, and the word "one", *together with all succeeding words*, are italicized. When you type things correctly, as

```
... italicize just {\it one\/} word in a sentence.
```

the instruction to use italic type is limited to the group `{\it one\/}` in which it occurs. To keep from making such mistakes, it might help to mentally pronounce `\it` as "switch to italics". (Of course, you won't have any problems if you've arranged for a single key stroke to produce `{\it }`.)

● **Exercise 2.10:**
Typeset the following:

> *When a sentence is typeset in slanted type, you might want to underline a <u>roman</u> word for emphasis.*

Now it's time to take what we've learned and see what TEX really does with our input file. Throughout Chapter 1 and this chapter, it's been assumed that you've been doing all the problems, and checking your answers with those in Appendix A. The final exercise of this chapter is somewhat different, because it calls for the creation of a computer file, which we will actually submit to TEX, in the next chapter.

On most computers, file names have two parts separated by a period, like 'file.ext', where the part after the period is called the "extension". Assuming that this is true for your computer, the file that you create for this final exercise should be called 'paper.tex'. It really isn't important for the first part of the file to be called 'paper', but the second part, the extension, should be 'tex'. (If the file names on your computer system don't conform to this pattern, consult your system's experts for additional details.)

● **Exercise 2.11:**
Make a computer file 'paper.tex' that TEX will use to print the following:

> Everyone will be happy when TEX finally arrives, and Dr. Treemunch can start typing his own so-called scholarly manuscripts. His last *opus*—which The Amer. Jour. Recr. Drugs recently published—created quite a sensation, particularly the material that he has expounded on pages 22–23. Including this material cost an extra $1,000, but it did make ¶¶ 1 and 2 quite popular.
>
> The head of the department, our own I. M. Stable, attributes Tree-munch's recent aberrant behavior to his "research" for this paper, but others point out that Treemunch's name isn't on many computers' databases, so his name often gets hyphenated quite strangely, which may account somewhat for his feeling of being ill-used.

Chapter 3. Your First TeX Experience

Although we've only covered the rudiments of TeXspeak, it's time to take a little break, lie back, and let the computer do some work. At the end of the last section you produced a file `paper.tex`. Now we'll ask TeX to process it and see what happens. We will spell out the various steps of this process in considerable detail, but it will definitely help if you follow along on your own terminal. Before doing this, however, be sure that you have the right input for `paper.tex`, by checking with the answer for Exercise 2.11.

It should be noted that the precise details involved in running TeX depend on the particular operating system you are using. [Because of the heavy demands that TeX may place on the computer's capabilities, your system might even require that TeX jobs be done in batch mode.] The local experts at your computer installation will be able to tell you about such things.

Before we begin, we need to add a few things to the file `paper.tex`, which is not yet in a suitable state to be submitted to $\mathcal{A}_{\mathcal{M}}\mathcal{S}$-TeX. To prepare it properly, first add the lines

```
\input amstex
\documentstyle{amsppt}
```

at the very beginning of the file. The first line tells TeX to read in a file that tells it about the special features of $\mathcal{A}_{\mathcal{M}}\mathcal{S}$-TeX. The second line specifies a certain style for the output (the desired page size, typeface, and so forth); we've requested a workaday style called 'amsppt', the "AMS preprint style". If we had typed

```
\documentstyle{bul}
```

then we would have instructed TeX to print things in the 'bul' style, the style of the *Bulletin of the American Mathematical Society*.

(Notice that in the first line we didn't say `\input{amstex}`. The instruction `\input` is one of TeX's fundamental control sequences, and TeX knows that its argument is simply everything up to the first space or ⟨carriage-return⟩. For TeXnical reasons, `\input` works in a special way—braces around `amstex` are not only unnecessary, they are actually *wrong*! Fortunately, `\input` is the only exceptional control sequence of this sort that you will ever have to worry about.)

Normally a paper will have things like a title and the author's name at the beginning. Such material would be specified right after the \documentstyle line. Ignoring such frills for the moment, we will simply instruct T_EX that the body of the document follows immediately, by adding the line

```
\document
```

So now the text proper starts on line 4. Finally, at the very end of the file, add the line

```
\enddocument
```

As you may have guessed, this tells T_EX that the document is over, and brings everything to a screeching halt—anything on succeeding lines will be ignored.

Now that the file **paper.tex** has been completed, you can leave the editor. Once again you are in communication with the operating system. It has given you a prompt sign—to be specific, let's say it's the symbol @—and now we're ready to go!

First you have to ask the operating system to run T_EX. To do this, you type **TeX** or **tex** or **run tex**, or something of that sort. After it has been invoked by the proper incantation, including the ⟨carriage-return⟩ at the end of the line, T_EX will sign on with a message such as

```
This is TeX, Version 1.1 (preloaded format=plain 84.8.1)
**
```

The ** is T_EX's way of asking you for the name of the input file you want it to process. At this point you can type **paper**. (Before typing the ⟨carriage-return⟩ after **paper** you can probably correct any typing errors with the DELETE key, or whatever other key you usually use.) Notice that we merely have to type **paper** to process the file named **paper.tex**; T_EX assumes that the file has the extension **tex** unless another extension is explicitly given.

On many systems this two-step process has a short-cut: typing

```
tex paper
```

after the @ prompt will have the same effect. Whichever method you use, as soon as you press the ⟨carriage-return⟩ after **paper**, T_EX will begin to process the file **paper.tex** and something like the following will appear on your screen:

```
(paper.tex (amstex.tex) (amsppt.sty)
Overfull \hbox (2.68718pt too wide) ...
\tenrm ers point out that ... databases,|
[1]
```

The first line tells you that TeX has begun to read `paper.tex` and that the instructions in this file have caused it to first read the file `amstex.tex`, where the special features of $\mathcal{A}_{\mathcal{M}}\mathcal{S}$-TeX are stored,[1] and then to read the file `amsppt.sty` where the details of the `amsppt` style reside. TeX may appear to be quite sluggish as it prints out this line, because reading in files involves interacting with the operating system.

Once TeX has finished reading in the files, it will probably print out the next, more mysterious lines, quite quickly:

```
Overfull \hbox (2.68718pt too wide) ...
\tenrm ers point out that ... databases,|
```

These lines seem to be saying that something is wrong, but we'll have to wait until we see the output in order to decipher them.

Next comes [1], which tells you that $\mathcal{A}_{\mathcal{M}}\mathcal{S}$-TeX has processed enough of your file to make one page, which has been numbered "1"; no other numbers appear since the whole paper fits on one page.

At this point TeX has constructed, and placed in your directory, a new file called `paper.dvi`. This is a <u>de</u>vice-<u>i</u>ndependent file that can be used, with suitable supplementary programs, to drive whatever printing device your computer uses to get the hard copy. In fact, something like

```
Output written on paper.dvi
```

has probably also appeared on the screen to tell you this, accompanied perhaps by other lines about a 'transcript file' named `paper.lst` or `paper.log`, which we'll worry about later.

At present our only worry is how to get the printed output. Your computer will have another program that takes the file `paper.dvi` and sends it off to the printer; you'll have to consult your system experts to find out just how printed output is obtained. We'll want to examine this printed output carefully—there will be some surprises in it—so you should go pick it up as soon as possible.

---

[1] Some computer installations may have a separate `amstex` program, in which the special features of $\mathcal{A}_{\mathcal{M}}\mathcal{S}$-TeX have already been added to TeX. If you use such a program you won't need the initial `\input amstex` line, and it will essentially be ignored if you do have it.

If you have made the file **paper.tex** correctly your output will not look like the original on page 19. Instead it will look like this:

Everyone will be happy when T_EX finally arrives, and Dr. Treemunch can start typing his own so-called scholarly manuscripts. His last *opus*— which The Amer. Jour. Recr. Drugs recently published—created quite a sensation, particularly the material that he has expounded on pages 22–23. Including this material cost an extra $1,000, but it did make ¶¶ 1 and 2 quite popular.

The head of the department, our own I. M. Stable, attributes Treemunch's recent aberrant behavior to his "research" for this paper, but others point out that Treemunch's name isn't on many computers' databases,■ so his name often gets hyphenated quite strangely, which may account somewhat for his feeling of being ill-used.

We can immediately see the reason for the `Overfull \hbox` message. The word "databases" (together with the comma attached to it) extends a little beyond the margin—the '`Overfull \hbox`' is the whole horizontal line

ers point out that Treemunch's name isn't on many computers' databases,

The `Overfull \hbox` message begins by telling us that this box is `2.68718pt` too wide; here `pt` stands for the printer's "point", which is approximately 1/72 of an inch. 2.68718 points isn't very much, but a word that protrudes this far into the right margin will be noticeable. Just to be sure that we *do* notice it, T_EX has placed a big ugly black mark right next to the offending word, so that our first attempt at typesetting isn't exactly something that you'd like to take home and show off to your friends. Information about this overfull box is also transmitted to your terminal: the next lines

    \tenrm ers point out that ... databases,|

describe the `Overfull \hbox` in more detail—first comes `\tenrm`, the name of the font being used (ten point roman), then comes a good portion of the actual letters being set, and finally we have the end of the line, `databases,` followed by |, which stands for the black box that T_EX put on the paper.

The reason for such miserable output is that T_EX doesn't know how to hyphenate the word "databases". T_EX has a very efficient procedure for finding hyphenation points, but it doesn't catch them all, and "database" slips through unaffected. Moreover, T_EX was not willing to move "databases" onto the next line because it would have to st·   out this line,

ers point out that Treemunch's name isn't on many computers'

to an extent that it considers intolerable.[1] T_EX would rather produce something that *you* will find intolerable, so that you will be forced to deal with the problem.

Well ..., having been forced to deal with the problem, one possibility is for *us* to force T_EX to break the line against its inclination. To force a linebreak we just type `\linebreak`. Thus, we can type

```
many computers'\linebreak databases ...
```

to force T_EX to break the line before the word "databases"—and to spread out the line so that it reaches to the right margin. If you leave a space before `\linebreak`, *A_MS*-T_EX will simply assume that you didn't want it, and still spread the line out to the margin.

● **Exercise 3.1:**
Add `\linebreak` to `paper.tex`, and run it through T_EX to see what you get. How bad did T_EX think it was to break the line in this way? (You don't have to bother deleting the file `paper.dvi`; T_EX will delete it when it needs to write a `dvi` file for the new `paper.tex`.)

There obviously ought to be a better solution to our problem than forcing T_EX to break the line in this way; we should be able to tell T_EX how to hyphenate "databases". In fact, we can do this by changing `databases` in the input to

```
data\-bases
```

The special control symbol `\-` represents a "discretionary hyphen"—it tells T_EX that a hyphen can be inserted here, without insisting on it. (So if we change the wording later on, we won't be forcing a hyphen in an unwanted place.)

Missing the hyphenation in "databases" was an unfortunate lapse on T_EX's part, but sins of commission are worse, and Dr. Treemunch would undoubtedly be quite incensed about the absurd way that T_EX *did* hyphenate his name in the second paragraph. We can fix this problem by typing

```
Tree\-munch
```

The `\-` not only informs T_EX of a possible hyphenation point for "Treemunch", it also prevents any other hyphenations, because T_EX will never insert hyphens into a word that already has either a hyphen or a discretionary hyphen.

---

[1] Actually, it's the `amsppt` style that determines how far T_EX will allow a line to be stretched; the text on page 19 was produced by modifying the `amsppt` style so that it would allow more stretching.

● **Exercise 3.2:**

Change `paper.tex` by removing the `\linebreak` and inserting discretionary hyphens in `databases` and `Treemunch` and `Treemunch's` and run the paper again, to see what you get.

Although the discretionary hyphen `\-` will save the day when an anomalous word occurs, it would be inconvenient to insert discretionary hyphens in the same word over and over again. If we are going to continue complaining about Treemunch for several pages, we can add the proper hyphenation of his name to TEX's database for the whole paper, simply by typing

```
\hyphenation{Tree-munch}
```

at the beginning.

● **Exercise 3.3:**

Take out all the discretionary hyphens `\-` in `paper.tex`—the ones that you inserted in `data\-bases` and `Tree\-munch` and `Tree\-munch's`—and add

```
\hyphenation{Tree-munch}
\hyphenation{data-base}
```

to the beginning of the paper (right after `\document`, say). For the purposes of this exercise we are explicitly not giving TEX the hyphenation for the forms "Treemunch's" and "databases". Run `paper.tex` through TEX again, and see what you get, consulting the Answers for further enlightenment.

Finally, let's get things right by adding the proper hyphenation of the words "Treemunch", "database" and "databases". It isn't necessary to add a separate `\hyphenation` line for each. We can combine them into one line

```
\hyphenation{Tree-munch data-base data-bases}
```

● **Exercise 3.4:**

Replace the old `\hyphenation` lines with this new one, and run `paper.tex` again.

Now that we know how to get TEX output, you can handle the Exercises in a different way. Instead of scribbling them down on a piece of paper, and checking with Appendix A, you can scribble them down in a computer file, and see what TEX does with them. Of course, you'll want to save up the answers for a chapter or two, rather than running TEX over again for each Exercise, unless you can afford to use lots of machine time. But sooner or later (perhaps already) you will make some errors that will get TEX even more confused than you are. So the very next step is to look at the sort of error messages that TEX gives you.

Chapter 4. TEX's Erroneous Zones

The file `paper.tex` was purposely contrived to produce bad hyphenations and `Overfull box` messages. After all, it's a commonplace that initial experiences of this sort are seldom entirely satisfactory. In practice, however, hyphenation problems almost never arise, and an `Overfull box` is also quite rare.

Until you become quite a TEX adept, you're much more likely to be greeted with "error messages"; these occur when you have done something that gets TEX confused, so that it has to stop and ask for clarification. You needn't get too uptight when you encounter an error mesage, because TEX can always be coaxed into making an informed guess about your intentions. You can think of an error message as a chance to figure out what TEX is thinking. Some people like such opportunities to psychoanalyze the computer, but if this doesn't appeal to you, then you can always let TEX try to figure out what *you* were thinking.

Leaving our file `paper.tex` intact for the present, let's begin by making another file, say `goof.tex`, in which we will purposely plant some errors:

```
\input amstex
\documentstyle{amsppt}
\document
Here is a word in {\It italics\/} and here is one
in {\Bf boldface} and one in {\It italics\/} again.
\enddocument
```

As in the previous chapter, we will be making various changes in this file; if you make the changes in your copy of `goof.tex` as we go along, you'll be able to see the results described here happening on your terminal.

First let's try running our initial version of `goof.tex` through TEX. When we do, TEX will shriek at us:

```
! Undefined control sequence.
l.4 Here is a word in {\It
                          italics\/} and here is one
?
```

The top line, beginning with !, is an error message, telling us that TEX has come upon a control sequence that it doesn't recognize. More information is given in the next pair of lines. On the first of these lines we see the undefined control

26

sequence \It, together with (a portion of) the line that comes before it. The succeeding input is printed one line lower, so that it is easy to see exactly how far TEX had gotten in the input file before it detected the error.

Finally, TEX has printed ? on the next line, indicating that it is asking us what to do. At this point we have several options. The most abject response would be to type X or x, followed by ⟨carriage-return⟩, in order to exit from TEX. Then we could return to our file and fix the error, try running it through TEX again, to discover the next error, return to our file and fix this error, etc., etc., etc. Instead of capitulating so quickly, however, we can simply type ⟨carriage-return⟩. Now TEX will try to fix the error as best it can; in the present situation it will simply ignore the control sequence \It and proceed. Of course, this means that the word "italics" won't appear in italics, but that's hardly worth worrying about, since we'll probably find some more errors anyway, and won't try to print anything this first time through.

Sure enough, we soon get the next error message,

```
! Undefined control sequence.
l.5 in {\Bf
            boldface} and one in {\It italics\/} again.
?
```

whose meaning should now be clear. This time let's try a somewhat more gutsy approach; we want to insert the correct control sequence \bf. To do this we can type i or I, followed by ⟨carriage-return⟩, to tell TEX that we want to insert something. (Go ahead, try it.) TEX will respond with

```
insert>
```

Now we can type \bf, followed by ⟨carriage-return⟩. As you can see, TEX accepts this and quickly presents us with the final error message:

```
! Undefined control sequence.
l.5 in {\Bf boldface} and one in {\It
                                      italics\/} again.
?
```

This time let's simply type x to exit, so that we can examine a few more types of errors.

If you go back to the editor, you'll see that \bf hasn't actually been inserted into your file—TEX merely inserted \bf into its own private copy of your file.

All the old errors remain in `goof.tex`, but for the moment don't correct them. Instead, add one new error: omit the { before the final \It, so that we have

```
in {\Bf boldface} and one in \It italics\/} again.
```

Now start TEX all over again. Naturally, we first get the old error message

```
! Undefined control sequence.
l.4 Here is a word in {\It
                          italics\/} and here is one
?
```

This time we'll insert the correction \it, but we'll do it in just one step. Try typing

```
        i\it    or    I\it
```

followed by ⟨carriage-return⟩. Now correct the next two errors in the same way. Finally, TEX will reach the fourth error:

```
! Too many }'s.
l.5 in {\Bf boldface} and one in \It italics\/}
                                                again.
?
```

The meaning of this error message should also be quite clear, but sometimes you may want to ask TEX for more help. We can do this by typing h or H, followed by ⟨carriage-return⟩, and in the present situation TEX will answer:

```
You've closed more groups than you opened.
Such booboos are generally harmless, so keep going.
```

Well, let's take TEX's advice: at this point it won't help to insert anything—the time for inserting the necessary { is long since past—so we'll just keep going by hitting ⟨carriage-return⟩ again. This causes TEX to take the only diversionary tactic possible—it simply omits the } and hopes for the best. Sure enough, TEX now gets to the end of the file, and produces a `dvi` file.

We wouldn't want to print the `dvi` file that TEX has produced because our final error wasn't really corrected: by omitting the } TEX has actually caused the word "again" to be printed in italics also. Now's the time to go back and correct all the errors at once. Have you forgotten them? Don't worry! Here's where we get to use the "transcript file" `goof.lst`; you'll find that the error messages that appeared on the screen have also been recorded there, so you can look them over at your leisure.

● **Exercise 4.1:**
Consult `goof.lst` to see what additional information it contains. Correct all
the errors in `goof.tex` and run it through TₑX once again, to check that you
get no error messages.

● **Exercise 4.2:**
Omit the { before the final \it, type h or H when you get the error message,
and then type it once again, to see what you get.

● **Exercise 4.3:**
Put back the { but leave out the space after the first \it, so that we have

```
{\ititalics\/}...
```

in the file. What error message do you get, and how should you respond?

● **Exercise 4.4:**
Correct the previous error, but now leave out the last *right* brace }, so that we
have something like

```
... and one in {\it italics\/ again.
\enddocument
```

with a { that has no matching }. Run this file through TₑX to see what happens.
If you get such a message in a big file, what should you do?

Although we've examined several kinds of errors in this chapter, they were all
rather simple to diagnose. That's to be expected, since we can presently typeset
only simple material, and consequently make only simple mistakes. As we learn
to typeset more interesting material we will also examine, perhaps inadvertently
at times, the more interesting mistakes that can be made when we really put
our minds to it.

There are a few other details of TₑX's error messages that you might be interested
in learning about now.

● **Exercise 4.5:**
Balance the braces again, but change the first \it to \It once more. This time,
when TₑX shrieks the error message at you, shriek right back by typing !, followed by
⟨carriage-return⟩, and see what happens.

● **Exercise 4.6:**
Leave out the very last line, \enddocument, in `goof.tex`, and see what happens when
you run it through TₑX. Figure out how to bring things to a satisfactory conclusion,
checking with Appendix A.

- **Exercise 4.7:**
See what happens when you mistype the name of the paper. For example, try

      @tex goofy

(assuming that you have no file called `goofy.tex`).

- **Exercise 4.8:**
Try telling $\mathcal{A}_{\mathcal{M}}\mathcal{S}$-T_EX to use your own (as-of-yet nonexistent) style `mystyle`, by changing

      \documentstyle{amsppt}

to

      \documentstyle{mystyle}

and see what happens.

Chapter 5. Spaces That Separate, Ties That Bind

Although the hyphenation problems in `paper.tex` have already been resolved, the output isn't ready to be "finalized". Why? Because the experienced eye would immediately note that the spacing in this paper isn't what you'd expect from high quality typesetting, where there is more space at the ends of sentences than between words. (This looks better and makes for easier reading.) TeX also follows this rule, but it doesn't always know where a sentence ends! One trouble is that TeX usually assumes that periods end sentences.

Of course, as you can readily see from the previous paragraph, TeX *does* know that ! and ? represent the end of a sentence, just as it knows that periods followed by quotation marks or parentheses also represent ends of sentences. TeX is even smart enough to know that periods after upper-case letters are probably initials, and thus *not* ends of sentences. So in the output for `paper.tex` the spacing in the name "I. M. Stable" was fine. But TeX doesn't know about abbreviations, so it can't figure out that input like `Dr.␣` doesn't signify the end of a sentence. Consequently, "Dr. Treemunch" and "The Amer. Jour. Recr. Drugs" were too spaced out.

$\mathcal{A}_{\mathcal{M}}\mathcal{S}$-TeX has the control symbol '`\.`' to represent a period that indicates an abbreviation rather than ending a sentence. So we can get the right spacing by typing `Dr\. Treemunch` and `The Amer\. Jour\. Recr\. Drugs`. Notice that the spaces after '`\.`' aren't ignored, since they follow a control *symbol*.

In addition to the poor spacing after the abbreviations, a couple of the line breaks in our output for `paper.tex` are also unsatisfactory, because they interrupt the flow of reading. It isn't ideal to have "pages" at the end of one line, with "22–23" on the next line, and the break between "¶¶" and "1 and 2" is even more disconcerting. TeX can't deal with such psychological questions, so you have to help it out here, also. Once again, there is a simple solution to the problem. If you type the "tie" ~ between two words, then TeX will insert a space, but prohibit a line break. Thus, you can type `pages~22--23` and `\P\P~1 and~2`. In the second example a second tie was used to prevent "2" from appearing at the beginning of a line.

By the way, if you have a space on either side of ~ it will simply be ignored by $\mathcal{A}_{\mathcal{M}}\mathcal{S}$-TeX. This makes it easier to insert ties later on, and also simplifies matters as you're typing: if you've typed `pages␣` and then suddenly realize that you ought to have a tie, you can just type ~ next, without bothering to go back to delete the ␣. (If you are missing the ~ key, you can use the control sequence

\tie instead; of course, in this situation, a space after \tie is ignored by TEX in any case.)

Unfortunately, there doesn't seem to be a good set of rules for deciding just when ties should be used. It's a matter of judgment and experience, wherein the TEXnical typist can show Eir mettle. After a while you won't have to insert ties on the second try, because the whole thing will become second nature. Further suggestions for using ties will be found in Part 3, and ties will also appear in the Answers to the Exercises, when appropriate.

Ties are often preferable to \␣ after abbreviations. For example, it is best to type Dr.~Treemunch, since this will still give an interword space, and also prevent a line break. And the best way to type the journal title might be

```
The~ Amer\. Jour\. Recr.~Drugs.
```

● **Exercise 5.1:**
Insert ~ and \. in the appropriate places in paper.tex and run it through TEX once again. This was the sixth try. Rest, and admire your handiwork.

● **Exercise 5.2:**
The first time the author tried Exercise 5.1, he got the strange combination '¶¶ĩ' in the output. What was his mistake?

● **Exercise 5.3:**
How would you type the following?

> Weird fruit (mangos, papayas, etc.) are avoided by farmers, fastidious eaters, et al.

In our final version of paper.tex we still have a possibly objectionable line break, at the en-dash between "22" and "23". TEX normally regards hyphens and dashes as reasonable places for line breaks, but $\mathcal{A}_\mathcal{M}\mathcal{S}$-TEX provides an easy way to specify hyphens and dashes where line breaks *can't* occur. If you type @- you will get a hyphen with a line break prohibited. Similarly, @-- and @--- give an en-dash and em-dash and prohibit a line break. (By the way, most document styles tell TEX to disallow line breaks after hyphens and dashes in bibliographies, so you usually don't have to bother with @- and @-- there.)

If you try replacing the -- by @-- in paper.tex, you'll find that TEX has to juggle the paragraph a bit to comply with all your specifications.

Chapter 6. Doing It With Élan

You can now use TEX to print about 95% of any ordinary text that you will ever encounter. But before you add TEXpertise to your résumé, we ought to resume our study of TEX, since you still can't typeset things like ..., well, like this paragraph.

First of all, as we have already intimated in Chapter 1, there are a few special symbols that sometimes appear in text:

Type	To get
\dag	† (dagger or obelisk)
\ddag	‡ (double dagger or diesis)
\S	§ (section number sign)
\P	¶ (paragraph sign or pilcrow)

And you might want \copyright to © your brilliant production.

More important, remember that the characters

$$\backslash \quad \{ \quad \} \quad \$ \quad \& \quad \# \quad \% \quad @ \quad \sim \quad \char94 \quad \_ \quad "$$

have special uses in $\mathcal{A}_{\mathcal{M}}\mathcal{S}$-TEX, so some finagling is required to make them appear in the output. We know that \$ stands for the dollar sign $. The other standard non-mathematical symbols are produced similarly:

\{	{
\}	}
\$	$
\&	&
\#	#
\%	%
\@	@

TEX also allows you to type _ to get a printed _, for things like "*first_letter*"; mathematicians seldom use such constructions but computer scientists are partial to them. (If you are missing the _ key, you can use \underscore instead of _.)

- **Exercise 6.1:**
The rule that TEX ignores everything on a line after a % sign isn't 100% accurate. What is the exception? *Hint*: See Exercise 6.1.

• **Exercise 6.2:**

How would you type the following sentence to TEX?

> My #1 solace is M & M's, though any candy is dandy; I agree
> 100% with O. Nash† that liquor is quicker, but a fifth of J & B
> @ $13.95 {price as of this writing} is beyond my means.

The undirected double quote mark " doesn't appear on our list of special
symbols for the simple reason that it really isn't a symbol at all—normal text
fonts have no such character, and you will always want either `` or ''. The
backslash \ is another symbol that doesn't appear in normal text. But \ is a
fairly common mathematical symbol; in fact, it is used in a couple of different
ways, and some fonts may even have a variant form, like ∖. There are special
control sequences for these symbols in mathematics formulas.

This leaves only the symbols ~ and ^ to be accounted for. These symbols
can occur in ordinary text, but only as accents ~ and ^ over letters. In fact, a
whole slew of special symbols and accents is needed for foreign languages that
still basically use the roman alphabet. If you are an English literary chauvinist,
you might not even want to bother learning about these accents right now—
for the time being you can type the usual sloppy approximation to non-English
words and names, and trust the journal editors to worry about details; when
your foreign colleagues fume, just tell them "¡Mañana is good enough for me!"

Each accent over a letter is indicated by a control sequence with an argument.
In the following table the same letter o will be used as the argument in all cases.

Type	*To get*	
\`o	ò	(grave accent)
\'o	ó	(acute accent)
\^o	ô	(circumflex or "hat")
\"o	ö	(umlaut or dieresis)
\~o	õ	(tilde or "squiggle")
\u o	ŏ	(breve accent)
\v o	ǒ	(háček or "check")
\H o	ő	(long Hungarian umlaut)
\B o	ō	(macron or "bar")
\b o	o̲	(bar-under accent)
\D o	ȯ	(dot accent)
\d o	ọ	(dot-under accent)
\c o	o̧	(cedilla)

$\mathcal{A}_{\mathcal{M}}\mathcal{S}$-TeX also has a "tie" accent indicated by \t, which is a control sequence with *two* arguments:

```
\t oo                          o͡o
```

(We've already mentioned that \lq can be used if the ` key is missing from your keyboard. But you can't replace \` by \\lq since TeX would interpret this as the control symbol \\ followed by the letters lq! Appendix D explains the alternative ways of typing \`, \', \~ and \^.)

Notice that spaces are needed after \u, ..., \c and \t since they are control *words*. Thus, to get the word "háček" you should type

```
h\'a\v cek
```

Admittedly, a word with a space in it looks strange, so you might find the input

```
h\'a\v{c}ek
```

less confusing. But this takes quite a bit more typing, and you'll probably get used to things like `h\'a\v cek`.

Of course, spaces are not needed after control *symbols* like \'. Indeed, you might think that a space after \', as in the input

```
h\' a\v cek
```

would be an error, for in Chapter 1 we said that spaces after control symbols are not ignored. However, this rule actually applies only to control symbols like \$, \␣ and \/ that do not have arguments. When a control symbol *has* an argument, there is a more general rule that takes precedence:

> TeX *always ignores spaces when looking*
> *for the argument of a control sequence.*

You should remember this rule for later use, but for accenting letters you can simply stick to things like \'a, which are easier to type anyway.

• **Exercise 6.3:**
What is wrong with typing the following?

```
The word ``h\'a\vc ek'' should be spelled
with a h\' a\v c ek.
```

• **Exercise 6.4:**
How would you type the following: belovèd protégé; rôle coördinator; soufflés, crêpes, pâtés, etc.

There's only one little detail of accenting that TEX won't take care of automatically. For accents over 'i' and 'j' one needs the dotless 'ı' and 'ȷ'; to obtain them you must type \i and \j.

● **Exercise 6.5:**
What's the non-naive way to type naïve?

● **Exercise 6.6:**
How would you type the names Ernesto Cesàro, Pál Erdős, Sergeĭ Ĩurév, Eduard Čech, Ṭâbit ibn Qorra, Muḥammad ibn Mûsâ al-Khwârizmî?

In addition to the accents that you can get with TEX, there are also a few special letters that TEX recognizes:

Type	*To get*
\oe, \OE	œ, Œ
\ae, \AE	æ, Æ
\aa, \AA	å, Å
\o, \O	ø, Ø
\l, \L	ł, Ł
\ss	ß

● **Exercise 6.7:**
Explain how to type the following: Æsop's Œuvres en français.

● **Exercise 6.8:**
How would you type the names Øystein Ore, Anders Jonas Ångström, Stanisław Świerczkowski?

Finally, the ¡ and ¿ that you need for Spanish aren't specified by control sequences, but are recognized as ligatures:

Type	*To get*
!`	¡
?`	¿

(¡This arrangement seems pretty safe, since it's hard to imagine a situation where you would want !` or ?` to occur in text!)

● **Exercise 6.9:**
How do you type the following:

¿What did you say, Señor? I said, "¡Mañana is good enough for me!"

All our examples so far have involved roman type, but everything that we've said also applies to the other text fonts. Each type style has its own accents and special letters, so that {\bf\"o} yields **ö** and {\sl \^a} yields *â*.

• **Exercise 6.10:**

Explain how to type the following sentence:

> *Commentarii Academiæ Scientiarum Imperialis Petropolitanæ* is
> now *Akademiĭa Nauk SSSR, Doklady.*

Well . . . , now that we've finally gotten accents out of the way, we musn't omit
𝒜ℳ𝒮-TₑX's way of handling an "ellipsis", the three dots (...) that indicate an
omission. If you simply type three periods in a row, the output is "...", with the
dots too close together. On the other hand, if you leave blank spaces between
the dots you will get too much space, and TₑX might even break a line between
them! So 𝒜ℳ𝒮-TₑX gives you the control sequence \dots to help you. The input

```
Hmm\dots how do you space the dots?
```

produces "Hmm ... how do you space the dots?" If you leave a space before
the \dots, 𝒜ℳ𝒮-TₑX will simply ignore it and insert the amount of space that
it thinks is proper. Of course, the space *after* \dots is certainly irrelevant, since
it follows a control word (but you do need at least one space between \dots and
how in our example). Don't worry if the dots happen to be followed by some
punctuation, TₑX will handle it just right ... ! Well . . . , actually you do have
to worry a little.

• **Exercise 6.11:**

What is wrong with typing the following?

```
Well \dots ,actually you do have to worry a little.
```

• **Exercise 6.12:**

What is the proper input for the first paragraph of this chapter?

Since several different topics have been covered in this chapter, a brief review
is in order:

(1) The printed characters {, }, $, &, #, % and @ are named by the obvious
control symbols—\ followed by the corresponding characters. The symbols †, ‡, §, ¶ and © have control words to name them. There's also _
for a printed _.

(2) Accents over a letter are produced by applying various control sequences
to the letter (or pair of letters in the case of \t). Spaces are unnecessary
(but allowed) after those that are control symbols. \i and \j are needed
for the dotless ı and ȷ.

(3) There are control sequences for special letters like œ, æ, å, ø, ł and ß, but
the Spanish ¡ and ¿ are obtained as ligatures.

(4) Use \dots for ' ... '.

We'll conclude this section by listing a few stray points that you might have to worry about now and then.

(i) As we've already mentioned, TEX assumes that periods after upper-case letters are initials, and hence do not indicate the end of a sentence. But sometimes a period, or other punctuation, after an upper-case letter *is* the end of a sentence:

> Perhaps you're wondering who concocts these silly illustrations about TEX. (You won't find the answer in Appendix A.) I cannot tell a lie—it is I. Supported by the NSF? Nope, nor any other such boondoggle.

In this case $\mathcal{A}_{\mathcal{M}}\mathcal{S}$-TEX gives you '@.' for a period that *is* the end of a sentence, with similar constructions @, @; @: @! and @? for other punctuation:

```
... about \TeX@.   ...   Appendix~A@.)
... It is I@.   ... by the NSF@?   Nope, ...
```

(ii) On the other hand, the rule about periods after upper-case letters doesn't apply when a period follows an *accented* upper-case letter, as in "É. Cartan". So here you would need \. (or preferably ~) to indicate an ordinary interword space: \'E.~Cartan.

(iii) Another special spacing problem occurs when you have quotes within quotes:

> "They call this 'typesetting'" he sneered.

It won't do to type

```
...'typesetting'{''} he sneered.
```

because not enough space will be left after the single quote—you'll get '" which looks almost like three equally-spaced single quotes—while '␣'' will leave too much space. The special construction @" will solve this problem. Type

```
...'typesetting' @" '' he sneered.
```

Spaces before and after @" are ignored, so your input doesn't have to look squashed. You will also get the correct spacing in any of the legitimate combinations

```
'' @" '                    '' '
'' @" '                    '' '
' @" ''                    ' ''
```

Chapter 7. The Consummation

We can now typeset just about anything that occurs in ordinary text, and TEX will arrange it in elegantly printed paragraphs, choosing the spacing between the words as evenly as possible. But every one knows that such bland perfection isn't very alluring, so papers usually have numerous embellishments to create a more provocative setting.

THE PRELIMINARIES
(Title, Author, Etc.)

A paper ought to begin with a snappy title, displayed prominently to entice the reader, and then the author(s) should receive (th)eir due recognition. The title of the paper is specified with $\mathcal{A}_\mathcal{M}\mathcal{S}$-TEX's \title...\endtitle construction. For example, in the amsppt style the input

```
\title Treemunch's Tribulations \\ Strange
 Names\\ And People
\endtitle
```

will produce the title

**Treemunch's Tribulations
Strange Names
And People**

Notice that \\ separates the various lines of the title; $\mathcal{A}_\mathcal{M}\mathcal{S}$-TEX won't break a title into separate lines for you, since this requires an æsthetic decision (including things like capitalizing the first letter of the word "And"). It isn't necessary to enclose the individual lines within braces, because $\mathcal{A}_\mathcal{M}\mathcal{S}$-TEX knows that the first line is everything between \title and the first \\, the second line is everything between that \\ and the next \\, and the third line is everything from there to \endtitle (no \\ is required after the final line). The special control sequence \\ is used in all $\mathcal{A}_\mathcal{M}\mathcal{S}$-TEX constructions of this sort, where line breaks are specified by the typist.

Authorship is established with \author...\endauthor. Line breaks (\\) are allowed here also, to accomodate threesomes, foursomes, and even more perverse arrangements.

This chapter could not have been completed without the aid of a good friend, but discretion forbids mentioning Eir name.

$\mathcal{AMS}$-TEX also takes care to disregard extraneous spaces in constructions like `\author` and `\title`. Although we typed

```
\title Treemunch's Tribulations \\ Strange
     . . .
```

the first two lines are taken to be 'Treemunch's Tribulations' and 'Strange Names', not 'Treemunch's Tribulations␣' and '␣Strange Names'. So you don't have to worry about extra spaces creeping in to interfere with the proper centering of each line.

• **Exercise 7.1:**
How do you think you would get the second and third lines to be set in ordinary roman type (to serve as a subtitle)?

Both `\title...\endtitle` and `\author...\endauthor` must appear within a special `\topmatter...\endtopmatter` region, which is used to segregate all the little bits of "topmatter" (some of which may actually end up at the bottom of the title page, or even at the end of the paper). The beginning of an $\mathcal{AMS}$-TEX file should thus look something like this:

```
\input amstex
\documentstyle{...}
\topmatter
\title...\endtitle
\author...\endauthor
\affil...\endaffil
\address{...}
\date{...}
\thanks{...}
\keywords{...}
\subjclass{...}
\abstract{...}
\endtopmatter
\document
```

The control sequences in the braces { } are all optional. They can be typed in any order, but they must go between `\documentstyle{...}` and `\document`— if you forget the `\topmatter...\endtopmatter` boundaries, all your topmatter will simply disappear.

The `\title`, `\author` and `\affil`(iation) are the only topmatter that call for specified line breaks (\\). In the amsppt style, the affiliation goes right below the author's name. Most journal styles will probably omit the affiliation, but they might use \address{...} to indicate a more complete address, which often appears at the very end of the paper; the amsppt style puts \address's at the end also. \address doesn't allow \\'s to indicate specific line breaks—you simply type \address{⟨the entire address⟩}, and $\mathcal{A}_\mathcal{M}\mathcal{S}$-TEX will set it as ordinary type, introducing line breaks in the usual way. But you can use \address more than once, to get different addresses for different authors; be sure to type them in the order they should appear in the output.

The \date{...} is another piece of information that may be eliminated, or changed, by a journal, which probably has its own "Date received" information. You can use \date with the amsppt style to establish priority on a particularly hot item.

Acknowledgement of support is made with \thanks{...}, whether you're thankful or not. In the amsppt style this acknowledgement appears on the first page, in the same position as a footnote.

Some journals ask for keywords and AMS subject classifications for a paper. These go in \keywords{...} and \subjclass{...}. The amsppt style simply prints these at the end of the paper, so that the author can proofread them. The label "*Keywords.*" automatically appears before the keywords that are typed in, and the label "1980 *Mathematics Subject Classification.*" appears before the subject classification. Journals may use different labels, but in any case these labels will appear automatically, so they shouldn't be typed in.

Finally, \abstract{...} is used for text that might be set in a separate style, to serve as an abstract for the paper. If the journal normally prefaces abstracts with the word "Abstract.", "Summary.", etc., this will be printed automatically, so it shouldn't be typed. If the journal doesn't print abstracts, the text itself will simply be ignored.

THE BODY OF THE PAPER

Even after the preliminaries are over, special techniques are used to engage the reader's attention.

(1) Headings and subheadings may be used to organize the material.

(2) Mathematicians like to state some things with fanfare, using special fonts to call attention to their THEOREMS and LEMMAS.

(3) Related things are often presented in lists.

(4) And, although it's generally considered bad style, mathematicians sometimes use footnotes.[1]

---

[1]Bet you were wondering when we'd come to that.

Headings. The first heading in this chapter was typed as

```
\heading The Preliminaries\\
\rm (Title, Author, Etc.)\endheading
```

And the subheading for this subsection was typed as

```
\subheading{Headings}
```

Notice that the syntax for \subheading{...} is different than the syntax for \heading...\endheading, because explicit linebreaks (\\) aren't called for in \subheading. Note also that the period after **Headings** was supplied automatically, so it shouldn't be typed in (other styles may use other punctuation).

Theorems and Proofs. Mathematicians like to \proclaim their statements in a grandiloquent manner. In the amsppt style the input

```
\proclaim{Theorem (Folk-theorem)} Two plus two is four, and
neither five nor three.
\endproclaim
```

will produce the output

Theorem (Folk-theorem). *Two plus two is four, and neither five nor three.*

Notice that the period after the label {Theorem (Folk-theorem)} gets printed as part of the style. The label was printed in the "small caps" font (\smc), but the statement of the proclamation was printed in slanted type. Extra space precedes the proclamation, and \endproclaim adds some extra space at the end also. But the most important function of \endproclaim is to turn off the slanted type. If you forget \endproclaim, then you'll be stuck in slanted type for the rest of the paper—or at least until you get to another \endproclaim. $\mathcal{A}_{\mathcal{M}}\mathcal{S}$-TEX has no way of knowing when the proclamation was really supposed to end, but if you forget the \endproclaim and have another \proclaim later on, $\mathcal{A}_{\mathcal{M}}\mathcal{S}$-TEX will realize that you must have goofed, and it will issue an error message.

    Sometimes the bombast of a \proclaim will be supported by a demonstration. If you type

```
\demo{Proof} See the {\it Collected Poems\/} of
A.~E.~Housman.
\enddemo
```

the `amsppt` style will render this as

PROOF: See the *Collected Poems* of A. E. Housman.

The colon, or other punctuation, gets printed automatically. `\demo`'s are usually printed in roman type, and `\enddemo` might do nothing more than leave a little extra space at the end. But certain styles might print `\demo`'s in a narrow width, for example, and then a missing `\enddemo` could be quite a disaster!

If you forget an `\endproclaim`, $\mathcal{A}_{\mathcal{M}}\mathcal{S}$-TeX will also give you an error message as soon as it reaches the next `\demo`. But a missing `\enddemo` never generates an error message, since there's no way to be sure that a `\demo` ought to be over— sometimes a `\demo` will include another `\proclaim` within it, and perhaps even the `\demo` for that `\proclaim`.

Other Devices. Here's an example of a theorem with a list of properties in its statement:

THEOREM. *Let us assume the following:*

   (1) *All the standard laws of Aristotelian logic hold, as they are stated in the classical treatises;*
   (2) *All men are mortal;*
   (3) *Socrates is a man.*

Then Socrates is mortal.

$\mathcal{A}_{\mathcal{M}}\mathcal{S}$-TeX has `\roster` to produce such lists, with each item in the `\roster` preceded by `\item`:

```
\proclaim{Theorem} Let us assume the following:
\roster
\item  All the standard ...
\item All men are mortal;
\item Socrates is a man.
\endroster
Then Socrates is mortal.
\endproclaim
```

Notice that `\roster` automatically labels the various `\item`'s. In the `amsppt` style, the labels are (1), (2), ..., but in other styles the labels might come out as (i), (ii), ..., or [a], [b] ..., etc.

Part 3 explains how you can override this automatic selection, and specify your own labels.

Finally, to get footnotes,[1] you just type

```
Finally, to get footnotes,\footnote{At last!}
you just type ...
```

and, sure enough, the footnote mark will appear right after the previous character, while the footnote text will appear at the bottom of the page (unless you are using a sneaky style that prints all the footnotes at the end of the paper). The particular style you are using will also determine which symbols are used as footnote marks. Further details about footnote marks will be found in Part 3.

\footnote ignores spaces and ⟨carriage-return⟩s that come before it, so that you can type the \footnote on a separate line:

```
Finally, to get footnotes,
\footnote{At last!}
you just type ...
```

But the space or ⟨carriage-return⟩ after the final } of the \footnote is not ignored; it provides the space that comes before the next word "you". If you don't want the space[2], you just omit it:

```
If you don't want the space
\footnote{As in this case.},
you just omit it:
```

BIBLIOGRAPHIES

Bibliographical references usually contain quite a few different types of information. Consequently, the control sequences for dealing with them are somewhat involved, and have been sequestered in Appendix B. Mathematicians setting their own papers might prefer to leave these details to some one else, and even the ambitious TEXnical typist will probably want to tackle these details some other time. But references also have to be cited within the paper itself. Most mathematical papers refer to a bibliographic entry by enclosing its number or other identification in brackets, often printing it in boldface type:

By Theorem 4 of [**10**] and results of [**K-N**] we have ...

Sometimes additional information is put in the brackets:

By [**10**, Theorem 4] and results of [**K-N**] we have ...

---

[1] At last!

[2] As in this case.

Although this is pretty easy to type by hand, $\mathcal{A}_{\mathcal{M}}\mathcal{S}$-TEX has the control sequence
\cite, which makes it even easier:

```
By \cite{10, Theorem 4} and results of \cite{K-N}
```
. . .

In the amsppt style, \cite sets anything after the comma, if there is one, in ordinary type; only the input before the comma gets set in boldface.

● **Exercise 7.2:**
Become a self-published author. Write a few thoughts of your own, and then add all that jazz to make it look like a real paper. Pick a catchy title, and don't be ashamed to tell people you are the author—let them know where your computer is located, perhaps even give them an address to write to *you* at. You might want to print the date this accomplishment was achieved, give thanks to all the people who put up with you as you played with the computer, or supply a brief summary for your busy friends. Find something outrageous to say and proclaim it in a grandiose way. Be creative, have fun.[1]

Keywords and phrases. \abstract, \address, \affil, \author, \cite, \date, \demo, \footnote, \heading, \item, \keywords, \proclaim, \roster, \subheading, \subjclass, \thanks, \title, \topmatter.
Questions about $\mathcal{A}_{\mathcal{M}}\mathcal{S}$-TEX may be addressed to the author (who is solely responsible for the contents of this book) $^{c}/_{o}$ American Mathematical Society, P. O. Box 6248, Providence, RI 02940.

---

[1] Maybe add a footnote.

Part 2

Main
Courses
which everyone needs

Chapter 2^3. TEX's Brand Of Mathematics

The real fun and challenge of technical typesetting comes from the horrendous formulas with which mathematicians routinely deal. Insiders know, of course, that the complexity of these formulas is somewhat misleading. Big formulas are made up of smaller formulas, and smaller formulas are made up of yet smaller formulas, and . . . . Fortunately, unlike Swift's hierarchy of back-biting fleas, this process does not go on *ad infinitum*—all formulas can be built up in a few steps from relatively simple ones. So the art of technical typesetting begins with the simplest formulas.

To tell TEX that the next part of the present paragraph is part of a mathematical formula, simply enclose it within $ signs—this causes TEX to enter "mathematics mode" and to process that input text specially. For example, you can get the formula $z < y = 3(x - 1.5)/(-2|x| + l)$ to appear in the output by typing

```
... get the formula $z < y=  3( x -1. 5) /( - 2 | x
|+1) $ to appear in the output by typing ...
```

This simple example illustrates several important points.

(1) Letters are automatically italicized in formulas, while numerals and punctuation symbols (like parentheses) are set in roman type. An l (lowercase L) gets set as l, which is even easier to distinguish from the numeral 1 than an ordinary typeset 'l'. Notice, by the way, that even a single symbol can be a "formula": if you type `$x$` in the input, you will get x in the output.

(2) The hyphen becomes a minus sign and the slash becomes a slanted fraction line. The symbol $|x|$ stands for the "absolute value of x", but it's not necessary to know what this means; the only important thing is that TEX will typeset | even if your keyboard has ¦ instead of |. Remember also that you can use `\vert` instead of | if your terminal lacks this symbol.

(3) Most important of all, within $ signs TEX completely ignores all spaces and ⟨carriage-return⟩s.

When setting a formula, TEX relies on its own spacing rules, which probably involve more details than you would want to keep track of. For example, in the formula $z < y = 3(x - 1.5)/(-2|x| + l)$ the < and = signs are "binary relations", which function as verbs, the + sign and the first − sign are "binary operators",

49

which function like conjunctions, and the second − sign functions like an adjective. Standard printing conventions use spacing that reflects these different roles: thus, there is a little more space around the < and = signs than there is around the + sign or the first − sign, while there is no space at all after the second − sign. Fortunately, you don't have to remember any of this, since TₑX does it all for you.

Despite the fact that TₑX ignores spaces within $ signs, they should not be regarded as useless, since they can make the input text a lot easier to read— for example, individual parts of long complicated formulas can be separated by several spaces. Initially, force of habit may lead you to use spaces even in short formulas, like

```
$z < y = 3(x - 1.5)/(-2|x| + 1)$
```

so as to approximate the spacing that will eventually appear in print. However, you'll soon come to realize that the spaces do nothing but slow down the typing, and you'll probably graduate to something like `$z<y=3(x-1.5)/(-2|x|+1)$`, reserving spaces for more complicated situations. In this manual we'll use spacing in a haphazard way, just to emphasize that it's an unnecessary good.

● **Exercise 8.1:**
What's wrong with typing the following?

```
If the formula$ y=x-1$ is true ...
```

● **Exercise 8.2:**
Explain how to type the following sentence:

Deleting an element from an n-tuple leaves an $(n-1)$-tuple.

● **Exercise 8.3:**
What is the proper way to type the following?

Consider the graph of $f - g + h$ in the x-y plane.

You should take advantage of the fact that TₑX is usually smart enough to choose correct spacing in mathematics formulas, but you needn't be taken in by TₑX's finesse at setting mathematics formulas. TₑX doesn't really "understand" formulas (any more than a human typesetter does). Technical typists should regard this as good news, for it means that they don't have to understand the formulas either. For example, it's not important to know why there are parentheses in the formula $z < y = 3(x-1.5)/(-2|x|+l)$—so long as they get typed in. Mathematicians actually use parentheses in many different ways, but again it is not necessary to understand these different uses. If you type $y=f(x)$ you will get the formula $y = f(x)$, in which the parentheses have a special mathematical use. Similarly, if you type $y=f[x\ ]$ and $z=f\ (x,y)$ you will get the formulas $y = f[x]$ and $z = f(x,y)$.

Mathematicians are usually fairly careful about putting the necessary parentheses in their manuscripts. But they sometimes get lazy, and stop counting parentheses in a formula like the following:

$$1 + 2(3 + 4(5 + 6(7 + x)))$$

Even if the parentheses don't match up, a catastrophe won't ensue—TₑX isn't very discriminating on this score, and will be quite happy to typeset the formula

$$1 + 2(3 + 4(5 + 6(7 + x))$$

even though it is mathematically unacceptable. This is fortunate, because TₑX mustn't object to a formula like $(x, x + 1]$, which doesn't look like it should be mathematically acceptable, but which actually is, because the parenthesis and bracket have special meanings.

Curly braces, as well as parentheses and brackets, are often used with special meanings, as in the following formula:

$$x + |x| + (x) + [x] + \{x\}$$

To set this formula you just have to remember that printed braces must be specified by the control sequences \{ and \}, since actual braces serve the special function of grouping things. Thus, you should type

```
$x +|x|+ (x)+[   x]+\{x\}$
```

In addition to \vert as a replacement for |, TₑX also has \lbrack and \rbrack as replacements for [and]; the latter work in math mode as well as in text. (And TₑX even has \lbrace and \rbrace to stand for the *printed* \{ and \}.)

Brackets and braces may also be used just like parentheses, in order to make the pairings clearer, as in the formula

$$1 + 2\{3 + 4[5 + 6(7 + x)]\}$$

Such constructions are becoming a little old-fashioned, since [ ] and { } frequently have special meanings, but they occur often enough in many branches of mathematics.

• **Exercise 8.4:**
How was the above formula typed?

• **Exercise 8.5:**
What output would the following input produce?

```
$1+2{3+4[5+6(7+x)]}$
```

Hint: Look closely.

• **Exercise 8.6:**
And how about the following?

```
$x {+} y$
```

(The answer is a little surprising—be sure to try it out, and consult Appendix A.)

A nasty surprise awaits you if you type the formula `$10x + 100 y +1,000 z$`. You will get $10x+100y+1,000z$ because TEX normally leaves a little space after commas in math mode.

• **Exercise 8.7:**
How do you think you can get around this?

So far we've only dealt with formulas involving letters, numerals and punctuation, together with the symbols $=$, $+$, $-$, $<$, $>$ and $|$ that appear on most keyboards.* But mathematicians routinely employ dozens of other symbols, like ∞, $\in$, $\leq$, etc. Each of these symbols has a control sequence to name it. The symbol ∞, which stands for "infinity" (more or less), is named by `\infty`; the shorter name `\inf` happens to be used for something else, which we'll learn about in a later chapter. And the symbol $\in$ occurs in formulas like $x \in A$, which is often read "x in A". To get the formula $x \in A$ you just type `$x\in A$`. Notice that the space after `\in` is needed, even though TEX "ignores" spaces in formulas.

By the way, some keyboards have special keys like **∞**, but you should not use them unless your TEX has been specifically tailored for that keyboard.

---

*We also ought to mention the $*$ key! In ordinary text this gives the asterisk $*$, which is normally used only for footnotes. Since $\mathcal{A}_{\mathcal{M}}\mathcal{S}$-TEX, together with the particular style you are using, determines what the footnote marks will be, and inserts them for you automatically, you will hardly ever use $*$ in text. But $*$ is sometimes used in math formulas. For example `$(f*g)(x)$` gives the math formula $(f * g)(x)$.

TₑX has the control sequence `\ell` to give the symbol ℓ, which mathematicians sometimes use with some special meaning. But before using `\ell` be certain that this is what is wanted, since many authors write something like ℓ in their manuscripts simply to indicate an *l*. (A symbol like ℓ is available on many typewriters, and conscientious typists often use it instead of `1`, to distinguish it from the typewriter's `1`, thereby adding one more layer of confusion!)

The names for all the esoteric math symbols are listed in Appendix E. Most of them should simply be learned as needed, but there are a few extremely common ones that you'll want to know about right away:

`\leq` or `\le`	$\leq$	("less than or equal")
`\geq` or `\ge`	$\geq$	("greater than or equal")
`\neq` or `\ne`	$\neq$	("not equal")
`\notin`	$\notin$	("not in")

By the way, the control sequence `\not` gives a $/$ that can be used to "negate" other binary operators besides $=$. For example, the control sequence `\equiv` gives the operator $\equiv$ in math mode, and `$\not\equiv$` gives $\not\equiv$; the control sequences `\ne` and `\neq` are, in fact, simply abbreviations for `\not=`. But notice that the $/$ in $\notin$ has a different slope from the $/$ in $\neq$. For this reason, you should always type `$\notin$` rather than `$\not\in$`, which gives the less pleasing symbol $\not\in$.

In addition to special symbols, mathematicians sometimes use accents, as in formulas like $\hat{A}$, and other fonts, as in formulas like $a\mathbf{x} + b\mathbf{y}$. Fonts and accents work completely differently in math mode than they do in ordinary text, and details have been relegated to Part 3, because these matters are rather specialized.

On the other hand, mathematicians have also supplemented their arsenal of specially concocted symbols with letters stolen from the Greeks, and these are used very frequently. For example, `$\alpha$` and `$\beta$` and `$\gamma$` and `$\delta$` produce the first four Greek letters α, β, γ and δ, while `$\Gamma$` produces Γ, which is an upper-case gamma, and `$\Delta$` similarly produces Δ, an upper-case delta. (There are no `\Alpha` and `\Beta`, since the corresponding upper-case letters just look like "A" and "B".)

The fifth letter of the Greek alphabet is produced by `$\epsilon$`, which gives ϵ. Notice that this is quite different from the membership symbol $\in$. Unfortunately, not all mathematicians are conscientious about distinguishing these symbols in their manuscripts, so some consultations may be in order before beginning a long job. Make sure also that the author has carefully distinguished the Greek letter `\nu` (ν) from v and `\kappa` (κ) from x or k. The Greek letter `\phi` (ϕ) should also be distinguished from the symbol $\emptyset$, called `\emptyset`.

Just to make matters a little worse, ϵ has the variant form ε, which is produced by `$\varepsilon$`, and four other Greek letters also have variant forms:[1] while the input `$(\theta, \pi, \rho, \phi)$` yields $(\theta, \pi, \rho, \phi)$, the input `$(\vartheta,\varpi,\varrho,\varphi)$` yields $(\vartheta, \varpi, \varrho, \varphi)$. All upper-case Greek letters also have variants: for example, `\varGamma` gives Γ and `\varDelta` gives Δ.

If you haven't had the benefits of a liberal education (studying the classics or belonging to a fraternity or sorority), you may not be familiar with the names of the Greek letters. That's no problem—they are all listed in Appendix E, together with all the other esoteric symbols. Still, you might think that it's going to be quite a pain to type `$\alpha$` every time you want an α if this symbol happens to appear frequently in a paper. Wouldn't it be nicer to type short names, like `$\a$` for `$\alpha$` and `$\b$` for β? And while we're at it, why does TEX have such funny names for some of the other funny symbols? Calling $\equiv$ `\equiv` may be helpful to mathematicians, who usually pronounce $\equiv$ as 'equivalent to', but it doesn't help the technical typist!

TEX has a rather conservative philosophy about terminology: it generally uses long descriptive names for most of its control sequences, since there is then at least some basis for common agreement about the names—any system of abbreviated names usually has both vigorous adherents and detractors. TEX can afford to take such a cavalier approach to the problem because TEX typists *can always define their own control sequences.* When an esoteric symbol occurs only once or twice in a paper, you might as well just look it up in Appendix E and use the name provided, but for symbols that appear frequently you can invent your own names—you can tell TEX that you want `\a` to mean `\alpha`, etc. The process of defining your own control sequences isn't covered until Part 3, because it's always easier to learn an established system, no matter how irritating it may sometimes seem, than it is to create your own special variant. But you can keep this possibility in the back of your mind every time you do an exercise that has you typing longer control sequences than you'd like.

- **Exercise 8.8:**
You've typed a long paper in which the author has used the letter x in numerous formulas. Now E tells you that Eir handwritten x was really supposed to be κ! So you are going to use your text editor to replace all x's with `\kappa`'s. How should you proceed?

- **Exercise 8.9:**
Now assume you have the opposite problem. The fickle author decides to replace all κ's with k's. What precautions do you need?

---

[1] For the fate of a fifth variant, $\varkappa$ (`\varkappa`) see Appendix F.

• **Exercise 8.10:**

Consulting Appendix E for the names of various symbols, explain how to typeset the following formulas:

(1) $X \setminus (A \cup B) = (X \setminus A) \cap (X \setminus B)$

(2) $x \notin A \not\subset B$

(3) $(X \times Y) \times Z \simeq X \times (Y \times Z)$

(4) $\omega \wedge (\eta \wedge \lambda) = (\omega \wedge \eta) \wedge \lambda$

(5) $V \oplus \Lambda(V)$

(6) $\|a(x + y)\| \leq |a| \cdot (\|x\| + \|y\|)$

(7) $2 \cdot \aleph = \aleph$

(8) $2 \cdot \omega \neq \omega$

(9) $\nabla R(X, Y)$

(10) $(100 \pm .001) \div 5$

(11) $\forall x \gg A$

(12) $f * g : A \rightarrow B$

(13) $x \mapsto \alpha + x$

(14) $f(x) \in o(x) \ \& \ g(x) \in O(x) \implies f \circ g(x) \in o(x)$

In this chapter we've explored only the rudiments of typesetting mathematical formulas—as of yet we're not even able to produce an interesting little formula like $8 = 2^3$. But we've already learned enough to begin making new and interesting mistakes! To see how TₑX copes with our new-found abilities, let's make a file containing the following (where we temporarily use \par instead of a blank line to make a few things clearer a little later on).

```
This paragraph contains a formula $x that we forgot to
end properly. It also contains a second formula y$ that
we forgot to start, and a final
formula $x+y that we also forgot to end.\par This
paragraph contains another formula \alpha+\beta$
that we forgot to start.
```

TEX can't read our minds when we make errors of this sort. As far as it is concerned, in the first two lines we are specifying the weird formula

$$xthatweforgottoendproperly.Italsocontainsasecondformulay$$

After all, there's nothing here that couldn't actually occur in a formula!

On the other hand, starting a new paragraph inside a math formula makes no sense at all, so it is specifically disallowed, and when TEX sees

```
formula $x+y that we also forgot to end.\par This
```

it knows that the formula *had* to end before the \par that ends the paragraph. In fact, when we run our paper through TEX we will get an error message like the following:

```
! Missing $ inserted.
```

```
      .  .  .
```

```
1.8 formula $x+y that we also forgot to end.\par
                                             This
```

with a ? on the next line, as usual. We've left out four lines of the actual message, which is a little more intimidating than any we've seen before, because the basic strategy in dealing with such error messages is to focus attention on the top line and the bottom two lines, and not worry overly much about the lines in between.

As before, the bottom two lines tell us that TEX detected an error when it got to the \par on line 8. And the top line

```
! Missing $ inserted.
```

tells us that TEX tried to recover by inserting a $ just before the \par (of course, TEX hasn't really inserted the $ into your original file, only in its own private copy). If we simply press ⟨carriage-return⟩ in response to the ? prompt, TEX will have recovered as best it can (TEX has no way of figuring out that the $ should really go after the +y, and it's too late for that, anyway). What we get next is an Overfull box message like

```
Overfull \hbox ...
[]\tenrm This para-graph con-tains a for-mula $\teni xthatwe
```

which comes about because the formula

$$x that we forgot to end properly. It also contains a second formula y$$

doesn't fit on a line!

Our next error message is more interesting:

```
! Missing $ inserted.
```

       . . .

```
1.9 paragraph contains another formula \alpha
                                     +\beta$
```

As this error message shows, TₑX is now inserting the $ sign necessary to *begin* the formula $\alpha + \beta$. So if we press ⟨carriage-return⟩ TₑX will not only proceed to the end of the file, it will actually have printed the right formula in this case.

TₑX was able to figure out that a $ was needed before the \alpha because TₑX has no regard for the glories of the Greek tongue—as far as it is concerned, Greek letters are just additional esoteric math symbols, so they are allowed only in math mode. In a pinch you could get $\tau\epsilon\chi$ in text by typing $\tau\epsilon\chi$, but if you're actually setting Greek text, you will be using a different version of TₑX, designed for a keyboard with Greek letters on it, and you shouldn't even be reading this manual, which is undoubtedly all English to you.

- **Exercise 8.11:**

See what happens when you give the following file to TₑX:

```
This paragraph has a formula $x that we forgot to end.

This paragraph has the formula 3\alpha+\beta

This is accurate within \pm.0003 percent.

This paragraph has only text.
```

- **Exercise 8.12:**

¿Señor, what happens when you have the following in your file?

```
The symbols < and > and | give
$<$ and $>$ and $|$ in math mode.
```

Chapter 9. Lousy Breaks? Try An Artful Display

TEX has a special method of finding the hyphenations that are needed to break a paragraph of text into lines of equal length, but line breaking becomes a more difficult chore when formulas are intermingled with text. TEX tries hard not to break a line in the middle of a formula, and when such breaks are unavoidable TEX will break only after binary relations (reluctantly), or after binary operators (as a last resort).

Thus, if TEX has to break a line in the middle of the formula $f(x, y) = (x+y)(x-y)$, it will try to break after the $=$ sign. But if a break after the $=$ sign doesn't turn out to be feasible, TEX will settle for a break like $f(x, y) = (x + y)(x-y)$ after the $+$ sign, or for a break after the $-$ sign, which will look equally bad. Fortunately, breaks after binary operators occur only rarely, but if you did get such a break, and it was unacceptable to the author, you might try to force a break after the $=$ sign with \mathbreak. $\mathcal{A}_{\mathcal{M}}\mathcal{S}$-TEX also has \nomathbreak to *prevent* a linebreak in a formula, so you could also try putting \nomathbreak after the + and the -, but then there's a good chance that you might get an Overfull box message. And, of course, you can easily get an Overfull box whenever a line of text just happens to end with a formula like $abc(def)ghi[jkl]mnp$ that simply can't be broken.

In most cases, the best solution to a bad line break or an Overfull box that comes from a math formula is to have the author do a little rewriting. In fact, many mathematicians will be glad to insert or delete a few words in their not-so-deathless prose in order to keep their treasured formulas intact; with TEX there are opportunities for rewriting that traditional printers can't spare the time for.

TEX's standard rules for breaking formulas only allows breaks *after* binary relations, not before. So TEX may break a formula after the equal sign, like $f(x, y) = (x + y)(x - y)$, but still produce an Overfull box because the first part of the formula "$f(x, y) =$" doesn't quite fit. In such a case, instead of rewriting, the author might be willing to have the $=$ sign appear on the next line, even though most printers regard this as bad printing style. You can force the break by typing f(x,y)\mathbreak =. Another possibility is to type \allowmathbreak=, which simply allows a break before the $=$ sign without forcing it (that way, if you change the paragraph later on, you won't have to worry about forcing a line break that is no longer appropriate).

Although TEX might break the formula $f(x, y) = (x+y)(x-y)$ after the $=$ sign, or even after the $+$ or $-$ sign, it will not choose to break the formula after the comma. That's because commas in math formulas usually separate parts of a single mathematical entity—few mathematicians would accept a linebreak like $f(x,$ $y) = (x+y)(x-y)$. TEX also uses spacing after the comma which reflects its special role: examine the formula $f(x, y) = (x+y)(x-y)$ closely, *yes*, you can see that the space after a comma in a math formula is less than the space after a comma that occurs in text.

For these reasons, *actual punctuation commas should always be left outside the $ signs*. For example, if you want

> We have $a < b$, $a = b$ or $a > b$ in this case.

you should type

```
We have $a<b$, $a=b$ or~$a>b$ in this case.
```

If you typed

```
We have $a<b, a=b$ or~$a>b$ in this case.
```

you would get

> We have $a < b, a = b$ or $a > b$ in this case.

The spacing doesn't look as good here, and a linebreak after "$a < b$," would be inhibited.

- **Exercise 9.1:**
  How should you type the following?

  > There exist such division algebras only for $n = 1$, 2, 4 or 8.

- **Exercise 9.2:**
  How would you type the following?

  > We have $f(x) = A$, B or C for $x = 0$, 1, ..., n.

- **Exercise 9.3:**
  Explain how to type the following:

  > For all a and b we have $a < b$, $a = b$, or $a > b$. We say that $<$ is a *partial ordering*.

- **Exercise 9.4:**
  How would you type the following?

  > If a, b, $c > 0$, then $f(a, b, c) > 0$.

Exercise 9.2 illustrated a use for `\dots` between formulas, but mathematicians frequently incorporate dots as a *part* of their formulas. For example, `$f(1,\dots,n)$` gives the formula $f(1,\dots,n)$; notice that the spaces after the commas are smaller here. And if you type `$1+\dots+n$` something magical happens: you get the formula $1 + \cdots + n$, with the dots centered (further details about the behavior of `\dots` in math mode will be found in Part 3).

● **Exercise 9.5:**

How would you typeset the following?

> We have shown that $f(1,\dots,n) \leq f(0,\dots,0) + f(1,\dots,1) + \cdots + f(n,\dots,n)$ for $n \geq 1$.

Sometimes, even punctilious adherence to the punctuation rules won't give truly satisfactory results, because of lapses on the author's part. Despite the dictates of good mathematical style, mathematicians frequently fail to supply a few words to separate mathematical formulas that belong to different clauses. Instead of saying

> If $x > 0$, then $y > 1$.

a mathematician may simply say

(*)   If $x > 0$, $y > 1$.

This sentence was typed as

    If $x>0$, $y>1$.

with the comma outside of the formulas, but (*) is still a little confusing when read quickly, because the two formulas tend to merge into one. To compensate for the author's bad style the savvy TEXnical typist will use `\␣` to put an additional space between the two formulas. Thus, you could type

    If $x>0$, \ $y>1$.   or   If $x>0$,\ \ $y>1$.

to get

> If $x > 0$, $y > 1$.

(This is one of those cases, referred to in the answer to Exercise 5.3, when you wouldn't want $\mathcal{A}_{\mathcal{M}}\mathcal{S}$-TEX to ignore the space before `\␣`, because you are purposely using the combination `␣\␣` or `\␣\␣` to get extra space.)

If long formulas appear in text, then bad breaks are almost inevitable. So long formulas are frequently "displayed"—they are set on a separate line like this:

$$1 + 1 = 2$$

In fact, formulas, even short ones, are often displayed simply to give them prominence. The art of displaying formulas is actually an important aspect of mathematical style, so TEX will never make a decision to display a formula on its own—you have to tell TEX to do this by enclosing the input in $$ signs instead of $ signs, so that it enters "display math mode". For example, the input

```
    ... If $f(x)=x+1$, then we will have $$f([x+1
]/[x+2])=\{[x+1]/[x+2]\}+1
        =(2x+3)/(x+2).$$
Consequently,...
```

produces the output

   ... If $f(x) = x + 1$, then we will have

$$f([x + 1]/[x + 2]) = \{[x + 1]/[x + 2]\} + 1 = (2x + 3)/(x + 2).$$

   Consequently, ...

Notice that everything between the $$ signs got set as a *one-line* formula—multi-line formulas don't get explained until Chapter 16. Notice also that although the comma was typed outside the $ signs, the period was typed **inside** the $$ signs—otherwise the period would have appeared at the beginning of the next line, right before "Consequently"!

   Just as in ordinary math mode, spaces and single ⟨carriage-return⟩s are ignored within $$ signs, so the displayed formula

```
    $$f(x)=(x+y)(x-y)$$
```

can also be typed as

```
    $$
    f(x)=(x+y)(x-y)
    $$
```

(I like to handle displayed formulas this way, because it makes them easy to spot when I'm looking through the file later on, but this is purely a matter of taste.)

• **Exercise 9.6:**
How would you type the following?

> After the unspeakable exertions of the previous chapter, we have finally succeeded in proving the fundamental result that

$$1 + 1 = 2,$$

> and now we are going to try to prove that

$$2 + 2 = 4.$$

> As a first step in that direction, we will prove the distributive law for multiplication.

• **Exercise 9.7:**
How would you get the following formula?

$$1 + 2 + 3 + 4 + 5 + 6 + 7 + 8 + 9 + 10 + 11 + 12$$
$$+ 13 + 14 + 15 + 16 + 17 + 18 + 19 + 20 = 190$$

And how about the following?

$$a + b = c$$
$$A + B = C$$

 Some journals don't center displayed formulas, but instead set them like

$$1 + 1 = 2$$

and

$$1 + 1 + 1 = 3$$

with some fixed indentation from the left margin. Although this is probably done merely to relieve the typesetter from the chore of centering the formula, TEX can also set displayed formulas this way when the style calls for it.

Chapter 10. The 2nd Level Of Complexity.

Technical typesetting wouldn't be such a big deal if spacing and line breaks were the only concern. But mathematical formulas also convey a lot of information through the positioning of text. Even if you're not a mathematician you probably know that a^2 and a^3 are used as abbreviations for $a \times a$ ("a squared") and $a \times a \times a$ ("a cubed"). And there are many other situations where mathematicians use superscripts $^{\text{set up high}}$ and subscripts $_{\text{set down low}}$. You can't use positioning on the terminal since the input just goes in line by line, so all this information has to be conveyed in some other way.

To tell TEX that you want a character set as a superscript, you simply have to type ^ before it:

Type	To get
x^2	x^2
x^a	x^a
x^α	x^α
2^x	2^x

Many keyboards have keys with an up-arrow ↑ on them. Sometimes these keys are simply used to move the cursor around, but if you are lucky you might have a key that actually produces ↑ on the screen; if so, this key will probably replace the ^ key. Chances are (though you'd better check with a local expert) that you can use ↑ instead of ^, which is pleasant, since x↑2 looks even nicer that x^2. Of course, you might be so unlucky as to have *neither* ^ nor ↑. In this case you will have to make do with the control sequence \sp to give you superscripts:

$x\sp2$	x^2
$x\sp a$	x^a
$x\sp\alpha$	x^α
$2\sp x$	2^x

Notice that now you have to be careful to have a space after the \sp when the next symbol is a letter.

It's something of a downer that most keyboards don't having anything that indicates "down" as surely as ^ or ↑ signifies "up". About the closest is the "underscore" key _. So TEX uses _ to get subscripts:

x_2	x_2
x_y	x_y

If you're lucky enough to have a key that produces ↓ on the screen, find out if
you can use it instead of _. If you have neither _ or ↓ you can use the control
sequence \sb instead:

`$x\sb2$`	x_2
`$x\sb y$`	x_y

The instructions ^ and _ apply only to the next single character, so there is
no ambiguity in the following:

`$x^2y^2$`	x^2y^2
`$x ^ 2y ^ 2$`	x^2y^2
`$x_2y_2$`	x_2y_2
`${}_2F_3$`	$_2F_3$

Notice the use of the empty group {} in the last example to get a "prescript",
by having it be a subscript to an empty formula. You could also type simply
`$_2F_3$` in this case, because TeX will assume that there is an empty group
at the beginning of the formula if it begins with ^ or _. But it's better always
to make your intentions clear, to TeX and to yourself, by supplying the empty
group.

• **Exercise 10.1:**
Try typesetting the two formulas `$x + {}_2F_3$` and `$x + _2F_3$`, to see if
there is any difference between them.

When you want a whole expression superscripted or subscripted, just enclose
it in braces:

`$z=x^ {2y}$`	$z = x^{2y}$
`$2^{32}$`	2^{32}
`$x_{10}$`	x_{10}
`$x^{\{3y\}}$`	$x^{\{3y\}}$

In the above examples, the superscripts and subscripts ^{32} and $_{10}$ have to be put
in braces because they are *two* printed symbols, even though 32 and 10 are, to
the reader, just one number. On the other hand, `$x^\alpha$` on the previous
page *didn't* require braces around \alpha, because \alpha is just one symbol,
even though the control sequence to name it is several characters long.

● **Exercise 10.2:**

Explain how to type the following sentence:

> If the $n-1$ numbers $x_1, \ldots, x_{\alpha-1}, x_{\alpha+1}, \ldots, x_n$ are all $\neq x_\alpha \pm 1$, then $f(x_1, \ldots, x_n) > 0$.

Since superscripts and subscripts are usually needed only in math mode, TEX absolutely prohibits them outside of math mode, in order to assist it in detecting omitted $ signs.

● **Exercise 10.3:**

Make a file with the following three paragraphs

```
This paragraph has the formula x^2$.

This paragraph has the formula $x^10}$
and the formula $x^{10$.

This paragraph has only text.
```

and see what error messages you get when you run it through TEX, hitting ⟨carriage-return⟩ whenever necessary.

When a sub or superscript applies to a whole expression, mathematicians will use parentheses (or brackets or braces) to indicate this:

`$(x+1)^3$`	$(x+1)^3$
`$(x^2)^3$`	$(x^2)^3$
`$[x^2]^3$`	$[x^2]^3$
`$\{x^2\}^{3y}$`	$\{x^2\}^{3y}$

Actually, mathematicians and experienced technical typists may be somewhat surprised that these simple inputs worked—how did TEX know, for example, that 3 was supposed to be a superscript to the whole expression $(x+1)$ or (x^2)? The answer is very simple: TEX didn't know—it just followed instructions very literally and set the 3 as a superscript to the right parenthesis! On the other hand, when you put a formula in braces, the exponent applies to the whole formula:

`${(x^2)}^3$`	$\left(x^2\right)^3$
`${[x^2]}^3$`	$\left[x^2\right]^3$
`${ \{x^2\} }^{3y}$`	$\left\{x^2\right\}^{3y}$
`${({(x^2)}^2)}^4$`	$\left(\left(x^2\right)^2\right)^4$

This might seem better from a logical point of view, but notation like $(x^2)^3$ is just as easy to read, so there's no point making things harder for yourself; in fact, this notation has been in use for hundreds of years, so the more "logical" notation will probably seem subtly wrong to mathematicians—save $(x^2)^3$ for special effects or emphasis.

- **Exercise 10.4:**
  Explain how to type the following:

  In a non-commutative group we have

  $$(ab)^{-1} = b^{-1}a^{-1}$$

  and

  $$(ab)^{-2} = [(ab)^{-1}]^2 = [b^{-1}a^{-1}]^2 = b^{-1}a^{-1}b^{-1}a^{-1},$$

  but

  $$(a^m)^2 = a^{m+m} = a^{2m}.$$

A more interesting problem arises when you want a formula like

$$a^{b^c}.$$

To a mathematician this is very different from $(a^b)^c$. In the formula a^{b^c} the a has a superscript, but the superscript is not b, rather it is the entire formula b^c:

$$a^{\boxed{b^c}}$$

TeX thinks of such formulas just as a mathematician does: it's the formula b^c that appears as the superscript, so we have to put the appropriate input b^c inside braces:

$$\texttt{\$\$a\^{}\{b\^{}c\}\$\$} \qquad\qquad\qquad a^{b^c}$$

Once you understand this principle, you will have no trouble producing all sorts of formulas that would make traditional typesetters tear their hair out:

`$a^{b^{c+1}}$`	$a^{b^{c+1}}$
`$2^{(2^x)}$`	$2^{(2^x)}$
`$2^{2^{2^{2^{2^x}}}}$`	$2^{2^{2^{2^{2^x}}}}$
`$2^{(a+b)^2}$`	$2^{(a+b)^2}$
`$x_{y_2}$`	x_{y_2}
`$x_{y^2}$`	x_{y^2}

Notice that in the formula a^{b^c} the a is in the normal size font used for text, called "t-size", the superscript b is in a smaller "s-size", and the c is in a still smaller "ss-size". But TEX doesn't reduce the size after this, since such tiny letters are already so difficult to read.

● **Exercise 10.5:**
Typeset the following displayed formula.

$$2^{x_1 + \cdots + x_{n+1}} = 2^{x_{n+1}} \cdot \left(2^{x_1 + \cdots + x_n}\right)$$

● **Exercise 10.6:**
Explain how to type the following:

Suppose that $x^{x^x} = (x^x)^x$. Prove that $x = 1$ or 2.

● **Exercise 10.7:**
Describe the difference between the output of `${x^y}^z$` and `$x^{y^z}$`.

● **Exercise 10.8:**
Some computer systems use a construction like `a^b^c` to indicate a^{b^c}, but TEX won't accept such input. See what happens when you try to TEX a file that has `$a^b^c$` in it.

Although TEX won't accept `$a^b^c$` or `$a_b_c$`, a formula can have both a superscript and a subscript, specified in either order.

`$A^a_b$`	A^a_b
`$A_b^a$`	A^a_b
`$x^{31415}_{92}+\pi$`	$x^{31415}_{92} + \pi$
`$\Gamma_{y^a_ b}^{z_c^d}$`	$\Gamma^{z^d_c}_{y^a_b}$

Formulas like $A^a{}_b$ are often resorted to by printers because A^a_b is hard to set on a Linotype machine. This is obviously not a problem for TEX, but many mathematicians still prefer staggered sub and superscripts in certain situations. For example, a formula like x_i^2 is probably an abbreviation for $x_i \times x_i$, where the i plays quite a different role from the 2. In such cases many mathematicians prefer $x_i{}^2$. You can force TEX to stagger by artfully barricading its path with empty groups {}:

`$x_i{}^2$` or `${x_i}^2$`	$x_i{}^2$
`$R_i{}^{jk}{}_l$`	$R_i{}^{jk}{}_l$

The second of these examples is not a weird product of the author's imagination; rather, it is a weird product of "tensor analysis", a branch of mathematics waggishly defined as the study of sub and superscripts, where exact positioning is important. If the author uses such notation, it should be up to Em to indicate Eir intentions clearly, but there's no harm checking first. You might also want to check about the author's preferences for x_i^2. If you aren't sure, remember that it is easy to change `x_i^2` and `x_i^3` to `x_i{}^2` and `x_i{}^3`—a good text editor can really facilitate replacing `^` by `{}^` in the necessary places—but it's not so easy to change `x^2_i` and `x^3_i` to `x_i{}^2` and `x_i{}^3`. For this reason, I always try to remember to type subscripts before superscripts.

- **Exercise 10.9:**
Explain how to type the following:

> Suppose that there is no λ with $x_i = \lambda y_i$, $i = 1, 2$. Then the equation $(\lambda y_1 - x_1)(\lambda y_2 - x_2) = 0$, i.e., the equation

$$\lambda^2({y_1}^2 + {y_2}^2) - 2\lambda(x_1 y_1 + x_2 y_2) + ({x_1}^2 + {y_1}^2) = 0$$

> has *no* solution λ.

As you may have noted from Exercises 10.2, 10.4 and 10.5, the extra spacing around binary operators like $+$ and $-$ disappears when they are in sub or superscripts. Binary operators can even occur as sub or superscripts all on their own. For example, $*$ is a binary operator when used in constructions like

$$\texttt{\$(f*g)(x)\$} \qquad\qquad\qquad (f * g)(x)$$

but you can also type

$$\texttt{\$z\_\{ij\}\^*\$} \qquad\qquad\qquad z^*_{ij}$$
$$\texttt{\$f\^*(x) \textbackslash cap f\_*(\textbackslash nu)\$} \qquad\qquad f^*(x) \cap f_*(\nu)$$

And you can even get things like

$$\texttt{\$f\_+\$} \qquad\qquad\qquad f_+$$
$$\texttt{\$f\_-\$} \qquad\qquad\qquad f_-$$

though this last input would probably look better with extra braces:

$$\texttt{\$f\_\{+\}\$} \qquad\qquad\qquad f_+$$
$$\texttt{\$f\_\{-\}\$} \qquad\qquad\qquad f_-$$

Of course, you probably don't want the bother of typing braces unnecessarily, but this is another situation where a customizable editor can make things a lot easier. You can arrange for a single key stroke to produce `^{}` or `_{}`, and then move the cursor back a character, so that you are ready to type the superscript or subscript and then skip over the right brace. This takes one extra stroke when you don't need braces, but it saves lots of typing whenever you do need them. Such an arrangement has the added advantage that you won't start a multi-symbol superscript with a left brace and then forget to supply the closing right brace (a very easy error to make).

In addition to superscripts and subscripts, mathematicians often use the notation f' ("f prime"). TeX has the control sequence `\prime`, but if you type `f\prime` you'll get $f\prime$, which isn't what you want at all! Instead, you have to treat primes just like any other superscript:

`$f^\prime$` $\qquad\qquad\qquad\qquad\qquad$ f'

Your initial reaction might be: Why does TeX have to treat primes in such a complicated way—why not have `\prime` be a smaller prime mark that's already shifted up into the superscript position? The answer to this is very simple: primes often occur together with subscripts, as in

`$f_2^\prime$` $\qquad\qquad\qquad\qquad\qquad$ f_2'

If the prime were simply a symbol on its own it would occur after the f_2, instead of right above the 2. Somewhat mollified, you still might think that it's going to be a bit of bother to type `^\prime` every time you need a $'$, and if you're thinking ahead you can imagine what a nuisance it's going to be to get f'''—you'll have to type `f^{\prime\prime\prime}}`! Fortunately, TeX has a special device to circumvent this problem. When TeX is in math mode, it will translate $'$ into `^\prime`; moreover, $''$ will be translated into `^{\prime\prime}` and $'''$ will be translated into `^{\prime\prime\prime}`, etc.

`$f'[g(x)]g'(x)$` $\qquad\qquad\qquad$ $f'[g(x)]g'(x)$

`$y_1'+y_2''+y_3'''$` $\qquad\qquad\qquad$ $y_1' + y_2'' + y_3'''$

This is a $'$ example of how easy it is to use TeX.

• **Exercise 10.10:**
Explain what is wrong with typing the following:

```
In the formula $``x+y''$ the $+$ sign is a binary operator.
```

$\mathcal{A}_{\mathcal{M}}\mathcal{S}$-TEX doesn't give you any special way of getting *subscript* primes, since they are used so rarely; for constructions like $F_{\prime}(w,z)$, you'll simply have to type `$F_\prime(w,z)$`. You might also want to use `\prime` in situations like this:

$g^{\prime 2}$ g'^2

But you can also manage with an empty group:

`$g'{}^2$` g'^2

• **Exercise 10.11:**
Why not type simply `$g'^2$`?

• **Exercise 10.12:**
Explain how to type the following displayed equation:

$$f^{(n+2)} = [f^{(n+1)}]' = [f^{(n)\prime}]' = [f^{(n)}]''$$

Before leaving this topic, we ought to acknowledge one possible pitfall when you are typing superscripts and subscripts: on rare occasions braces are needed even though they would *seem* to be unnecessary. For example, suppose that we wanted the symbol $A_{\neq}$. You might think that it would be safe to type

`$A_\ne$`

since it's perfectly OK to type `$A_\alpha$` to get A_α. But if you type `$A\ne$` you'll get the strange result '$A_{/}=$'! That's because `\ne` isn't really a single symbol at all. It's simply an abbreviation for `\not=`. Thus TEX takes your input `$A_\ne$`, translates it into `$A_\not=$`, and then dutifully sets the $/$ as a subscript to the A! If you are blessed with a customizable editor, and always have braces around your sub and superscripts, you won't have to worry about such anomalies. But even if you aren't, you shouldn't worry very much. Such situations occur rarely enough and it's sufficient to be aware of them, so that you won't be totally freaked when they do arise.

• **Exercise 10.13:**
See what happens when you try to TEX a file that contains the following.

```
This file contains only the formula $A_\notin$.
```

Chapter 11. Our Problems Mount

In a formula with superscripts and subscripts, the symbols still go in "from left to right". But many formulas involve more critical dislocations, with one subformula placed on top of the other. $\mathcal{AMS}$-TEX has several control sequences to deal with these problems.

The most important such control sequence is \frac, which produces

$$(*) \qquad \frac{n+1}{n+3}$$

and similar fractions. \frac is a control sequence with two arguments, the numerator above the fraction line, and the denominator below the line; the fraction ($*$) was produced by typing

```
$$\frac {n+1}{n+3}$$
```

This displayed fraction is set in TEX's "d-size", with the numerator and denominator each in the usual t-size. If we type $\frac {n+1}{n+3}$ we get $\frac{n+1}{n+3}$. Now the whole fraction is in t-size, which means that its numerator and denominator are in the smaller s-size.

Notice that ($*$) could also have been typed as

```
$$\frac{n+1} {n+3}$$
```

The space isn't required after the \frac in this case, since it is followed by the non-letter {; and the space before {n+3} is ignored, not only because we are in math mode, but also because TEX always ignores spaces when looking for any arguments of a control sequence.

Fractions produced by \frac are automatically positioned correctly with respect to binary operators and relations,

```
$$z=\frac{x+y^2}{x-y^2}-1$$
```
$$z = \frac{x+y^2}{x-y^2} - 1$$

so you don't have to worry about adjusting their position. Notice also that fractions like

$$\frac{1}{n+1} \qquad \text{and} \qquad \frac{N-1}{2}$$

occur quite frequently, so you often get the opportunity to omit some braces.

$$\verb|\frac23|\qquad\qquad\qquad \frac{2}{3}$$

$$\verb|\frac1{n+1}|\qquad\qquad\qquad \frac{1}{n+1}$$

$$\verb|\frac{N-1}2|\qquad\qquad\qquad \frac{N-1}{2}$$

Since the numerator and denominator of displayed fractions are in t-size, when you put fractions within fractions you get results like

$$\verb|\frac x{1+\frac x2}|\qquad\qquad \frac{x}{1+\frac{x}{2}}$$

$$\verb|\frac {\frac x2+1}2|\qquad\qquad \frac{\frac{x}{2}+1}{2}$$

In both of these cases it would probably be better to convert the fraction $\frac{x}{2}$ to the "slashed form" $x/2$:

$$\verb|\frac x{1+x/2}|\qquad\qquad \frac{x}{1+x/2}$$

$$\verb|\frac {x/2+1}2|\qquad\qquad \frac{x/2+1}{2}$$

But some authors will prefer $\frac{x}{2}$, and others might insist on having

$$\frac{x}{1+\frac{x}{2}} \qquad \text{and} \qquad \frac{\frac{x}{2}+1}{2}$$

with the $\frac{x}{2}$ in d-size. $\mathcal{A}_{\mathcal{M}}\mathcal{S}$-TeX has the control sequence \dsize to force a formula into d-size. For example, we got $\frac{x}{2}$ to appear in text by typing

$$\verb|$\dsize\frac x2$|$$

And to get $\frac{x}{2}+\frac{x}{2}$ to appear we just have to type

$$\verb|$\dsize\frac x2+\frac x2$|$$

—note that \dsize causes a switch to d-size for the *whole formula*; in this respect it is analogous to \rm, \it, \bf and \sl, except that its effects are limited to the formula within which it appears.

• **Exercise 11.1:**
How were the displayed formulas

$$\frac{x}{1 + \dfrac{x}{2}}$$

and

$$\frac{\dfrac{x}{2} + 1}{2}$$

typed?

• **Exercise 11.2:**
Typeset the following:

> *Hölder's Inequality:* Let $0 \leq p, q \leq \infty$ with $\dfrac{1}{p} + \dfrac{1}{q} = 1$. If $f \in L^p(\mu)$ and $g \in L^q(\mu)$, then $fg \in L^1(\mu)$ and
>
> $$\|fg\|_1 \leq \|f\|_p \|g\|_q.$$

The answers to Exercises 11.1 and 11.2 should explain why \dsize has been designed to work the same way that \rm, \it, \bf and \sl work in text, rather than as a control sequence with an argument: when you have to force a fraction into d-size it's usually necessary simply to insert \dsize before it—extra braces will be needed only rarely. But $\mathcal{A}_{\mathcal{M}}\mathcal{S}$-TEX actually provides you with a much better way of getting d-size fractions, one that will eliminate all worries about braces. The control sequence \dfrac will automatically produce a fraction in d-size; thus, typing \dfrac ab is equivalent to typing {\dsize\frac ab}. You'll find \dfrac especially convenient when you type \frac the first time through, and then after seeing the output decide that a d-size \frac was really needed— all you have to do is type an extra d before the f. You can save \dsize for rare occasions when d-size is needed for some other type of construction.

• **Exercise 11.3:**
Redo Exercise 11.1 using \dfrac.

As you might suspect, $\mathcal{A}_{\mathcal{M}}\mathcal{S}$-TEX also has the control sequence \tsize, to force a formula into t-size.

• **Exercise 11.4:**
Explain how to type the following displayed formula.

$$fg = \tfrac{1}{2}[(f+g)^2 - f^2 - g^2]$$

It turns out that t-size fractions are often desired within displays, so $\mathcal{A}_{\mathcal{M}}\mathcal{S}$-TEX also has \tfrac to get a t-size \frac, thereby eliminating any concern about braces.

- **Exercise 11.5:**
Redo Exercise 11.4 without using \tsize.

When a fraction appears in a superscript, it is in s-size, which means that its numerator and denominator are even smaller, in ss-size:

$e^{-n+\frac1{12n}}$ $e^{-n+\frac{1}{12n}}$

In superscripts, the slashed form of a fraction is almost always preferred, but once again, some authors may be picky, and the non-slashed form may be standard in certain situations. (Traditional typesetters have a terrible time with fractions in s-size, but TEX won't complain about them—only the poor readers will complain about the tiny symbols.)

$\mathcal{A}_{\mathcal{M}}\mathcal{S}$-TEX also has \ssize and \sssize to force a formula into s-size or ss-size, but you will hardly ever need them. Naturally, \dsize, \tsize, \ssize and \sssize all work the same way, forcing a change of size for a whole formula, and thus behaving analogously to the font changes \rm, \it, \sl and \bf; so you should think of them as "switch to d-size", etc. You don't have to worry about running into similar anomalies later on—these are the only $\mathcal{A}_{\mathcal{M}}\mathcal{S}$-TEX control sequences that work like this.

In addition to fractions, mathematicians frequently use the special concoction

$$\binom{n}{k}$$

which is called a "binomial coefficient". You don't have to have any idea what that means, just remember that \binom is used to produce it, so that the above display was produced by typing

    `$$\binom nk$$`

Aside from the fact that the output looks a little different, \binom works exactly like \frac, with the same conventions for the size of the top and bottom formulas:

    `$$\binom n{\frac k2}$$` $\binom{n}{\frac k2}$

    `$$\frac{\binom nk}2$$` $\dfrac{\binom nk}{2}$

• **Exercise 11.6:**

Explain how to improve the first example to either

$$\binom{n}{k/2} \qquad \text{or} \qquad \binom{n}{\frac{1}{2}k}$$

and the second example to

$$\frac{\binom{n}{k}}{2}$$

As you might have guessed, $\mathcal{A}_{\mathcal{M}}S$-TEX also has \dbinom and \tbinom to produce a \binom that is in d-size or t-size.

• **Exercise 11.7:**

Redo the last part of Exercise 11.6 without using \dsize.

Fractions and binomial coefficients are by far the most common constructions where one formula is stacked on top of another. But there are several others you may come across. For example, in certain situations the author might want a fraction with a thicker fraction line, like

$$\frac{\dfrac{(u' \circ u^{-1})(v'' \circ u^{-1})}{(u' \circ u^{-1})} - \dfrac{(v' \circ u^{-1})(u'' \circ u^{-1})}{(u' \circ u^{-1})}}{(u' \circ u^{-1})^2}.$$

$\mathcal{A}_{\mathcal{M}}S$-TEX has \thickfrac for such fractions, and it's also possible to vary the thickness of the fraction line. And then there's the "Legendre symbol" $\left(\frac{a}{b}\right)$, which is like a binomial coefficient, except that it has both a fraction line and parentheses, not to mention the "Euler number" $\left\langle\frac{n}{k}\right\rangle$, which is like a binomial coefficient, except that it has "angle brackets" $\langle$ and $\rangle$ instead of parentheses. $\mathcal{A}_{\mathcal{M}}S$-TEX doesn't have special control sequences for these and similar combinations that mathematicians may concoct, but it does have a "generalized fraction" mechanism by which you can produce any such special symbols that you will need. Details will be found in Part 3.

$\mathcal{A}_{\mathcal{M}}S$-TEX's control sequence \frac is constructed from TEX's control sequence \over, which could also be used to produce fractions, but $\mathcal{A}_{\mathcal{M}}S$-TEX users aren't supposed to know about \over, because \frac is easier to use. When you *misuse* \frac, however, things can get more complicated, because TEX first translates \frac into its own terms before figuring out what has gone amiss.

• **Exercise 11.8:**

Make a file containing the following three paragraphs

```
This paragraph has $\frac1{a+b$ and $\frac 1a+b}$.

This paragraph has $\frac1{a+b$.

This paragraph has only text.
```

and run it through TEX. Hit ⟨carriage-return⟩ for the first two error messages, but when you get a

Runaway argument?

message, which we've never seen before, type h or H for help before hitting ⟨carriage-return⟩ once again.

Chapter 12. Benefitting From TₑX's Largess

Although $+$ is a "binary operator", which connects two terms in formulas like $a + b$, this same binary operator can be used to connect several terms, as in the formula $a + b + c + d$—the sum of a, b, c and d. But when mathematicians want to indicate the sum of many numbers a_1, a_2, ..., a_n, they usually use a special expression like $\sum_{i=1}^n a_i$. Although it isn't necessary to understand exactly what this means, certain features of such a formula are important. The $\sum$ sign is basically an upper-case Greek sigma, but it's usually larger and in a different type-style from the Greek Σ. To get this special $\sum$ symbol you type \sum (in math mode). Of course, it's often hard to distinguish Σ from $\sum$ in a handwritten or typewritten manuscript, but one of the tell-tale signs of a $\sum$ are sub and superscripts like the $_{i=1}^n$. These smaller formulas are called the "limits" of the $\sum$, and something special happens when you display a formula with $\sum$. When you type $\sum_{i=1}^n a_i$ you get $\sum_{i=1}^n a_i$ in text, but when you type the displayed formula

$$\sum_{i=1}^n a_i$$

you get

$$\sum_{i=1}^n a_i$$

Notice that the $\sum$ has gotten even larger, and the "limits", though they have been typed as sub and superscripts, magically migrate to positions below and above the $\sum$ sign.

$\sum$ is called a "large operator", and several other binary operators have "large" counterparts. For example, the binary operators \cup ($\cup$) and \cap ($\cap$) have corresponding large operators \bigcup and \bigcap. In text these control sequences give $\bigcup$ and $\bigcap$, but in displayed formulas they will give $\bigcup$ and $\bigcap$, and "limits" that were typed as sub and superscripts will end up below and above the symbols. Other large operators will be found in Appendix E.

• **Exercise 12.1:**
How would you type the following formulas?

(1)
$$(f \cdot g)^{(n+1)}(a) = \sum_{k=0}^{n+1} \binom{n+1}{k} f^{(k)}(a) g^{(n+1-k)}(a)$$

$$(2) \qquad 0 = (1 + -1)^n = \sum_{j=0}^{n} (-1)^j \binom{n}{j}$$

$$(3) \qquad \sum_{i=1}^{n} {x_i}^2 \cdot \sum_{i=1}^{n} {y_i}^2 = \sum_{i=1}^{n} {x_i}^2 {y_i}^2 + \sum_{i \neq j} {x_i}^2 {y_j}^2$$

$$(4) \qquad \sum_{i=1}^{p} \sum_{j=1}^{q} \sum_{k=1}^{r} a_{ij} b_{jk} c_{ki}$$

$$(5) \qquad \Sigma^2 : [X, S_0(\infty)] \rightarrow [\Sigma^2 X, S_0(\infty)]$$

$$(6) \qquad \bigcup_{n=1}^{m} (A_n \cup B_n)$$

$$(7) \qquad X \setminus \bigcup_{i \in I} A_i = \bigcap_{i \in I} X \setminus A_i$$

Sometimes a large operator has a multi-line limit, like

$$\sum_{\substack{0 \leq i \leq m \\ 0 < j < n}} P(i, j)$$

While _ or \sb is used to get a single-line limit, you would get this formula by typing

```
$$\sum \Sb 0\le i\le m\\ 0<j<n \endSb  P(i,j)$$
```

Between \Sb and \endSb each \\ indicates a new line. Similarly, there's \Sp ... \endSp to get multi-line upper limits.

- **Exercise 12.2:**
Reset formula (4) in Exercise 12.1 as

$$\sum_{\substack{1 \leq i \leq p \\ 1 \leq j \leq q \\ 1 \leq k \leq r}} a_{ij} b_{jk} c_{ki}$$

- **Exercise 12.3:**
See what happens when you have

```
$$\sum\Sb 0\le i\le m\\0<j<n $$
```

```
\enddocument
```

in your file, with \endSb missing from the displayed formula.

There's another "large operator" that acts rather differently from `\sum`. If you type `\int` in math mode, you will get the symbol $\int$ that mathematicians call an "integral sign", and in a displayed formula the integral sign grows larger, just like a `\sum` sign. But the "limits" won't move to the bottom and top of the $\int$ sign.

$\int_a^b$

$$\int_a^b$$

$$\int_a^b$$

$$\int_a^b$$

In addition to `\int`, $\mathcal{A}_{\mathcal{M}}\mathcal{S}$-TEX also has `\oint`, which produces $\oint$ and $\oint$.

And `\int`'s often occur in groups, like $\iint$ and $\iiint$. But you shouldn't type something like `$\int\int$` because this gives $\int \int$ with too much space between the symbols. Instead use the special symbols

$$\iint$$

$$\iint$$

$$\iiint$$

$$\iiint$$

$$\iiiint$$

$$\iiiint$$

$$\idotsint$$

$$\int \cdots \int$$

The proper treatment of "limits" on `\sum` and `\int` is not actually decided by TEX, but is determined by the particular style you are using. Some journals set limits on `\sum` as sub and superscripts even in displays, and some set limits above and below $\int$ signs in displays. Even when a journal normally sets limits on $\int$ signs to the right, it is possible to force the limits on an `\int` to be set below and above when particular formulas seem to demand this. For example, in the equation

$$(*) \qquad \int_{\partial(M-\cup_{i=1}^n U_i)} r^*\Pi = -\sum_{i=1}^n \int_{\partial U_i} r^*\Pi$$

the long limit was set at the bottom of the first integral because this looks better than

$$\int_{\partial(M-\cup_{i=1}^n U_i)} r^*\Pi$$

If you type `\int\limits`, then TEX will set any sub and superscripts the `\int` may have as "limits".

- **Exercise 12.4:**
How was equation (∗) typed?

- **Exercise 12.5:**
Explain how the displayed formula

$$\iiint_M d\omega = \iint_{\partial M} \omega$$

should be typed.

Although TEX conveniently selects a different style for large operators in text and in displays, authors sometimes want formulas like $\sum_{n=1}^{\infty} \dfrac{(-1)^n}{n}$ to appear in text, because the usual text style formula $\sum_{n=1}^{\infty} \frac{(-1)^n}{n}$ looks a little too squashed. Of course, you can do this simply by typing

```
$\dsize\sum_{n=1}^\infty\frac{(-1)^n}n$
```

Such constructions are often used in books, but journal editors aren't fond of them, because of the paper that they waste, not to mention the uneven appearance that they give to the page. A pleasant compromise is to type

```
$\sum\limits_{n=1}^\infty\frac{(-1)^n}n$
```

which gives $\sum\limits_{n=1}^{\infty} \frac{(-1)^n}{n}$; such constructions often make formulas a lot more readable without sacrificing too many trees.

$\diamondsuit$ `\limits` has its obverse `\nolimits`, which causes the sub and superscripts on a large operator not to be re-positioned, even if they ordinarily would be. `\limits` and `\nolimits` should be used only for special occasions, however. If you don't like the conventions used by the **amsppt** style for limits on `\sum`'s and `\int`'s, you shouldn't use `\limits` and `\nolimits` to correct each formula. The right thing to do is to change the conventions permanently, thereby creating a somewhat new style of your own. Part 3 explains how this can be done.

Chapter 13. Creating Your Own Space

Although TEX can usually figure out the correct spacing in formulas, it sometimes needs a little coaching. For example in the formula

$$\int_a^b f(x)\,dx$$

the dx ought to be separated from the other symbols by a small amount of space, a little gap that printers call a "thin space". This little space is so useful for adjusting math formulas that TEX has the extremely simple control sequence \,, to specify it. Thus, the proper way to get the formula above is to type

    `$$\int_a^bf(x)\,dx$$`

You will also want to put a thin space before dx or dy or $d$whatever in calculus formulas like the following:

    `$dx\,dy=r\,dr\,d\theta$` $dx\,dy = r\,dr\,d\theta$

But don't use \, for expressions like $\dfrac{dy}{dx}$ or dy/dx.

- **Exercise 13.1:**
How should the following formulas be typeset?

(1) $y\,dx - x\,dy$

(2) $x\,dy/dx$

(3) $\displaystyle\int_1^x \frac{dt}{t}$

(4) $\displaystyle\int dy = \int \frac{dy}{dx}\,dx$

- **Exercise 13.2:**
How can you get the formula

$$\frac{dz}{dx} = \frac{\dfrac{dz}{dy}}{\dfrac{dy}{dx}}$$

with the $\dfrac{dz}{dy}$ and $\dfrac{dy}{dx}$ separated by a slightly longer fraction line?

AMS-TEX allows you to use \, outside of math mode also, but you will seldom need it, except for special effects. One such case is an expression like '55 mi/hr'—this looks best when the space after '55' is just \, instead of an ordinary interword space.

• **Exercise 13.3:**
How would you typeset each of the following?

(1)   1 ml equals 1.000028 cc

(2) $g = 9.8 \, \text{m/sec}^2$

(3) $0°$ C equals $32°$ F

Quite a different sort of spacing problem occurs when you have a display containing a main formula with a side condition, like

$$F_n = F_{n-1} + F_{n-2}, \qquad n > 1.$$

In addition to the thin space, printers have a much larger amount of space called a "quad space", and tradition has established that two quad spaces should be inserted between a main formula and its side condition. TEX has the control sequence \quad to specify a quad space, and it even has the special abbreviation \qquad to stand for \quad\quad, so you can type the above formula as

```
$$
F_n=F_{n-1}+F_{n-2},\qquad n>1.
$$
```

• **Exercise 13.4:**
Explain how to get the following displayed formula.

$$\int_0^\infty \frac{t - ib}{t^2 + b^2} e^{iat} \, dt = e^{ab} E_1(ab), \qquad a, b > 0.$$

TEX is capable of producing spaces of any amount, but in this chapter we haven't even bothered to introduce the various measurements that TEX knows about (they include inches, centimeters, the printers' points and picas, and many others), because the control sequences \, and \quad and \qquad usually provide just the sort of spacing you need. There are a few other situations where formulas can be improved by the judicious insertion or removal of a thin space, and AMS-TEX has lots of cute devices to deal with all sorts of other special spacing problems. But such subtleties can be postponed until Part 3. Some people are a little superstitious, so let's just think of this chapter as a \, between Chapters 12 and 14.

Chapter 14. Fascinating Things That Expand By Themselves

When you type a `\frac`, the fraction line automatically grows to the proper length, sufficient to encompass both the numerator and denominator. TeX has many other control sequences that select symbols whose size depends on the context. For example, you can `\underline` or `\overline` a formula:

`$$\underline 4$$`	$\underline{4}$
`$$\underline{\underline{4+x}}$$`	$\underline{\underline{4+x}}$
`$$x^{\underline n+m}$$`	$x^{\underline{n}+m}$
`$$\overline{\overline{x^3}+x^{x^3}}$$`	$\overline{\overline{x^3}+x^{x^3}}$

And you can put arrows of various sorts over a formula:

`$$\overrightarrow{x+y}$$`	$\overrightarrow{x+y}$
`$$\overleftarrow{x-y}$$`	$\overleftarrow{x-y}$
`$$A^{\overleftrightarrow{x+y}}$$`	$A^{\overleftrightarrow{x+y}}$

You can also get arrows under your formulas with `\underrightarrow`, `\underleftarrow` and `\underleftrightarrow`. The most common arrows, `\overrightarrow` and `\underrightarrow`, have the shorter names `\overarrow` and `\underarrow`. Of course, if you were using such arrows frequently you would want to define your own shorthand names, as explained in Chapter 19.

Arrows over and under formulas shouldn't be confused with other arrows that act like binary relations. We've already come across `\rightarrow`, and `\Longrightarrow`; other arrows are listed in Appendix E.

● **Exercise 14.1:**
Explain how to type each of the following:

(1)

The sum of the vectors $\overrightarrow{OA}$ and $\overrightarrow{OB}$ is defined by

$$\overrightarrow{OA} + \overrightarrow{OB} = \overrightarrow{OP},$$

where $OAPB$ is a parallelogram.

(2)

In any triangle ABC we have

$$\overline{AB} + \overline{BC} > \overline{AC}.$$

(3)

The Pythagorean Theorem: If $\angle C$ of $\triangle ABC$ is a right angle, then

$$\overline{AB}^2 = \overline{AC}^2 + \overline{BC}^2.$$

● **Exercise 14.2:**
How do you type the following formula?

$$B_{i,j} \longleftrightarrow A_{i+j,\overline{i+j}}$$

More interesting size changes occur when you take the square root of a formula, with \sqrt:

    `$$\sqrt2$$` $\sqrt{2}$

    `$$\sqrt{\frac ab+1}$$` $\sqrt{\dfrac{a}{b}+1}$

The output from

    `$$\sqrt{1+\sqrt{1+\sqrt{1+`
                    `\sqrt{1+\sqrt{1+\sqrt{1+\sqrt{1+x}}}}}}$$`

shows a variety of available square-root signs:

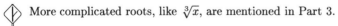

$$\sqrt{1+\sqrt{1+\sqrt{1+\sqrt{1+\sqrt{1+\sqrt{1+\sqrt{1+x}}}}}}}$$

The four smallest square-root signs are made up of distinct characters, together with overlines of the appropriate length, but the three largest signs are all essentially the same, except for a vertical segment ' | ' that gets repeated as often as necessary to reach the desired size.

More complicated roots, like $\sqrt[3]{x}$, are mentioned in Part 3.

• **Exercise 14.3:**

Explain how to type the following:

The solutions to $ax^2+bx+c = 0$ are given by the *quadratic formula*:

$$x = \frac{-b \pm \sqrt{b^2 - 4ac}}{2a}.$$

• **Exercise 14.4:**

Suppose that you want the formulas $2^{\overline{y}}$ and $2^{\sqrt{x}}$ in your file. What happens if you type `$2^\overline y$` and `$2^\sqrt x$`, omitting the braces around `\overline y` and `\sqrt x`?

Large parentheses are constructed in a manner similar to large square-root signs: once TEX gets beyond a certain size, it combines standard tops and bottoms with a repeatable extension:

There is one important difference between parentheses and square roots, however. TEX will not choose the appropriate size parentheses unless you formally request them. To get a formula enclosed in parentheses of the right size, type

    \left(formula   \right)

For example,

    $$\left(\frac1{1-x^2}\right)^2$$ $\left(\dfrac{1}{1-x^2}\right)^2$

• **Exercise 14.5:**

Typeset the following:

(1)

For $F = 0$ we have the "degenerate hyperbola"

$$x + \frac{B}{2A} = \pm\sqrt{\frac{-C}{A}}\left(y + \frac{D}{2C}\right).$$

(2)

The nth Fibonacci number F_n is given by

$$F_n = \frac{\left(\dfrac{1+\sqrt{5}}{2}\right)^n - \left(\dfrac{1-\sqrt{5}}{2}\right)^n}{\sqrt{5}}.$$

Similarly, by typing

`\left[`   formula   `\right]`

you will get variable size brackets around the formula:

`$$\left[\frac{a+b}2\right]$$`
$$\left[\frac{a+b}{2}\right]$$

(If you are using `\lbrack` for [and `\rbrack` for], you can also type things like `\left\lbrack` and `\right\rbrack`.)

- **Exercise 14.6:**
  Typeset the following:

  For $0 < x \leq 1$ we have

  $$f(x) = \frac{1}{\left[\dfrac{1}{x}\right]}.$$

Variable size curly braces are also available—remember to type `\{` and `\}`:

`$$\left\{\frac1{1-x^2}\right\}$$`
$$\left\{\frac{1}{1-x^2}\right\}$$

- **Exercise 14.7:**
  Typeset the following displayed formula:

  $$\|f\|_p = \left\{\int_0^1 |f|^p\right\}^{\frac{1}{p}}$$

Parentheses, brackets and braces are only a few of the "delimiters" that can go after \left and \right. Among the other delimiters there are

vertical line: |	| or \vert
double vertical line: ||	\\| or \Vert
left floor bracket: ⌊	\lfloor
right floor bracket: ⌋	\rfloor
left ceiling bracket: ⌈	\lceil
right ceiling bracket: ⌉	\rceil

(less frequently used delimiters will be found in Part 3). When used alone, the control sequences on the right produce the normal text size symbols on the left, but when used with \left and \right they produce variable size symbols.

- **Exercise 14.8:**

How is the displayed formula

$$\left\|\frac{x}{a}\right\| = \frac{\|x\|}{|a|}$$

typeset?

You can actually put any delimiters you want after \left and \right—they don't have to be the left and right members of a matching pair. For example, you can type

$$x\in\left(\frac ab,\frac cd\right]$$ $x \in \left(\dfrac{a}{b}, \dfrac{c}{d}\right]$

or even (yukk)

$$x\in\left]\frac ab,\frac cd\right[$$ $x \in \left]\dfrac{a}{b}, \dfrac{c}{d}\right[$

When you have weird constructions like the second of these examples, \left and \right do more than simply select the correct size for the delimiters; they also help provide the proper spacing in formulas. TEX normally treats] as a right delimiter, and if you typed $x\in]a,b[$ you would get $x \in]a, b[$, because TEX doesn't leave any extra space between a binary relation and a right delimiter. But \left] tells TEX to treat the] that it selects as a left delimiter, so if you type $x\in\left]a,b\right[$ you will get $x \in]a, b[$; in this particular situation the brackets are ordinary size, of course, but now the spacing comes out right.

- **Exercise 14.9:**

For mathematicians who insist on using such yukky notation, explain the right way to type the following formula: $]-\infty, T[\times]-\infty, T[$.

There are two delimiters that are rather special:

left angle bracket ⟨   \langle
right angle bracket ⟩   \rangle

These symbols are not constructed with repeatable extensions and therefore have a maximum size; in the font used for this book the largest angle brackets you can get are

$$\Bigg\langle \qquad \Bigg\rangle$$

If your formula happens to be enormously tall, TEX will simply settle for the largest pair available. By the way, TEX allows you to type \left< and \right> as well as \left\langle and \right\rangle, even though < and > aren't the same as ⟨ and ⟩.

- **Exercise 14.10:**
Typeset the following:

The connection ∇ is compatible with the metric if and only if

$$\frac{d}{dt}\langle V,W\rangle = \left\langle \frac{DV}{dt},W \right\rangle + \left\langle V,\frac{DW}{dt} \right\rangle.$$

In a \left...\right construction, TEX figures out the proper size for the delimiters by first looking at the formula between the \left and the \right. So \left's and \right's have to pair up correctly, just like curly braces.

- **Exercise 14.11:**
Typeset the following:

We derive the quadratric formula by "completing the square":

$$ax^2 + bx + c = a\left(x^2 + \frac{b}{a}x + \frac{c}{a}\right) = a\left[\left(x + \frac{b}{2a}\right)^2 + \left(\frac{c}{a} - \frac{b^2}{4a}\right)\right].$$

As a matter of fact, TEX mentally inserts braces around \left...\right pairs, so the effect of the size changes \dsize, \tsize, ... is restricted by such pairs.

• **Exercise 14.12:**
Typeset the formula

$$\left(\frac{1}{\sqrt{A}}+\sum_{i=1}^{n}a_i\right)\left(\frac{1}{\sqrt{B}}+\sum_{i=1}^{n}b_i\right)$$

using as few strokes as possible.

The requirement that \left's and \right's match up might cause you some consternation when you have to typeset a formula like

$$\left.\frac{dx^2}{dx}\right|_{x=a}=2a$$

where there *aren't* matching delimiters. To handle such cases, TEX allows a period after \left and \right, to produce the "empty" delimiters '\left.' and '\right.' that keep TEX well-balanced, but that don't produce any symbol in the output. Thus, you can type

```
$$\left.\frac{dx^2}{dx}\right|_{x=a}=2a$$
```

• **Exercise 14.13:**
What happens if you type

```
$$\left,\frac{dx^2}{dx}\right|_{x=a}=2a$$
```

with a comma mistakenly typed instead of a period?

• **Exercise 14.14:**
What happens if you omit the \left. completely and simply type the following?

```
$$\frac{dx^2}{dx}\right|_{x=a}=2a$$
```

• **Exercise 14.15:**
How do you get the following displayed formula?

$$\left[\frac{dy}{dx}\right|_{x=a}\right]^2$$

You will also want to use a blank delimiter along with one other delimiter, the last that we will mention here. This is a variable size $/$, which has a largest size, just like the delimiters $\langle$ and $\rangle$. This delimiter can be obtained with either \left/ or \right/.

```
$$\left.\frac{c+1}d\right/x^2$$
```                    $$\frac{c+1}{d}\bigg/x^2$$

It is important for the \left/ or \right/ to enclose the large part of the formula, since the size of the delimiters is based on what goes between \left and \right.

• **Exercise 14.16:**
How should the displayed formula

$$x^2 \left/ \frac{c+1}{d} \right.$$

be typeset?

Despite the convenience of \left...\right constructions, there are certain occasions when you will want to specify the exact size of delimiters yourself. For example, TeX has \bigl and \bigr to give delimiters just slightly bigger than ordinary ones:

$\bigl(x-s(x)\bigr)\bigl(y-s(y)\bigr)$ $\bigl(x - s(x)\bigr)\bigl(y - s(y)\bigr)$

$\bigl[x-s[x]\bigr]\bigl[y-s[y]\bigr]$ $\bigl[x - s[x]\bigr]\bigl[y - s[y]\bigr]$

$\bigl|\ |x|+|y|\ \bigr|$ $\bigl\|\,|x| + |y|\,\bigr\|$

$\bigl\lfloor\sqrt A\bigr\rfloor$ $\bigl\lfloor\sqrt A\bigr\rfloor$

Here \left and \right would not have the same effect, since they don't make things any bigger than necessary; the input

$\left[x-s[x]\right]\left[y-s[y]\right]$

would simply yield $[x - s[x]]\,[y - s[y]]$.

(There's one other important difference between \bigl and \bigr and \left and \right: Although the constructions \bigl] and \bigr[cause TeX to regard the big] as a left delimiter, and the big [as a right delimiter, \bigl and \bigr *do not* group things; you can even have a \bigl in a formula without a matching \bigr.)

Although \big delimiters can do wonders for the readability of certain formulas, they may not go over too big with the copy editors of mathematical books and journals, where standard size parentheses have been nestling next to each other for ages. In a formula like $(x + f(x))^2$ there's really no need to use bigger parentheses for the outer pair, just as there is no need to raise the superscript ^{2} any higher. So use \big delimiters with restraint. Mathematicians are so used to the old style that they may discomforted by the "improvements".

There are also times when \left...\right gives delimiters that are too *big*, namely when you use \left and \right to enclose a \sum with limits:

$$\left(\sum_{k=1}^n A_k \right)^2$$

It usually looks better to let the limits protrude slightly beyond the parentheses,

$$\biggl(\sum_{k=1}^n A_k\biggr)^2$$

so you need to request a specific size. In addition to the `\bigl` and `\bigr` delimiters, which are just a little bigger than ordinary ones, TEX also has `\biggl` and `\biggr` delimiters. These delimiters are the size that TEX would choose around a formula that is two lines tall:

```
$$\left[\frac bd\right]$$
$$\biggl[\frac bd\biggr]$$
```

$$\left[\frac bd\right]$$

and they are also the ones you should usually use around `\sum`:

```
$$\biggl( \sum_{k=1}^n A_k \biggr)^2$$
```

$$\biggl(\sum_{k=1}^n A_k\biggr)^2$$

• **Exercise 14.17:**
Typeset the following:

(1)
$$\biggl(\sum_{i=1}^n x_iy_i\biggr)^2 = \sum_{i=1}^n (x_iy_i)^2 + \sum_{i\neq j} x_iy_ix_jy_j$$

(2)
$$\pi(n) = \sum_{m=2}^n \Biggl\lfloor\biggl(\sum_{k=1}^{m-1} \lfloor(m/k)/\lceil m/k\rceil\rfloor\biggr)^{-1}\Biggr\rfloor$$

(3)
$$m^*\Biggl(A\cap\biggl[\bigcup_{i=1}^n E_i\biggr]\Biggr) = \sum_{i=1}^n m^*(A\cap E_i)$$

• **Exercise 14.18:**
How would you typeset the following?

(1)
$$\left(\sqrt{\frac{A}{B}} + \sum_{i=1}^N a_i\right)^2$$

(2)
$$f\left(\sum_{i=1}^n p_ix_i\right) \le \sum_{i=1}^n p_if(x_i)$$

Chapter 15. A Roman Orgy

In math formulas, TEX automatically sets letters in italics, but sometimes you want ordinary roman letters, as in the formula

$$y = f(x + \text{constant})$$

$\mathcal{A}_{\mathcal{M}}\mathcal{S}$-TEX allows you to duck out of math mode for a moment by means of \text: you can get the above formula by typing

```
$$y=f(x+\text{constant})$$
```

In this formula the whole construction \text{constant} is treated simply as an ordinary symbol like x or y, and the spacing is determined accordingly.

Notice that \text is a control sequence with an argument, and only the argument is returned to ordinary text; things that come after the argument are back in math mode. So if you type

```
$$f(x)=x^{17}+\text{lower order terms}+e^x$$
```

you'll get

$$f(x) = x^{17} + \text{lower order terms} + e^x$$

- **Exercise 15.1:**
Typeset the following:

$$g(x) = f(x + \text{constant}) + f(x - \text{constant})$$

Within \text you can change fonts, just as in ordinary text. For example, if you type

```
$$f(x)=x^{17}+\text{terms of {\it different\/} order.}$$
```

you will get

$$f(x) = x^{17} + \text{terms of } \textit{different} \text{ order.}$$

Here {\it different\/} occurs within \text, so the result is no *different* from what you get when you type {\it different\/} in text. On the other hand, if you simply typed $different$ you'd get the formula $different$, which looks quite weird, partly because the italic letters used in math formulas are a little wider, but mainly because the spacing, appropriate for formulas rather than text, is *quite different* in many cases.

● **Exercise 15.2:**

What is wrong with typing the following?

    $$y=f(x+{\text constant})$$

(For some reason this is a very common error among beginning $\mathcal{A}_{\mathcal{M}}\mathcal{S}$-TEX users.)

When you are mixing formulas with \text'ual stuff, it's important to remember that spaces always die of exposure in math mode. So if you want to typeset the displayed formula

$$\Gamma(n) = (n-1)! \qquad \text{when } n \text{ is an integer}$$

you'd better not type

    $$\Gamma(n)=(n-1)!\qquad\text{when} n \text{is an integer}$$

or you will get

$$\Gamma(n) = (n-1)! \qquad \text{when} n \text{is an integer} \qquad !$$

Instead you have to type

    $$\Gamma(n)=(n-1)!\qquad\text{when }n\text{ is an integer}$$

Now the space after **when** and the space before **is** both survive, since they were typed within the protective environment of \text.

Fortunately, there's a much more straightforward way to get the spacing right in such situations. Not only can you switch fonts within \text, you can also switch right back into math mode, so that you can have math within \text within math! Thus, you can type

    $$
    \Gamma(n)=(n-1)! \qquad \text{when n is an integer}
    $$

At first this may be a little confusing, but you'll soon get used to the idea of nesting modes inside of each other like those

● **Exercise 15.3:**

Typeset the following:

$$F_n = F_{n-1} + F_{n-2} \qquad \text{for every } n > 1.$$

• **Exercise 15.4:**

Typeset formula (1) of Exercise 13.3 as $1\,\mathrm{ml} = 1.000028\,\mathrm{cc}$ and typeset formula (3) as $0°\,\mathrm{C} = 32°\,\mathrm{F}$.

• **Exercise 15.5:**

What do you think happens if you compound the mistake of Exercise 15.2, and type the following?

```
$$\Gamma(n)=(n-1)!\qquad{\text when $n$ is an integer}$$
```

There's one important difference between math formulas `$...$` that appear in ordinary text and those that appear in the `\text` of a displayed formula: in the latter case, math formulas are automatically set in d-size. Thus, if you type

```
$$
f(a)>f(b)\qquad\text{provided that $\frac a{b+1}>\sqrt3$}.
$$
```

you'll get

$$f(a) > f(b) \qquad \text{provided that } \frac{a}{b+1} > \sqrt{3}.$$

Since we're in a display, which already takes up extra space, there's really not much point trying to save space by setting the formula $\frac{a}{b+1} > \sqrt{3}$ in t-size. So $\mathcal{A}_{\mathcal{M}}S$-TEX automatically gives you d-size (though you can always get t-size by using `$\tsize...$` within `\text`).

• **Exercise 15.6:**

Typeset the following:

> We have

$$\frac{(n+1)^{p+1}}{p+1} = \sum_{k=1}^{n} k^p + \text{terms involving} \sum_{k=1}^{n} k^r \text{ for } r < p.$$

> It follows by induction that

$$\frac{\sum_{k=1}^{n} k^p}{n^{p+1}} = \frac{1}{p+1} + \text{terms involving negative powers of } n.$$

Mathematicians often allow text to wander quite freely within their displayed formulas, so you sometimes have to use considerable judgment to choose proper spacing. Authors ought to help out, by indicating where larger and smaller spaces are appropriate, but TEXnical typists still have to express their intentions in terms of standard TEX spacing.

● **Exercise 15.7:**
Decide how the displayed formulas

$$X_n = X_k \quad \text{if and only if} \quad Y_n = Y_k \quad \text{and} \quad Z_n = Z_k$$

and

$$Y_n = X_n + 1 \quad \text{and} \quad Z_n = X_n - 1 \qquad \text{for all } n \geq 0.$$

can be typeset.

There's one other important difference between \text and ordinary text: \text{...} creates just *one line* of text, an unbreakable unit that can't be re-arranged into a paragraph. This is usually just what you want in a display, but sometimes a side condition is so long that it has to be set as a small paragraph of text; this contingency is discussed in Part 3.

If you use \text within non-displayed formulas, any math formulas $...$ within \text just get set in t-size. But it isn't a very good idea to use \text this way, since you get an unbreakable line of text, with a good chance of creating an Overfull box. Usually the best strategy is to slip in and out of math mode.

● **Exercise 15.8:**
What would be the best way to typeset the following?

Everyone would like to know whether or not the set $\{p : p$ and $p + 2$ are prime $\}$ is infinite or not!

(Use a plain : for the colon in this formula, but put thin spaces between the braces and the rest of the formula—this "set notation" is discussed in Part 3.)

Although \text isn't very useful for in-line formulas, \text can be extremely useful in superscripts and second order superscripts, because the roman letters change size in the same way that italic letters of math formulas change size. (The bold face letters also change size, but slanted letters don't, because the fonts don't include slanted letters of the appropriate size.)

● **Exercise 15.9:**
How can the phrase "the nth Fibonacci number F_n" be typeset?

• **Exercise 15.10:**

Typeset the following displayed formula:

$$\sum_{l \text{ odd}} \binom{n}{l} = 2^{n-1}$$

• **Exercise 15.11:**

Although the notation f', f'' and f''' is standard, many printers use $f^{(\mathrm{iv})}$, $f^{(\mathrm{v})}$, $f^{(\mathrm{vi})}$, ... instead of f'''', f''''', f'''''', ..., because it gets too hard to count so many ′s. How would you typeset such formulas?

• **Exercise 15.12:**

See what happens if you have `$2^\text {nd}$` in your file, instead of the correct input `$2^{\text {nd}}$`.

We've been pretending that `\text` always puts things in roman type, but that's not quite correct. When you use `\text` in a display, or for an in-line formula, the font it chooses is actually the "current font". For example, if you are displaying a formula in the statement of a theorem, and you are using the `amsppt` style, so that `\proclaim` selects slanted type, then `\text` will set things in slanted type also. If you switch to another style, which uses a different font for `\proclaim`, the font for `\text` will change automatically. This is usually the sort of behavior that's expected when you use `\text` in a side condition. If roman letters are definitely desired, you can type `\text{\rm...}` when `\text` appears in a construction that might change the font. On the other hand, when you use `\text` in a superscript, the roman font is automatically selected, since in this case you are probably using `\text` explicitly to get smaller roman letters in math mode.

By now it might seem that `\text` allows you to get just about any sort of roman type into formulas that you would ever need. But roman letters have an important special use in mathematical formulas, one that works quite differently than ordinary text. Although the operators "summation" and "integration" are indicated by the symbols $\sum$ and $\int$, many common mathematical operators, like "sine", "cosine" and "logarithm" are simply indicated by abbreviations—"sin", "cos" and "log". Roman type is usually used in such cases, but it would be a nuisance to type `\text{sin}` every time you wanted "sin" to appear in a formula. And it would be more than a mere nuisance to try to specify the proper spacing in the formulas $\sin 2x$ and $\sin(2x)$ [there is a thin space after the 'sin' in the first case, but not in the second]. So $\mathcal{A}\mathcal{M}\mathcal{S}$-TEX has the control sequences `\sin`, `\cos` and \log that do all this for you:

$\sin2\theta=2\sin\theta\cos\theta$	$\sin 2\theta = 2\sin\theta\cos\theta$
$\sin(2x)=2\sin x\cos x$	$\sin(2x) = 2\sin x \cos x$
$x=e^{\,\log x}$	$x = e^{\log x}$

(The last formula shows a situation where a thin space can be helpful.)

The operators in the above examples are treated like $\int$ rather than $\sum$: any subscripts and superscripts are placed to the side of the operator, even in displays:

$$\sin^2x+\cos^2x=1$$	$\sin^2 x + \cos^2 x = 1$
$$\log_2x=(\log_2 e)(\log x)$$	$\log_2 x = (\log_2 e)(\log x)$

Notice that $\sin^2$, $\cos^2$ and $\log_2$ are automatically treated as new mathematical operators, so that there is a thin space in the expression $\sin^2 x$.

There are other common mathematical operators that are treated like $\sum$, with sub and superscripts appearing below and above in displays:

$$\max_{1<n<m}\log_2P$$	$\displaystyle\max_{1<n<m}\log_2 P$
$$\lim_{x\to 0}\frac{\sin x}x=1$$	$\displaystyle\lim_{x\to0}\frac{\sin x}{x}=1$
$$\frac{\max_{1<n<m}\log_2P_n}{\lim_{x\to0}(\sin x/x)}$$	$\dfrac{\max_{1<n<m}\log_2 P_n}{\lim_{x\to0}(\sin x/x)}$

* **Exercise 15.13:**
Explain how to change the last of these examples to the following.

$$\frac{\displaystyle\max_{1<n<m}\log_2 P_n}{\displaystyle\lim_{x\to0}\frac{\sin x}{x}}$$

* **Exercise 15.14:**
Explain how to typeset the following formulas.

(1)
$$\lim_{x\to0}\frac{\sin^2 ax}{\sin^2 bx}=\left(\frac{a}{b}\right)^2$$

(2)
$$\lim_{x\to\infty} x\sin\frac{1}{x}=\lim_{x\to\infty}\frac{\sin\dfrac{1}{x}}{\dfrac{1}{x}}=\lim_{x\to0^+}\frac{\sin x}{x}$$

(3)
$$\frac{1}{2} + \cos x + \cos 2x + \cdots + \cos nx = \frac{\sin(n+\frac{1}{2})x}{2\sin\frac{x}{2}}$$

(4)
$$(\log \circ f)' = f'/f$$

(5)
$$\lim_{x \to 0^+} x(\log x)^n = 0$$

(6)
$$\lim_{h \to 0^+} \int_{-1}^{1} \frac{h}{h^2 + x^2} = \lim_{h \to 0^+} \arctan \frac{x}{h}\Big|_{-1}^{1} = \pi$$

(7)
$$\arctan \tfrac{1}{2} + \arctan \tfrac{1}{3} = \arctan \left(\frac{\frac{1}{2}+\frac{1}{3}}{1-\frac{1}{6}}\right) = \frac{\pi}{4}$$

(8)
$$l - m = \lim_{\substack{n \to \infty \\ n \text{ even}}} \frac{2 - a_n^2}{1 + a_n} = \frac{2 - m^2}{1 + m}$$

● **Exercise 15.15:**
How could you typeset the following horrendous formula (which actually occurs in the answer book for a calculus text)?

$$\delta = \min \left(\sin^2 \left(\frac{[\min(1, \varepsilon/10)]^2}{9} \right) + \min(1, \varepsilon/10), \; [\min(1, \varepsilon/6)]^2 \right)$$

● **Exercise 15.16:**
Speaking of horrendous formulas, how would the formulas

$$\int_{k\pi+\pi/2-\delta}^{k\pi+\pi/2+\delta} \left| \frac{\sin x}{x} \right| dx \geq \frac{\delta}{k\pi + \pi/2}$$

and

$$\lim_{x \to \infty} \frac{\int_x^{x+\frac{\log x}{2x}} e^{t^2} dt}{e^{x^2}} = \lim_{x \to \infty} \frac{e^{\left(x+\frac{\log x}{2x}\right)^2} - e^{x^2}}{2xe^{x^2}} = \frac{1}{2}$$

be typeset?

You can use \limits and \nolimits after \max or \lim, with the same effect they would have after \sum. (But \limits and \nolimits have no effect after \sin, \cos and \log; these operators *never* have subscripts and superscripts set as limits.)

● **Exercise 15.17:**
Redo Exercise 15.13, using \limits.

Here are some of the operators that $\mathcal{A}_{\mathcal{M}}\mathcal{S}$-TEX knows about; those that can have subscripts and superscripts set as "limits" are preceded by (L):

\arccos	\cot	\exp	(L)\lim	\sec
\arcsin	\coth	(L)\gcd	\ln	\sin
\arctan	\csc	\hom	\log	\sinh
\arg	\deg	(L)\inf	(L)\max	(L)\sup
\cos	(L)\det	\ker	(L)\min	\tan
\cosh	\dim	\lg	(L)\Pr	\tanh

All of these control sequences produce just what their names say. $\mathcal{A}_{\mathcal{M}}\mathcal{S}$-TEX also has \liminf, \limsup, \injlim and \projlim, which produce the operators 'lim inf', 'lim sup', 'inj lim' and 'proj lim'. Some mathematicians use the variant forms

`$\varliminf$`	$\varliminf$
`$\varlimsup$`	$\varlimsup$
`$\varinjlim$`	$\varinjlim$
`$\varprojlim$`	$\varprojlim$

This list may look impressive, but it's hardly inclusive, because mathematicians are continually inventing new operators of their own. If a manuscript seems to have recurrent abbreviations in the formulas, like 'trace', 'Tor', 'ISO' or 'Res', there's a good chance that the author is using these as new operators. To get TEX to typeset Tor in roman type and also treat it as a new operator, just type

    \operatorname{Tor}

And use \operatornamewithlimits if you want an operator 'Res' which has "limits":

    $$\operatornamewithlimits{Res}
      _{x=0}\frac{f(x)}x$$

$$\operatorname*{Res}_{x=0}\frac{f(x)}{x}$$

Of course, you don't want to keep typing such monstrosities over and over again. If 'Tor' or 'Res' occur several times in a paper, you'll want to define your own control sequences \Tor and \Res, as explained in Part 3.

When an `\operatorname` has two parts, like 'lim inf' and 'lim sup', it usually looks better when there is only a thin space `\,` between the two parts.

● **Exercise 15.18:**
Some authors use 'arg sinh' instead of $\sinh^{-1}$. How should you typeset this?

Although spaces have to be inserted specifically within `\operatorname` and `\operatornamewithlimits`, any ` or ' or * or - or / will be treated as in text, with `` and '' giving " and " and -- and --- giving – and — . Periods, commas and colons will be followed by a small amount of space.

Aside from the proper spacing produced by `\sin`, `\cos`, ..., and any new gadgets that you produce with `\operatorname`, there's another important way that these operators differ from `\text`: they are normally set in roman type even if the current font is something different.

● **Exercise 15.19:**
Sometimes operator names are set in different fonts. For example, many mathematicians use $SO(n)$ and $SU(n)$ instead of $\mathrm{SO}(n)$ and $\mathrm{SU}(n)$, while others prefer $\mathbf{SO}(n)$ and $\mathbf{SU}(n)$. How would you obtain these?

Chapter 16. Keeping Them In Line

We can now specify most of the combinations of math symbols that are needed in formulas, and we can use double dollar signs \$\$ to get displayed formulas. But mathematical works often contain various combinations of formulas in displays, and this requires special treatment.

First of all, mathematicians frequently like to give their formulas a number, or some other kind of tag. Some journals place these tags to the left of the formula:

(3-1) $$x = y$$

while others put them on the right:

$$x = y \tag{3-1}$$

To produce the above formulas with a tag, just type

```
$$x=y\tag3-1$$
```

$\mathcal{A}_{\mathcal{M}}\mathcal{S}$-TEX will automatically choose the appropriate placement for the tag, and it will put the tag on a separate line if the formula is too long:
(3-1)
  a very long formula ...   ... ending here

Notice that it is not necessary to type `...\tag{3-1}$$` with braces around the tag: $\mathcal{A}_{\mathcal{M}}\mathcal{S}$-TEX knows that the tag is everything between `\tag` and the \$\$. Notice also that the parentheses around the tag are put in automatically; some formats might have something different, like [3-1] or **3-1**, etc. Finally, notice that tags are processed as ordinary text, rather than as formulas in math mode, so that - and -- give a hyphen and an en-dash, rather than one or two minus signs.

• **Exercise 16.1:**
The mathematician I. Settit liked to have punctuation after Eir displayed formulas, but when E tried to type the formula

(3-2) $$x = y,$$

it came out as:

((3-2),) $$x = y$$

What mistakes did E make?

● **Exercise 16.2:**
What should you do if you need a tag like A'?

● **Exercise 16.3:**
And how about tags like $(*)$, $(**)$ and $(***)$?

> The `amsppt` style places tags on the left, but in Part 3 we explain how to get tags
> on the right if you prefer.

Frequently, a display will contain several formulas in which certain symbols
are aligned. For example, consider the following displayed formulas:

$$(1) \qquad \max(f,g) = \frac{f+g+|f-g|}{2},$$

$$(2) \qquad \max(f,-g) = \frac{f-g+|f+g|}{2}.$$

Here the $=$ signs are aligned, and the two formulas are centered as a unit. This
output was produced using $\mathcal{A}_{\mathcal{M}}\mathcal{S}$-TEX's \align:

```
$$\align
  \max(f,g)   &=\frac{f+g+|f-g|}2,  \tag1  \\
  \max(f,-g)  &=\frac{f-g+|f+g|}2.  \tag2
\endalign$$
```

Between \align and \endalign the individual formulas are separated by \\
(no \\ is needed after the final formula). Each formula also contains an &
that goes between the part of the formula that will be on the left hand side &
the part that will be on the right. The \tag on any formula is optional.

When you use \align...\endalign, TEX lines up the individual formulas,
and then sets each one as a line the whole width of the page (although such a
"line" might have a lot of white space in it). Consequently, TEX will issue an
error message if you try to type something like

```
$$
A\align...\endalign B
$$
```

No printed symbols should be specified between the first **$$** and the \align, or
between the \endalign and the final **$$** sign.

In the above example we tried to type things nicely aligned, to make the file
easier to read, but of course that's all unnecessary (and not very practical if the
formulas involve lots of symbols). But to help \align get the spacing just right,
you should remember to type the &'s right *before* the symbols that are being
lined up. Notice also the placement of the comma and period.

- **Exercise 16.4:**
How should you typeset the following?

(1_l)
$$Q^l = Q_1 \left\{ \sum_k (-1)^k (PQ_1 - I)^k \right\}$$

(1_r)
$$Q^r = \left\{ \sum_k (-1)^k (Q_1 P - I)^k \right\} Q_1$$

- **Exercise 16.5:**
See what happens when you leave out the **&** in the second formula.

- **Exercise 16.6:**
Typeset the following.

$$\alpha_4 = \sqrt{\frac{1}{2}}$$

$$\alpha_8 = \sqrt{\frac{1}{2} + \frac{1}{2}\sqrt{\frac{1}{2}}}$$

$$\alpha_{16} = \sqrt{\frac{1}{2} + \frac{1}{2}\sqrt{\frac{1}{2} + \frac{1}{2}\sqrt{\frac{1}{2}}}}$$

etc.

Aligned formulas are usually thought of as a unit, so $\mathcal{A}_{\mathcal{M}}\mathcal{S}$-TEX normally doesn't allow a pagebreak between the formulas of an \align...\endalign construction. However, as we'll see in Part 3, there are numerous ways to tell $\mathcal{A}_{\mathcal{M}}\mathcal{S}$-TEX to allow breaks in a display.

\align enables you to deal with aligned formulas that take up the whole width of the page, but mathematicians sometimes like to squeeze several alignments into a single display:

$$\left\{ \begin{aligned} \alpha &= f(z) \\ \beta &= f(z^2) \\ \gamma &= f(z^3) \end{aligned} \right\} \qquad \left\{ \begin{aligned} x &= \alpha^2 - \beta \\ y &= 2\gamma \end{aligned} \right\}.$$

To handle displays of this sort, $\mathcal{A}_{\mathcal{M}}\mathcal{S}$-TEX gives you \aligned...\endaligned. Unlike \align, which tells TEX to align a sequence of lines the width of the page, the construction \aligned...\endaligned creates a single aligned unit, which is just wide enough for all the formulas involved, and which can be manipulated like any other symbol. For example, the above display was typed as

```
$$
\left\{
\aligned \alpha&=f(z)\\ \beta&=f(z^2)\\
\gamma&=f(z^3)\endaligned
\right\}\qquad\left\{
\aligned x&=\alpha^2-\beta\\ y&=2\gamma\endaligned \right\}.
$$
```

• **Exercise 16.7:**
Typeset the following display.

$$k_1, k_2 = H \pm \sqrt{H^2 - K} \qquad \text{where} \qquad \begin{cases} K = \dfrac{eg - f^2}{EG - F^2} \\ H = \dfrac{Eg - 2Ff + Ge}{2(EG - F^2)}. \end{cases}$$

When \aligned...\endaligned appears all by itself in a display, it looks just like the result of \align...\endalign. But \tag's work quite differently in the two constructions. In an \align you can put a \tag after each formula, and you *can't* put a \tag after the \endalign. In an \aligned, the situation is exactly the opposite: since it's all one unit, you can't \tag individual lines, but you *can* put a \tag after the \endaligned. For example, the input

```
$$\aligned \alpha&=f(z)\\
     \beta&=f(z^2)\\
        \gamma&=f(z^3)\endaligned\tag 22
  $$
```

gives

$$
\begin{aligned}
\alpha &= f(z) \\
\beta &= f(z^2) \\
\gamma &= f(z^3)
\end{aligned}
\tag{22}
$$

Notice that the tag is now centered on the whole \aligned unit.

- **Exercise 16.8:**

How should the following numbered two-line display be typeset?

$$(23) \qquad \begin{aligned} K &= \frac{eg - f^2}{EG - F^2} \\ H &= \frac{Eg - 2Ff + Ge}{2(EG - F^2)} \end{aligned}$$

- **Exercise 16.9:**

See what happens when you have a file containing

```
$$\aligned A&=B \\ C&=D$$
```

with the `\endaligned` missing, as the only line of text.

Every once in a while an author wants to gather together several formulas and display them all centered, instead of aligned:

$$a = b + c$$
$$d = e$$
$$f + g = h$$

If you typed this as three separate displayed formulas,

```
$$a=b+c$$  $$d=e$$  $$f+g=h$$
```

there would be too much space between them. So instead use `\gather`:

```
$$
\gather a=b+c\\  d=e\\
    f+g=h\endgather
$$
```

As usual, `\\` indicates line breaks, but within `\gather` the formulas must not have `&`'s in them, since nothing is being aligned. As with `\align`, you can use `\tag` on any formula.

- **Exercise 16.10:**

Typeset the following:

$$(3\text{-}2) \qquad g = \det(g_{ij})$$

$$(3\text{-}3) \qquad g^{kl} = (k, l) \text{ entry of the inverse matrix of } (g_{ij})$$

$\mathcal{A}_{\mathcal{M}}\mathcal{S}$-TEX also gives you `\gathered...\endgathered`, which bears the same relation to `\gather` as `\aligned` bears to `\align`. In other words, the construction `\gathered...\endgathered` produces a unit that can be treated as a new symbol—it can be used within other formulas, and can be given a `\tag`, which is centered with respect to the whole unit.

• **Exercise 16.11:**

Typeset the following:

We have $(a + bi)^2 = \alpha + \beta i$ if and only if

$$a^2 - b^2 = \alpha$$

(*)

$$2ab = \beta,$$

which can be solved to give

$$\left. \begin{array}{l} a = \sqrt{2\alpha + 2\sqrt{\alpha^2 + \beta^2}} \\[2ex] b = \dfrac{\beta}{2\sqrt{2\alpha + 2\sqrt{\alpha^2 + \beta^2}}} \end{array} \right\} \quad \text{or} \quad \left\{ \begin{array}{l} a = -\sqrt{2\alpha + 2\sqrt{\alpha^2 + \beta^2}} \\[2ex] b = \dfrac{-\beta}{2\sqrt{2\alpha + 2\sqrt{\alpha^2 + \beta^2}}}. \end{array} \right.$$

Chapter 17. Too Much Of A Good Thing

Sometimes a displayed formula can't be printed on a single line because it just won't fit, no matter how much TEX tries to squeeze things:

$$(a+b)^{n+1} = (a+b)(a+b)^n = (a+b)\sum_{j=0}^{n}\binom{n}{j}a^{n-1}b^j = \sum_{j=0}^{n}\binom{n}{j}a^{n+1-j}b^j + \sum_{j=1}^{n}\binom{n}{j-1}a^{n-j}b^j$$

This formula is really a lot of smaller formulas concatenated, and in such cases it is customary to break the long formula by lining up some of the relational symbols. In this way, we can fit even longer formulas into a single display:

$$(a+b)^{n+1} = (a+b)(a+b)^n = (a+b)\sum_{j=0}^{n}\binom{n}{j}a^{n-1}b^j$$
$$= \sum_{j=0}^{n}\binom{n}{j}a^{n+1-j}b^j + \sum_{j=1}^{n}\binom{n}{j-1}a^{n-j}b^j$$
$$= \sum_{j=0}^{n}\binom{n+1}{j}a^{n+1-j}b^j.$$

● **Exercise 17.1:**
How do you think you could typeset this display?

Exercise 17.1 shows how a little ingenuity can go a long way, but matters become more complicated when a split formula of this sort needs to be given a tag. If tags are placed on the left, it is customary for the formula to be typeset as

$$(1\text{--}2) \qquad (a+b)^{n+1} = (a+b)(a+b)^n = (a+b)\sum_{j=0}^{n}\binom{n}{j}a^{n-1}b^j$$
$$= \sum_{j=0}^{n}\binom{n}{j}a^{n+1-j}b^j + \sum_{j=1}^{n}\binom{n}{j-1}a^{n-j}b^j$$
$$= \sum_{j=0}^{n}\binom{n+1}{j}a^{n+1-j}b^j$$

but when tags are placed on the right it would be typeset as

$$(a+b)^{n+1} = (a+b)(a+b)^n = (a+b)\sum_{j=0}^{n}\binom{n}{j}a^{n-1}b^j$$

$$= \sum_{j=0}^{n}\binom{n}{j}a^{n+1-j}b^j + \sum_{j=1}^{n}\binom{n}{j-1}a^{n-j}b^j$$

$$= \sum_{j=0}^{n}\binom{n+1}{j}a^{n+1-j}b^j \tag{1--2}$$

So $\mathcal{A}_{\mathcal{M}}\mathcal{S}$-TEX gives you \split, which enables you to typeset the tags on a split formula without worrying about the conventions that the format will use: If you type

```
$$
\split
(a+b)^{n+1}
  &=(a+b)(a+b)^n=(a+b)
    \sum_{j=0}^n\binom nj a^{n-1}b^j\\
  &=\sum_{j=0}^n\binom nja^{n+1-j}b^j+
    \sum_{j=1}^n\binom n{j-1} a^{n-j}b^j\\
  &=\sum_{j=0}^n\binom{n+1}j
      a^{n+1-j}b^j\endsplit\tag1--2
$$
```

then $\mathcal{A}_{\mathcal{M}}\mathcal{S}$-TEX will automatically produce whatever output is appropriate for your format.

Note that the \tag comes after the **entire** construction \split...\endsplit; if you try to put the \tag on a particular line, you'll get an inscrutable error message, because $\mathcal{A}_{\mathcal{M}}\mathcal{S}$-TEX treats the \split...\endsplit construction as a single unit. Notice also that our line breaks are made *before* binary relations, whereas formulas in text are usually broken *after* binary relations.

- **Exercise 17.2:**
Suppose that you want to have TEX typeset

(1) $$(a+b)(a+b) = a^2 + 2ab + b^2,$$

(2) $$(a+b)(a-b) = (a+b)a - (a+b)b$$
$$= a^2 + ab - ab - b^2$$
$$= a^2 - b^2.$$

when tags are set on the left, but

$$(a+b)(a+b) = a^2 + 2ab + b^2, \tag{1}$$

$$(a+b)(a-b) = (a+b)a - (a+b)b$$
$$= a^2 + ab - ab - b^2$$
$$= a^2 - b^2. \tag{2}$$

when tags are set on the right. What input do you think you should you use?

Sometimes a formula has to be split in ways that don't seem to involve any alignment:

$$(f \circ g)'''(x) = \left[f'''(g(x)) \cdot g'(x)^3 + 2f''(g(x)) \cdot g'(x)g''(x) \right]$$
$$+ \left[f''(g(x)) \cdot g'(x)g''(x) + f'(g(x)) \cdot g'''(x) \right]$$

In such cases it is customary to leave at least two quads of space before the second part of the formula. The above formula was typed as

```
$$\split
(f\circ g)'''(x)&=\bigl[f'''(g(x))\cdot g'(x)^3+
                 2f''(g(x))\cdot g'(x)g''(x)\bigr]\\
  &\qquad+\bigl[f''(g(x))\cdot g'(x)g''(x)
         +f'(g(x))\cdot g'''(x)\bigr]
\endsplit
$$
```

so that the `\bigl[` is aligned with the invisible `\qquad`. Notice, again, that such a split is normally made *before* binary operators, although formulas in text are usually broken *after* binary operators.

• **Exercise 17.3:**
How do you think the following was typeset?

$$\Delta = [a+b+c]^n (a_{11} + b_{11} + c_{11}$$
$$+ a_{12} + b_{12} + c_{12} + a_{22} + b_{22} + c_{22}).$$

Elaborate sets of rules for breaking and setting displayed formulas can be compiled, but they vary from printer to printer, and in any case they are never really adequate. TeX doesn't even attempt to break long displayed formulas, because this is an art—the author of a mathematical manuscript should really determine all breaks, since they depend on subtle factors of mathematical exposition. (Of course, it's often difficult for the author to foresee the need for breaks, so the judgment of the experienced TeXnical typist can also be invaluable.)

The following display illustrates one other printing convention that you should know about:

$$
\int_a^b \left\{ \int_a^b [f(x)^2 g(y)^2 + f(y)^2 g(x)^2 - 2f(x)g(x)f(y)g(y)\, dx \right\} dy
$$

$$
= \int_a^b \left\{ g(y)^2 \int_a^b f^2 + f(y)^2 \int_a^b g^2 - 2f(y)g(y) \int_a^b fg \right\} dy
$$

Here the first line was placed almost flush left and the second line was placed almost flush right. This was typed using $\mathcal{A}_{\mathcal{M}}\mathcal{S}$-TEX's \multline:

```
$$
\multline
\int_a^b\biggl\{\int_a^b[f(x)^2g(y)^2+f(y)^2g(x)^2
  -2f(x)g(x)f(y)g(y)\,dx\biggr\}\,dy  \\
   =\int_a^b\biggl\{g(y)^2\int_a^bf^2+f(y)^2
       \int_a^b g^2-2f(y)g(y)\int_a^b fg\biggr\}\,dy
\endmultline
$$
```

The precise distance from the margin is determined by the format. In the amsppt style it is one quad of space; some formats may leave no space at all.

You can put a \tag after \multline...\endmultline, just as you can after \split...\endsplit. For example,

```
$$
\multline
\int_a^b\biggl\{\int_a^b[f(x)^2g(y)^2+f(y)^2g(x)^2
  -2f(x)g(x)f(y)g(y)\,dx\biggr\}\,dy  \\
   =\int_a^b\biggl\{g(y)^2\int_a^bf^2+f(y)^2
       \int_a^b g^2-2f(y)g(y)\int_a^b fg\biggr\}\,dy
\endmultline\tag 17
$$
```

gives either

$$
(17) \qquad \int_a^b \left\{ \int_a^b [f(x)^2 g(y)^2 + f(y)^2 g(x)^2 - 2f(x)g(x)f(y)g(y)\, dx \right\} dy
$$

$$
= \int_a^b \left\{ g(y)^2 \int_a^b f^2 + f(y)^2 \int_a^b g^2 - 2f(y)g(y) \int_a^b fg \right\} dy
$$

or

$$\int_a^b \left\{ \int_a^b [f(x)^2 g(y)^2 + f(y)^2 g(x)^2 - 2f(x)g(x)f(y)g(y)\, dx \right\} dy$$
$$= \int_a^b \left\{ g(y)^2 \int_a^b f^2 + f(y)^2 \int_a^b g^2 - 2f(y)g(y) \int_a^b fg \right\} dy \quad (17)$$

As in the case of \split, you mustn't try to put the \tag on any particular line, it must go after the entire \multline...\endmultline construction. Moreover, \multline creates lines the width of the whole page, just like \align, so you can't put it inside any other construction: nothing should come between the first $$ and the \multline or between the \endmultline and the second $$.

- **Exercise 17.4:**
Typeset the display

$$f^{(k)}(x) = e^{-1/x^2} \left[\sum_{i=1}^{3k} \frac{a_i}{x^i} \sin \frac{1}{x} + \sum_{i=1}^{3k} \frac{b_i}{x^i} \cos \frac{1}{x} \right]$$
for some numbers $a_1, \ldots, a_{3k}, b_1, \ldots, b_{3k}$.

As the name suggests, \multline can be used to create displays with several lines. All lines except the first and last are centered, although there is also a provision for shoving any of these to the left or right. Details of this sort will be found in Part 3.

Of course, mathematicians actually like to create even more perverse displays than any of the ones we've dealt with so far. But that, fortunately, can be left to the next, and final, chapter of this Part.

Chapter 18. Sophisticated Positions

Mathematicians like to have a computer typesetting system that makes it easy for them to produce all sorts of displays, but what really turns them on is the possiblity of typesetting "matrices". These are the rectangular arrays that appear in formulas like

$$A = \begin{pmatrix} x-\lambda & 1 & 0 \\ 0 & x-\lambda & 1 \\ 0 & 0 & x-\lambda \end{pmatrix}.$$

A matrix can be produced painlessly using $\mathcal{A}_{\mathcal{M}}\mathcal{S}$-TEX's \matrix...\endmatrix construction: to get the above formula you simply type

```
$$
A=\left( \matrix
x-\lambda & 1 & 0\\
0 & x-\lambda & 1\\
0 & 0 & x-\lambda
\endmatrix \right).
$$
```

Notice that \matrix is a bit like \aligned—in each row you put & between the 1st & 2nd & 3rd & ... elements, and you use \\ to separate the various rows. But there are also important differences: in a \matrix the elements within each column are centered, and there is a \quad of space between the columns. In addition, the entries of a \matrix are normally set in t-size and the space between the lines is the same as the space between lines of text, while the entries of an \align or \aligned are normally set in d-size and the lines are spread apart a little more.

Mathematicians seldom use matrices without enclosing them in parentheses or some other delimiters, and $\mathcal{A}_{\mathcal{M}}\mathcal{S}$-TEX has several other control sequences to provide these delimiters for you. The above display could also have been typed as

```
$$
A=\pmatrix
x-\lambda & 1 & 0\\
0 & x-\lambda & 1\\
0 & 0 & x-\lambda
\endpmatrix.
$$
```

And there's \bmatrix...\endbmatrix to get brackets\left[...\right] around the matrix, \vmatrix...\endvmatrix to get vertical lines \left|...\right|, and \Vmatrix...\endVmatrix to get the double vertical lines you would get with \left\|...\right\|. Caution: If you start with \pmatrix, but end with \endmatrix, then you have essentially specified a formula with \left(at the beginning, but no matching \right⟨delimiter⟩ at the end, so you will get an error message.

- **Exercise 18.1:**
Typeset the following:

$$(\text{I}.3) \qquad \begin{pmatrix} a & b \\ c & d \end{pmatrix} \cdot \begin{pmatrix} 0 & 1 \\ 1 & 0 \end{pmatrix} = \begin{pmatrix} a \cdot 0 + b \cdot 1 & a \cdot 1 + b \cdot 0 \\ a \cdot 0 + d \cdot 1 & c \cdot 1 + d \cdot 0 \end{pmatrix}$$
$$= \begin{pmatrix} b & a \\ d & c \end{pmatrix}$$

- **Exercise 18.2:**
Typeset the following matrix of matrices,

$$\begin{pmatrix} 1 & 0 \\ 0 & 0 \end{pmatrix} \qquad \begin{pmatrix} 0 & 1 \\ 0 & 0 \end{pmatrix}$$

$$\begin{pmatrix} 0 & 0 \\ 1 & 0 \end{pmatrix} \qquad \begin{pmatrix} 0 & 0 \\ 0 & 1 \end{pmatrix}$$

where there are *two* quads of space between the columns, and two blank rows between the printed rows.

- **Exercise 18.3:**
How can you typeset the following matrix? *Hint:* $\mathcal{A}_{\mathcal{M}}\mathcal{S}$-TEX has \hdots for horizontal dots, \vdots for vertical dots, and \ddots for diagonal dots.

$$\begin{pmatrix} a_{11} & a_{12} & \cdots & a_{1n} \\ a_{21} & a_{22} & \cdots & a_{2n} \\ \vdots & \vdots & \ddots & \vdots \\ a_{m1} & a_{m2} & \cdots & a_{mn} \end{pmatrix}$$

In some situations it may not be desirable to center the entries of a \matrix within each column. For example, in the parenthesized matrix

$$\begin{pmatrix} \cos\theta & \sin\theta \\ -\sin\theta & \cos\theta \end{pmatrix}$$

some printers might prefer to have the columns set flush right, and in the matrix

$$\begin{matrix} x & .1 & 1 \\ x+y & .11 & 11 \\ x+y+z & .111 & 111 \end{matrix}$$

the decimals in the second column are set flush left, while the numbers in the third column are set flush right. $\mathcal{A}_{\mathcal{M}}\mathcal{S}$-TeX has a special \format...\\ construction to specify a matrix with some new format. The above matrix was typed as

```
$$\matrix \format\c&\quad\l&\quad\r\\
x&.1&1\\
   . . .
\endmatrix$$
```

The \format "row" \format\c&\quad\l&\quad\r\\ specifies the new format; \c indicates a column in which the elements are centered, while \quad\l indicates a column in which the elements are set flush left, with the whole column preceded by a \quad of space, and \quad\r indicates a column with elements set flush right, again preceded by a \quad of space. You can also use \format with \pmatrix, etc.

- **Exercise 18.4:**
Typeset the following formula:

$$\begin{pmatrix} \cos\theta & \sin\theta \\ -\sin\theta & \cos\theta \end{pmatrix}\begin{pmatrix} \cos\phi & \sin\phi \\ -\sin\phi & \cos\phi \end{pmatrix} = \begin{pmatrix} \cos\rho & \sin\rho \\ -\sin\rho & \cos\rho \end{pmatrix}, \qquad \rho = \theta + \phi.$$

- **Exercise 18.5:**
Typeset the following column of numbers:

$$3.14159$$
$$2.71828$$
$$1.61808$$
$$.57701$$

• **Exercise 18.6:**

Typeset the following, where the columns are flush left.

$$
\det\begin{vmatrix}
c_0 & c_1 & c_2 & \cdots & c_n \\
c_1 & c_2 & c_3 & \cdots & c_{n+1} \\
c_2 & c_3 & c_4 & \cdots & c_{n+2} \\
\vdots & \vdots & \vdots & \ddots & \vdots \\
c_n & c_{n+1} & c_{n+2} & \cdots & c_{2n}
\end{vmatrix} > 0.
$$

• **Exercise 18.7:**

Typeset the following:

$$
\omega = \begin{pmatrix}
0 & \omega_{12} & 0 & & & \cdots & 0 \\
-\omega_{12} & 0 & \omega_{23} & 0 & & \cdots & 0 \\
0 & -\omega_{23} & 0 & \omega_{34} & 0 & \cdots & 0 \\
\vdots & & & & \ddots & & \vdots \\
0 & & \cdots & & 0 & & \omega_{n-1,n} \\
0 & & \cdots & 0 & -\omega_{n-1,n} & & 0
\end{pmatrix}
$$

$\mathcal{A}_{\mathcal{M}}\mathcal{S}$-TeX doesn't have a special control sequence to produce a matrix with braces { } around it, because this is almost never needed. But mathematicians very often define things by cases, using a construction like

$$
f(x) = \begin{cases} x+1, & \text{for } x > 0 \\ x-1, & \text{for } x \leq 0. \end{cases}
$$

You could get this with an appropriate \format and a \left\{ and \right. but $\mathcal{A}_{\mathcal{M}}\mathcal{S}$-TeX has the special construction \cases...\endcases to do it all for you. Just type

```
$$
f(x)=\cases x+1,&\text{for $x>0$}\\
    x-1,&\text{for $x\le0$}.\endcases
$$
```

taking care to get the punctuation right, and remembering to use \text when necessary. Notice, by the way, that the first element should *not* be typed as $x+1$: $\mathcal{A}_{\mathcal{M}}\mathcal{S}$-TeX is already processing the elements of a \matrix or \cases in math mode, and a naked $ sign will lead to complete havoc.

• **Exercise 18.8:**

Typeset the following:

$$f^{(k)}(x) = ax^{m-k}\sin\frac{1}{x}$$

$$+ \sum_{l=k+1}^{2k-1}\left(a_l x^{m-l}\sin\frac{1}{x} + b_l x^{m-l}\cos\frac{1}{x}\right) \pm \begin{cases} x^{m-2k}\sin\frac{1}{x}, & k\text{ even} \\[2ex] x^{m-2k}\cos\frac{1}{x}, & k\text{ odd.} \end{cases}$$

Part 3

Sauces &
Pickles
for special occasions

Chapter 19. Practicing Self Control

$\mathcal{A}_{\mathcal{M}}\mathcal{S}$-TEX comes equipped with dozens of control sequences to handle almost any conceivable mathematical formula. But you can also create new control sequences of your own, which can serve as abbreviations for complicated expressions that occur frequently within a paper. For example, if the formula $\alpha^2 + \beta^2$ occurs over and over again, you might find yourself wishing that you could type some short-hand expression like \ab to stand for it. To do this you simply have to insert

```
\define\ab{\alpha^2+\beta^2}
```

into your input file. Thenceforth, TEX will substitute \alpha^2+\beta^2 whenever it sees \ab, so $\ab$ will give the formula $\alpha^2 + \beta^2$, and $$\ab.$$ will give the displayed formula

$$\alpha^2 + \beta^2.$$

- **Exercise 19.1:**
Assuming that \ab has been \define'd in this way, how would you typeset the formula

$$\sqrt{\alpha^2 + \beta^2} + \sqrt{\gamma^2} \le x + \frac{\alpha^2 + \beta^2}{\gamma}$$

with the least amount of typing?

- **Exercise 19.2:**
And (this is trickier) how about the formulas $2^{\alpha^2+\beta^2}$ and $\Gamma_{\alpha^2+\beta^2}$?

- **Exercise 19.3:**
What happens if you have

```
\define\ab{ \alpha^ 2 +\beta^ 2 }
```

in your file?

The only thing you can \define is a control sequence, so you will get an error message if you mistakenly type

```
\define ab{\alpha^2+\beta^2}
```

In fact, $\mathcal{A}_{\mathcal{M}}\mathcal{S}$-TeX is quite picky about \define, and you will get an error message even if you type

```
\define{\ab}{\alpha^2+\beta^2}
```

—braces aren't allowed around that first control sequence! If you get an error message for one of these reasons and try to coax $\mathcal{A}_{\mathcal{M}}\mathcal{S}$-TeX into continuing by hitting ⟨carriage-return⟩, TeX will do its best to ignore the \define and press onward. But then when you use \ab later, TeX will complain that this is an undefined control sequence—an incorrectly executed \define is usually catastrophic, so you should probably exit immediately and fix things up.

There's nothing special about the name \ab, of course, and many typists will think of some entirely different abbreviation. You might simply use \1 if this is the first abbreviation you make, and you think that \1 will be easy enough to remember. But if you choose this control *symbol* there is one other precaution to be observed: Be sure to type

```
\define\1{\alpha^2+\beta^2}
```

without any extra space between the \1 and the {; an extra space would really louse things up, in ways that we'll discuss later.

Even in ordinary text you might find it useful to \define special control sequences. For example, if the names "de Rham" and "É. Cartan" occur frequently in a paper, you might

```
\define\deRham{de~Rham}
\define\Cartan{\'E.~Cartan}
```

to save yourself a lot of typing and thinking.

- **Exercise 19.4:**
How would you use these control sequences to typeset the following?

> The de Rham cohomology ring $H^*(G)$ had, of course, already essentially been computed by É. Cartan.

- **Exercise 19.5:**
You intend to tell people that there are lots of things that they **must** do, so you'd like to have a control sequence \must that will automatically produce the boldface '**must**'. How should you \define it? (Like Exercise 19.2, this is also a little tricky.)

Substituting a new control sequence for a complicated combination isn't the only use for \define; you can also use it to substitute a new control sequence for a standard control sequence that you don't like the name of. For example, you can type

>   \define\a{\alpha}

so that the short name \a can now be used for \alpha. By the way, this definition illustrates another way that $\mathcal{A}_\mathcal{M}S$-TEX is picky about \define. Even though we are \define'ing \a to stand for the single control sequence \alpha, we *must* have braces around the \alpha; the braces are essential in order for \define to figure out just what the definition is, and if you typed \define\a\alpha it would cause havoc.

- **Exercise 19.6:**

Assuming that you have the correct definition \define\a{\alpha} in your file, how can you type the following formula?

$$\alpha^\alpha + \alpha^{\alpha+\alpha} + \alpha^{\alpha^\alpha} + \sqrt{\alpha^2 + \alpha^3}$$

- **Exercise 19.7:**

And what would happen if you put

>   \define\ab{\a^2+\beta^2}

into your file?

- **Exercise 19.8:**

You might be tempted to

>   \define\a{α}

so that you could simply type \a in text and get α in text. Why would this be a real bad idea?

Although it was easy to tell TEX to use \a to mean \alpha, we're in for a surprise if we try to

>   \define\b{\beta}

When $\mathcal{A}_\mathcal{M}S$-TEX gets to this \define it will issue an error message,[1]

>   ! AmS-TeX error: \b is already defined.

---

[1] This error message comes with a little pronouncement, to inform you that it is produced by $\mathcal{A}_\mathcal{M}S$-TEX, rather than by TEX itself, but you can treat it just like any other error message.

Ah, yes, \b is indeed already defined: it's the control sequence that we use to get the 'bar-under' accent. (Perhaps you never read about \b because it's in Chapter 6, which you skipped, you snob. Never mind, you can also find \b in the index.)

If you type h or H after you get this error message, you'll find that $\mathcal{A}_{\mathcal{M}}\mathcal{S}$-TEX has ignored your \define, to prevent any conflict. That's sort of a shame, because β's occur frequently, while you may never come upon a single bar-under accent. So $\mathcal{A}_{\mathcal{M}}\mathcal{S}$-TEX also gives you \redefine. If you put

```
\redefine\b{\beta}
```

in your file, then all subsequent occurrences of \b will be replaced by \beta, even though \b originally had a different meaning. If you also want to be able to deal with an occasional bar-under accent, there's a way to arrange that too: if you put

```
\predefine\barunder{\b}
\redefine\b{\beta}
```

in your file, then \barunder will become a new name for the control sequence that produces a bar-under accent, and \b will become a new name for \beta. So you can type $\b$ to get β, and you can type

```
\barunder T\^abit ibn Qorra
```

to get the name 'Tâbit ibn Qorra'. It's essential for the \predefine to occur somewhere before the \redefine (that's why it's called \predefine, right?), but it needn't precede it immediately. Notice also that \predefine is a lot more special than \define and \redefine—within the curly braces you should have nothing but a *single control sequence*.

● **Exercise 19.9:**
You probably also want to have an abbreviation for \gamma, the third letter of the Greek alphabet. Technical typists often choose \g, but if you relish a reputation as an unregenerate logical type, like a mathematician, then you ought to opt for \c. How do you get $\mathcal{A}_{\mathcal{M}}\mathcal{S}$-TEX to accept \c as an abbreviation for \gamma, so that you can keep up this façade?

You might be tempted to use \redefine instead of \define at the very outset, instead of waiting to find out whether $\mathcal{A}_{\mathcal{M}}\mathcal{S}$-TEX accepts your \define, but this would be a very bad idea, because \define allows $\mathcal{A}_{\mathcal{M}}\mathcal{S}$-TEX to save you from errors that you might not be aware of. For example, suppose that we have some large complicated mathematical expression and we decide to call it simply \box, so that we put

```
\define\box{...}
```

into our input file. When $\mathcal{A}_{\mathcal{M}}\mathcal{S}$-TeX gets to this line, it will again issue an error message

```
! AmS-TeX error: \box is already defined.
```

You probably don't remember \box, because it hasn't ever been mentioned before, so let's look in the index. Guess what? It's not there either! That's because \box isn't a control sequence that you are ever supposed to use—it's a control sequence that TeX uses internally, in all sorts of important ways. If you were to \redefine the control sequence \box, then total chaos would ensue. So **always** use \define first, and if you happen to stumble upon a control sequence that doesn't appear in the index, then **don't** \redefine it under any circumstances. (A few of the control sequences that appear in the index are also used internally, but they all bear the annotation '[do not \redefine]' as a warning.)

Actually, \box is a rather exceptional case: most of the control sequences that you mustn't \redefine have strange names that you'd never think of anyway. Of course, there aren't as many control *symbols*, and quite a few are already defined, like \, and \' and \&; but there are still some left for the picking, including \0, \1, ..., \9.

(Despite the warnings just issued, there is one situation where it is safe, and even advisable, to use \redefine on the first try—namely, when you're trying to redefine a control sequence that you yourself originally produced with \define. If you typed

```
\define\ab{\alpha^2+\beta^2}
```

because there seemed to be a lot of $\alpha^2+\beta^2$ combinations in a paper, but suddenly they've disappeared, and $\alpha^3+\beta^3$ is popping up frequently, then you might decide to

```
\redefine\ab{\alpha^3+\beta^3}
```

A \redefine is necessary, since \ab has already been \define'd.)

Although $\mathcal{A}_{\mathcal{M}}\mathcal{S}$-TeX's \define tries to save you from errors, there are still a few precautions that you must attend to yourself. It's quite all right to \define control sequences in terms of other control sequences, but **don't** \define a control sequence in terms of itself! If your input file contains

\define\regress{infinite \regress}

then something horrible will happen the first time you use \regress: TEX will first replace \regress by infinite \regress, then it will replace \regress again, obtaining infinite infinite \regress, then it will replace \regress again, ... Soon TEX will run out of room to store all this stuff, and you'll get a dreaded error message

! TeX capacity exceeded, sorry. ...

 Something even worse occurs when you

\define\selfreference{\selfreference}

If you now use \selfreference in your file, TEX will look up the way it was \define'd, and then replace it with its definition, namely \selfreference. Then it will replace *this* \selfreference with \selfreference, and then replace *this* \selfreference with \selfreference, . . . ! In this case, TEX never runs out of room to store things, so it just keeps recycling—after several billion cycles, you'll probably start to wonder why nothing is happening on the screen. At this point, TEX can be stopped only by using the operating system's interrupt.

● **Exercise 19.10:**
What happens if you

\define\vicious{\circle}
\define\circle{\vicious}

and use \vicious in your file?

We also ought be more specific about where our \define's go. First of all, you must \define a new control sequence before using it. So one possibility is to collect all the \define's at the beginning of the paper, say right after the \document line. That way, you'll know just where to look in order to recall what's been \define'd. But sometimes you realize that you want to \define something as you're typing, and instead of jumping back to the beginning, you might prefer to insert the \define when the time is ripe. In such cases you might \define things right before the paragraph in which they are needed. You can even \define something smack in the middle of a paragraph, but if you do this, you need to be quite careful about spaces. If you typed something like

If we have \define\ab{\alpha^2+\beta^2} the
condition $\ab+1>0$,
then $\frac\ab\gamma>0$.

you would get

If we have the condition $\alpha^2 + \beta^2 + 1 > 0$, then $\frac{\alpha^2+\beta^2}{\gamma} > 0$.

with *two* spaces after 'have', one from the space after '**have**' and one from the space after '\define\ab{...}'. So one of those spaces would have to be eliminated, probably making the output look a little cramped. Even if you typed

```
If we have \define\ab{\alpha^2+\beta^2}
the condition $\ab+1>0$, then $\frac\ab\gamma>0$.
```

you would get two spaces, since the ⟨carriage-return⟩ at the end of the first line counts as a space. I like to keep all my \define's on separate lines, with a % at the end of the line, to obliterate the ⟨carriage-return⟩:

```
If we have
\define\ab{\alpha^2+\beta^2}%
the condition $\ab+1>0$, then $\frac\ab\gamma>0$.
```

Aside from keeping the spacing correct, you should also be aware that a \define inside a group gets forgotten when that group ends. If you type

```
{\bf If we have
\define\ab{\alpha^2+\beta^2}%
the condition $\ab+1>0$, then $\frac\ab\gamma>0$.}
```

then \ab will be undefined after the closing }. Of course, you're unlikely to put a \define within a group like that, but you might try putting a \define inside a math formula, especially since this eliminates worries about extra spaces. But it's important to know that \define inside a math formula also gets forgotten once the formula ends. In practice, this feature of \define is usually very convenient—it means that you can \define a control sequence for temporary use within a formula, and you can \define it to be something completely different inside a later formula.

We've covered several precautions that need to be observed for \define's, but there's also the more practical question of when a new \define is really expedient—you wouldn't want to use this new-found power to overwhelm yourself with a plethora of useless gadgets.

First of all, there are probably going to be a lot of special \define's and

\redefine's that you'll want to use all the time, like

```
\define\a{\alpha}
\predefine\barunder{\b}
\redefine\b{\beta}
\predefine\cedilla{\c}
\redefine\c{\gamma}
\predefine\dotunder{\d}
\redefine\d{\delta}
\define\e{\epsilon}
```

and any other shorthand names for Greek letters, or other common math symbols, that you use frequently. You can keep these permanently in a special file, say defs.tex, and use your text editor to dump the contents of the file into any other file that you happen to be working on. My own file of standard \define's contains

```
\define\({\left(}
\define\){\right)}
\define\[{\left[}
\define\]{\right]}
```

so that I can type things like

$$\left(\frac{1+\sqrt{5}}{2} \right)^{n}$$

simply as

```
$$\( \frac {1+\sqrt5}2 \)^n $$
```

In addition to constantly used \define's, there are frequently a few special \define's that can save a lot of typing in a particular file. You shouldn't be overly zealous in making new \define's for each paper—after all, it takes time to type the proper \define for a symbol, and if you have too many new control sequences to worry about you can be slowed down just trying to remember which one to use. But it makes sense to look through a paper before you start typing, to see if there are any formulas that occur dozens of times, or any particularly complicated formulas that occur at least 5 or 6 times, say. In particular, if the author introduces new operators like Tor and Res (compare page 99), then you will probably want to

```
\define\Tor{\operatorname{Tor}}
\define\Res{\operatornamewithlimits{Res}}
```

Finally, every once in a while it might pay to make a few definitions on the fly, to take care of some one-time monstrosity.

● **Exercise 19.11:**

The author once had to typeset the display

$$a_n = a_{n-1} + a_{n-2}$$

$$= \frac{\left(\dfrac{1+\sqrt{5}}{2}\right)^{n-2} - \left(\dfrac{1-\sqrt{5}}{2}\right)^{n-2} + \left(\dfrac{1+\sqrt{5}}{2}\right)^{n-1} - \left(\dfrac{1-\sqrt{5}}{2}\right)^{n-1}}{\sqrt{5}}$$

$$= \frac{\left(\dfrac{1+\sqrt{5}}{2}\right)^{n-2}\left(1 + \dfrac{1+\sqrt{5}}{2}\right) - \left(\dfrac{1-\sqrt{5}}{2}\right)^{n-2}\left(1 + \dfrac{1-\sqrt{5}}{2}\right)}{\sqrt{5}}$$

$$= \frac{\left(\dfrac{1+\sqrt{5}}{2}\right)^{n-2}\left(\dfrac{1+\sqrt{5}}{2}\right)^{2} - \left(\dfrac{1-\sqrt{5}}{2}\right)^{n-2}\left(\dfrac{1-\sqrt{5}}{2}\right)^{2}}{\sqrt{5}}$$

$$= \frac{\left(\dfrac{1+\sqrt{5}}{2}\right)^{n} - \left(\dfrac{1-\sqrt{5}}{2}\right)^{n}}{\sqrt{5}}.$$

a virtual mine field of potential typing errors, especially because of all those `\frac`'s within `\frac`'s. What possibilities for avoiding errors could be used (the control sequences `\(` and `\)` were already available)?

If you're an exerienced mathematical typist you've probably already begun to ask yourself how to get new control sequences *with arguments*, since a paper will often have many formulas with exactly the same form, except that different sub-formulas occur in various places. For example, if you're typing a calculus book, then you may encounter zillions of "derivatives" like

$$\frac{dy}{dx}, \qquad \frac{dz}{dx}, \qquad \frac{dw}{dx}$$

Although you could `\define` several new control sequences like `\derivy` and `\derivz` and `\derivw`, it would be a lot nicer to have a single control sequence `\deriv` so that `$$\deriv y$$` produces $\dfrac{dy}{dx}$ and `$$\deriv z$$` produces $\dfrac{dz}{dx}$, etc. To produce such a control sequence `\deriv` with one argument, you type

```
\define\deriv#1{\dfrac{d#1}{dx}}
```

Here #1 stands for the argument, so `\deriv f` gets replaced by `\dfrac{df}{dx}`, etc.

• **Exercise 19.12:**
How would you type the formulas

$$\frac{dx^2}{dx}$$

and

$$\frac{d(x^2 + x^3)}{dx}$$

using \deriv?

• **Exercise 19.13:**
Suppose a manuscript talks about many 'vectors' like $(x_1, \ldots, x_n)$, $(y_1, \ldots, y_n)$, etc. How can you conveniently abbreviate all of these formulas?

• **Exercise 19.14:**
And how would you then get $(\alpha_1, \ldots, \alpha_n)$ and $(x'_1, \ldots, x'_n)$?

• **Exercise 19.15:**
Finally, how about the formulas $(x'_1, \ldots, x'_n)$ and $(x_1', \ldots, x_n')$?

• **Exercise 19.16:**
Define a control sequence with one argument \power, such that $\power x$ produces 2^x and $\power\alpha$ produces 2^α, etc.

• **Exercise 19.17:**
How might you use a control sequence with an argument to avoid typing most of the \frac's in the display in Exercise 19.11?

If we progress from calculus to advanced calculus, we'll encounter "partial derivatives" like

$$\frac{\partial f}{\partial x}, \qquad \frac{\partial f}{\partial y}, \qquad \frac{\partial g}{\partial x}, \qquad \frac{\partial h}{\partial z}$$

which are certainly no fun to type. Now we'd like to have a control sequence \pd with *two* arguments, so we could type these formulas as $$\pd fx$$, $$\pd fy$$, $$\pd gx$$, $$\pd hz$$, etc. As you might expect, we can do this with

```
\define\pd#1#2{\dfrac{\partial#1}{\partial#2}}
```

(Notice that we don't need a space before the # in \partial#1 and \partial#2, even though we may be substituting letters for #1 and #2; once TEX has read the \define, it regards the \partial and the #1 as permanently separated.)

● **Exercise 19.18:**

Some authors use x_1, x_2, ... instead of x, y, ... in expressions like $\dfrac{\partial f}{\partial x_1}$, $\dfrac{\partial g}{\partial x_2}$, etc. How would you get these formulas with \pd as \define'd above? How could you modify the definition to make the typing easier?

● **Exercise 19.19:**

Suppose that a manuscript has lots of formulas of the form $\sqrt{a} + \sqrt{b}$, $\sqrt{a} + \sqrt{z}$, $\sqrt{c} + \sqrt{d}$, etc., and you want to have a control sequence \sqrts so that you can type these as $\sqrts ab$, $\sqrts az$, $\sqrts cd$, etc. Explain what is wrong with the following definition.

```
\define\sqrts#1#2{\sqrt#1+\sqrt#2}
```

● **Exercise 19.20:**

It's probably not good enough to have a control sequence with one argument to produce vectors like $(x_1, \ldots, x_n)$, $(y_1, \ldots, y_n)$, etc. You'll probably have to deal with things like $(x_1, \ldots, x_m)$, $(y_1, \ldots, y_{n+1})$ as well. Explain how to define \vec so that we can type these as $\vec xm$ and $\vec y{n+1}$.

● **Exercise 19.21:**

You've typed a 50 page manuscript in which the author has used formulas like $R_i{}^{jk}{}_l$ a couple of hundred times. Now E decides that the notation $R^i{}_{jk}{}^l$ would really be better; with some trepidation E asks if you could make all the changes, perhaps by using that nifty little text editor of yours. You can't, but you still smile at Em graciously. Why?

● **Exercise 19.22:**

You're typing manuscripts for several authors at the same time. Some of them want notation like x_i^2, y_j^3, ..., while others prefer $x_i{}^2$, $y_j{}^3$, ... How could you use a control sequence to keep things straight?

Since some precautions were required to \define a control sequence, you shouldn't be too surprised to learn that there are a couple of other precautions that are required for control sequences with arguments.

First of all, if you \define\cs where \cs is a control sequence with arguments, then after \define\cs the 'arguments' #1, #2, ... must appear in that order, and you can only go up to #9. TEX will issue an error message if they appear in the wrong order.

● **Exercise 19.23:**

In Exercise 19.20 we defined \vec so that $\vec xn$ produces $(x_1, \ldots, x_n)$, etc. But perhaps you don't like this, perhaps you'd prefer to type $\vec nx$, with the 'n' first, and the 'x' second. How can you arrange this?

When you \define a control sequence with an argument there is a second
precaution that is very important, though a little surprising. If we've made the
definition

\define\pd#1#2{\dfrac{\partial #1}{\partial#2}}

then we can get $\dfrac{\partial f}{\partial x}$ by typing $\pd fx$, and we can also type $\pd f x$ since
TEX always ignores spaces while looking for the arguments of a control sequence.
But you **must not** leave spaces after #1 and #2 when \define'ing \pd! If you
were to type

\define\pd#1 #2 {\dfrac{\partial #1}{\partial#2}}

then TEX would think that you were *demanding* that there be a space after the
first and second arguments. So if you typed

\pd fx =3 +x

TEX would not regard f and x as the first and second arguments. Instead it
would assume that fx is the first argument, since fx is the shortest thing with
a space after it. Similarly, TEX would assume that =3 is the second argument.
The results would be strange indeed!

So if you want to avoid anomalies when you \define control sequences with
arguments, just be sure not to have any extraneous spaces after the #1, #2,
#3, ..., and you shouldn't have any problems. If you find this rather mysterious,
and insist on learning more about the subtleties involved, you will find them
explained in the sidetrip that ends this chapter.

Since TEX ignores spaces when looking for the arguments of a control sequence,
the prohibition against leaving spaces in the *definition* of a control sequence with
arguments might seem like a bad inconsistency. But this is actually a special case of a
general feature of TEX, one that allows you to \define control sequences that behave
in rather special ways.

For example, let's consider the definition

\define\pd#1#2{\dfrac{\partial#1}{\partial#2}}

once again, and suppose that we are going to need symbols like $\dfrac{\partial x^2}{\partial x}$, $\dfrac{\partial f(x,y)}{\partial y}$, etc.
Then we will need braces:

$$\pd {x^2}x$$
$$\pd {f(x,y)}y$$

We might find it more convenient to type something like

```
$$ \pd x^2.x $$
$$ \pd f(x,y).y $$
```

with a period separating the arguments. We can arrange for this by typing

```
\define\pd#1.#2{\dfrac{\partial #1}{\partial#2}}
```

This \define tells TEX that a . *must* follow argument #1. (When you leave a space after an argument, TEX reasons similarly that this argument must be followed by a space.)

• **Exercise 19.24:**
How would you \define the control sequence \vec so that you type $\vec x,n.$ to get $(x_1, \ldots, x_n)$, and $\vec y,m+1.$ to get $(y_1, \ldots, y_{m+1})$, etc.

• **Exercise 19.25:**
Suppose you make the definition

```
\define\powers#1,#2.{2^{#1}+3^{#2}}
```

How would you type $2^3 + 3^4$ and $2^{10.03} + 3^{1,034}$ and, finally, $2^{1,034} + 3^{10.03}$?

Here's another example where you can make good use of this special feature of the \define process. Previously, we considered the definitions

```
\define\deRham{de~Rham}
\define\Cartan{\'E.~Cartan}
```

and we noted that you have to be careful to type \␣ when you need a space after the names. Well, here's a way of avoiding that distraction. Suppose that instead we adopt the definitions

```
\define\deRham/{de~Rham}
\define\Cartan/{\'E.~Cartan}
```

Now TEX expects \deRham and \Cartan to be followed by /, so you always have to type \deRham/ and \Cartan/. But these \.../ combinations don't take much more typing—and look rather nice anyway—and now you don't have to worry about TEX gobbling up extra spaces: if you leave a space after the / then TEX will leave a space there also.

• **Exercise 19.26:**
Redo Exercise 19.4, assuming that \deRham and \Cartan have been \define'd in this new way.

• Exercise 19.27:

Here's a somewhat trickier question. Suppose you decide that **\AmSTeX** isn't a good name for the $\mathcal{A}_{\mathcal{M}}\mathcal{S}$-TEX logo, you think it should be called **\AmS-TeX** instead. So you

```
\define\AmS-TeX{\AmSTeX}
```

What happens?

• Exercise 19.28:

What happens when you make the following definitions?

```
\define \ab  {\alpha^2+\beta^2}
\define \1   {\alpha^2+\beta^2}
```

• Exercise 19.29:

What happens if you leave out the braces in **\define\a{\alpha}**, so that you have

```
\define\a\alpha
```

in your file?

Chapter 20. ℰX-rated Features

In the previous chapters we've learned how to deal with almost all standard mathematical fare. This chapter covers everything else—the few topics that we didn't get to before, and all those little tricks that you will sometimes need to produce special effects or improve the appearance of a formula. This information has been sorted into various entries that are listed alphabetically. Assisted by the index (Appendix I), you should be able to find out about any special TEXniques you might need. But it's probably a good idea to browse through this chapter now, to get an idea what sort of things it contains, and then learn it all little by little. It may take quite some time to assimilate all this information, but this extra attention to detail will enable you to typeset formulas that even a master printer would be proud of.

ACCENTS IN MATH MODE

The usual accents for text, like \', \^, etc., are not allowed in math mode, which has the following accents instead:

`$\hat a$`	$\hat a$
`$\check a$`	$\check a$
`$\tilde a$`	$\tilde a$
`$\acute a$`	$\acute a$
`$\grave a$`	$\grave a$
`$\dot a$`	$\dot a$
`$\ddot a$`	$\ddot a$
`$\dddot a$`	$\dddot a$
`$\ddddot a$`	$\ddddot a$
`$\breve a$`	$\breve a$
`$\bar a$`	$\bar a$
`$\vec a$`	$\vec a$

It's usually a good idea to define special control sequences for accented letters that you need frequently. If $\hat A$, $\hat c$, $\check s$, $\tilde x$ and $\bar z$ occur a half dozen times or more in

133

a paper, you can put

```
\define\Ahat{{\hat A}}
\define\chat{{\hat c}}
\define\scheck{{\check s}}
\define\xtilde{{\tilde x}}
\define\zbar{{\bar z}}
```

at the beginning of your file. This not only saves a lot of typing, it also makes the input easier to read. Notice that we used an extra set of braces so that we can type things like `$2^\Ahat$` (compare page 70 and Exercise 19.2).

As in text, when an accent is placed over an i or j, you should use the dotless forms $\imath$ and $\jmath$. You get these by typing `\imath` and `\jmath` in math mode. For example, `$\hat\imath$` gives $\hat\imath$.

TₑX won't object if you put a math accent over an entire formula, but there's usually not much point in doing this, because the accent just gets centered over the formula. For example, `$\hat{I+M}$` would produce $\hat{I+M}$. When mathematicians need to indicate an accent over a whole formula, they usually resort to one of several devices.

First of all, some of the accents have wider versions. For example, there are `\widehat` and `\widetilde`:

`$\widehat x,\widetilde x$`	$\widehat x, \widetilde x$
`$\widehat{xy},\widetilde{xy}$`	$\widehat{xy}, \widetilde{xy}$
`$\widehat{xyz},\widetilde{xyz}$`	$\widehat{xyz}, \widetilde{xyz}$

The third line shows the maximum sizes presently available, but wider versions will probably be provided in later implementations of $\mathcal{A}_{\mathcal{M}}\mathcal{S}$-TₑX.

Another possibility is to use notation like $(I + M)^{\widehat{\ }}$ with a $\widehat{\ }$ accent in the position of a superscript. To get the hat accent in this position you can't type `^\hat` or `\sp\hat`, since `\hat` isn't a symbol, it's an instruction to put an accent over something. But $\mathcal{A}_{\mathcal{M}}\mathcal{S}$-TₑX has `\sphat`, which works just the way one would wish `\sp\hat` worked, and there's also `\spcheck`, ..., `\spvec`.

In a sense, the `\vec` accent also has wider versions, since you can always use `\overarrow`. On single letters `\vec` usually looks a bit better than `\overarrow`: compare $\vec z$ (`$\vec z$`) and $\overrightarrow{z}$ (`$\overarrow z$`).

Similarly, for the `\bar` accent you can use `\overline` on a long formula. Again, there is a difference between `\bar` and `\overline` on single letters. For example, `$\bar z$` gives $\bar z$, while `$\overline z$` gives $\overline z$. The `\bar` accent is a specific symbol, the same that is used for the `\B` accent in text. On the other hand,

accents in math mode]

\overline is a line of a certain thickness (usually not quite the same as the thickness of the \bar accent), and it grows to cover the entire formula. In a formula like $\overline{z}$ ($\overline z$) it may look a little too long, and $\overline\phi$ and $\overline A$ are even more unsettling: $\overline{\phi}$ and $\overline{A}$. On the other hand, the accent on $\bar M$ ($\bar M$) may look a little too small, so that $\overline{M}$ ($\overline M$) may be preferred.

When you are beginning a manuscript, you might not know whether \bar or \overline would be best over a particular letter, so you may have to go back and change an occasional \bar M to \overline M or *vice versa*. Of course, if the manuscript has lots of $\bar M$'s, then you've \define'd a control sequence \Mbar as an abbreviation for it, so all you have to do is change the definition.

TₑX can actually be instructed to draw a line of any thickness and any length, at any particular location, so that you can get an $\overline{M}$ that looks just right. But this takes some TₑXpertise, and a lot of trial and error. The smart way to deal with the problem, if you find both $\bar M$ and $\overline M$ unsatisfactory, is to temporarily \define\Mbar{\bar M} and then ask someone in the know to make a more sophisticated definition.

Now comes the fun part: double accents. Journals normally discourage, or even prohibit, the use of double accents, like $\hat{\hat A}$, which the printer may have to fashion out of tiny pieces of type. If a mathematician is using lots of double accents, like $\hat{\hat A}$, $\hat{\hat A}$, $\tilde{\tilde A}$, ..., then the readers of Eir paper will probably be as unappreciative as the printer, and E might to be advised to seek more felicitious notation. But occasionally double accents are appropriate, and mathematicians will probably squeal with delight at the thought that computer typesetting will make all this easy.

But the fact of the matter is, even TₑX has problems with double accents. When you type $\hat A$ you get $\hat A$ with the accent right over the peak of the A, but when you type $\hat{\hat A}$ you get $\hat{\hat A}$ (yeccch), with the top hat centered over the whole formula $\hat A$. So $\mathcal{A}_{\mathcal{M}}S$-TₑX has the variant \Hat, which makes TₑX work harder and get things right: If you type $\Hat{\Hat A}$, then you get $\hat{\hat A}$. There are also corresponding \Check, \Tilde, \Acute, \Grave, \Dot, \Ddot, \Breve, \Bar and \Vec; few of these should ever be required in any reasonable paper, and $\mathcal{A}_{\mathcal{M}}S$-TₑX doesn't even bother to give you \Dddot or \Ddddot.

$\mathcal{A}_{\mathcal{M}}S$-TₑX provides both \hat and \Hat because \Hat really gobbles up computer time. You should **always** use \hat for single accents, resorting to \Hat only when you really need to make TₑX work harder to get double accents right. How much harder does TₑX have to work when you use \Hat instead of \hat?

Well, if you have six or seven $\hat{\hat{A}}$'s on a page it might double the time TEX takes to typeset that page! If you

      `\define\Ahathat{\Hat{\Hat A}}`

then it'll be very easy for you to type the input, but it won't make things any easier for TEX, since your `\Ahathat` just gets translated into `\Hat{\Hat A}`. So AMS-TEX provides a special feature to help out in situations like this. What you ought to type is

      `\accentedsymbol\Ahathat{\Hat{\Hat A}}`

When you do this, TEX first goes through all the work involved in typesetting `\Hat{\Hat A}`, but then it stores that information away permanently, so that whenever you type `\Ahathat` in your file it can retrieve it instantly, without going through all the work again. It's as if a printer had a special $\hat{\hat{A}}$ character made up, so that E could always use this single piece of type instead of laboriously joining together smaller pieces of type. Once you have `\Ahathat` produced by `\accentedsymbol` you can use it as often as you like without worrying about slowing TEX down.

You shouldn't resort to `\accentedsymbol` too often, because TEX has only a limited space for storing new symbols; if you need to use `\accentedsymbol` to produce more than about 10 new symbols in a single paper, the author's notation is probably hopelessly inappropriate. And there's also one little catch: the new symbol `\Ahathat` that you create with `\accentedsymbol` really is like a printer's piece of type—it *won't* change size in a superscript or subscript. If you need many superscript $\hat{\hat{A}}$ symbols, you might create a smaller symbol with

      `\accentedsymbol\smallAhathat{{\ssize\Hat{\Hat A}}}`

(notice the extra set of braces), and then type things like

      `$\Gamma_1^\smallAhathat$` $\Gamma_1^{\hat{\hat{A}}}$

See also **fonts in math mode**.

ALIGNING FORMULAS

You can get vertical spacing between the lines of an `\align` with `\vspace` and `\spreadlines` (*see* **vertical spacing**).

Page breaks are usually not allowed within a display containing an `\align`... `\endalign` construction. But you can type `\allowdisplaybreak` after any `\\`

aligning formulas]

to allow a page break after that line of the display, and you can even force a page break after some line of the display with \displaybreak. You can also type \allowdisplaybreaks [*sic*] before the \align, and this will have the same effect as if you typed \allowdisplaybreak after each line. \allowdisplaybreaks is allowed only between $$ signs, and affects only the display in which it appears.

You can also put

```
\intertext{...}
```

between two lines of an \align to produce text that will go between the lines of the \align'ed formulas, without interrupting their alignment. For example, if you type

```
We have
$$
\align X&= (-1)^{i+j-k/3+*[\alpha,\beta]}Z_1
             +(-1)^{\alpha/\beta-*[i+j/2,i+k/3]}Z_2\\
\intertext{which by properties (a)--(d) of $*$,
together with commutativity of the ring,}
     &=\alpha Z_1+\beta Z_2,
\endalign
$$
which is the desired formula.
```

you will get

We have

$$X = (-1)^{i+j-k/3+*[\alpha,\beta]} Z_1 + (-1)^{\alpha/\beta-*[i+j/2,i+k/3]} Z_2$$

which by properties (a)–(d) of $*$, together with commutativity of the ring,

$$= \alpha Z_1 + \beta Z_2,$$

which is the desired formula.

with the = signs nicely aligned. You can't have a \par or blank line within \intertext, because \par's are always disallowed in a math formula, but there is the substitute control sequence \endgraf, which can be used instead. The first line of an \intertext always starts flush left (unless you precede it with \endgraf).

It would be bad style to use \intertext except on rare occasions. Even when two different \align's are closely related, it is *not* customary to have them line up with each other; use \intertext to achieve this effect only under special circumstances. (If you do use \intertext in this way, to combine two or more \align's into one long one, it's probably a good idea to put \allowdisplaybreak before and after the \intertext. Even then, the \intertext itself will be a single unit where page breaks can't occur.)

In an \aligned, which is a unit, you can't use \allowdisplaybreak[s], nor can you use \displaybreak or \intertext. But you can use \vspace; and \spreadlines does affect an \aligned within the displayed formula where it appears.

As illustrated on page 103, different \aligned's line up along their center lines. However, there are also \topaligned and \botaligned, which line up along their top or bottom lines, in case you can think of a need for such things.

Sometimes you need to align formulas at more than one place. For example, the display

$$(23) \qquad V_i = v_i - q_i v_j, \qquad X_i = x_i - q_i x_j, \qquad U_i = u_i, \qquad \text{for } i \ne j;$$

$$(24) \qquad V_j = v_j, \qquad\qquad X_j = x_j, \qquad\qquad U_j = u_j + \sum_{i \ne j} q_i u_i.$$

has = signs aligned at three places. You can get this by using $\mathcal{A}_{\mathcal{M}}\mathcal{S}$-TEX's \alignat. The above display was typed as

```
$$
\alignat 3
V_i & =v_i-q_iv_j,   & \qquad X_i & =x_i-q_ix_j,
   & \qquad  U_i & =u_i,\qquad\text{for $i\ne j$;} \tag 23\\
V_j & =v_j,           & \qquad X_j & =x_j,
   & \qquad  U_j & =u_j+\sum_{i\ne j}q_iu_i. \tag 24
\endalignat
$$
```

Right after \alignat you must specify the number of pairs of formulas that will be aligned.[1] Since we have \alignat 3, each line contains 3 pairs of formulas, with an & between the formulas in each pair. In addition, an & is needed between the first pair of formulas and the second pair, and between the second pair and

---

[1] You would type \alignat{10} if you wanted 10 pairs, but you probably wouldn't be able to fit them on the page.

aligning formulas]

the third pair, so there is a total of 5 &'s per line. Notice also that the space, \qquad, between the various columns of formulas, was specified explicitly.

The most common use for \alignat is for things like

$$
\begin{aligned}
x &= y & \text{by (1)}\\
x' &= y' & \text{by (2)}\\
x + x' &= y + y' & \text{by Axiom 1.}
\end{aligned}
$$

This was typed as

```
$$
\alignat2
x&=y &&\qquad\text{by (1)}\\
x'&=y'&&\qquad\text{by (2)}\\
x+x'&=y+y'&&\qquad\text{by Axiom 1.}
\endalignat
$$
```

Notice that we used && because we wanted the side conditions to be considered as the second formula of a pair, so that they would be lined up on the left. Within \alignat you can use the subsidiary control sequences \vspace, \allowdisplaybreak, \intertext, etc., just as within \align.

\alignat also has an "expanded" version, \xalignat, where the various columns are spaced evenly across the page, so that it isn't necessary to specify any particular spacing between the columns. And \xxalignat is even more expanded—the first and last columns are spread all the way to the margin; \tag's wouldn't make sense, and aren't allowed, in this construction.

There's also \alignedat, which is just like \alignat, except that it creates a single unit. Within \alignedat you can use the same subsidiary control sequences as within \aligned. There's no \xalignedat, since that wouldn't make any sense.

There's one important way that \alignat and \xalignat differ from \align and similar constructions. If there isn't enough room on a line for both the formulas and the tag in an \alignat, the tag will not automatically be placed on a separate line. In fact, it might even *overlap* the formula (!) without an Overfull box message being given. Fortunately, these constructions are sufficiently rare so that you can just check for yourself that everything came out all right; if you do have problems, you'll have to force the tag to go on a separate line by setting it as the tag to an empty formula.

Actually, even \align behaves a little strangely when a formula is too long: the ugly black box will not occur at the end of the particular line that is too long, but at the end of the last line of the set. Moreover, not one, but *two* Overfull \hbox messages will be given; however, they are nearly identical, and you shouldn't let yourself be bothered by it.

Finally, there's one special alignment problem for which $\mathcal{A}_{\mathcal{M}}\mathcal{S}$-T$_{\mathrm{E}}$X has a special feature. Occasionally you need something like

$$
\begin{aligned}
a + b &= c \\
f(a) + f(b) &= f(c) \\
\alpha &= \beta + \delta \\
\alpha' &= \beta' + \delta' \\
A + B &= C + D + E
\end{aligned}
$$

where several formulas are \gather'ed, but various groups of the formulas must be aligned (and each of the formulas might have tags). Normally you can't put an \align or \gather inside any other construction, but $\mathcal{A}_{\mathcal{M}}\mathcal{S}$-T$_{\mathrm{E}}$X allows you to type

```
$$
\gather a+b=c\\
 f(a)+f(b)=f(c)\\
{\align \alpha&=\beta+\delta\\
 \alpha'&=\beta'+\delta' \endalign}\\
 A+B=C+D+E\endgather
$$
```

with tags on any formula you want. For this very special usage, each \align . . . \endalign subgroup **MUST** be put inside braces.

$\mathcal{A}_{\mathcal{M}}\mathcal{S}$-T$_{\mathrm{E}}$X LOGO

If you're using the amsppt style, but can't stand having $\mathcal{A}_{\mathcal{M}}\mathcal{S}$-T$_{\mathrm{E}}$X print "Typeset by $\mathcal{A}_{\mathcal{M}}\mathcal{S}$-T$_{\mathrm{E}}$X" at the bottom of the page, put \nologo at the beginning of your paper.

ARROWS

$\mathcal{A}_{\mathcal{M}}\mathcal{S}$-T$_{\mathrm{E}}$X gives you a general way of placing small formulas over others, to get new relations like $\stackrel{\mathrm{def}}{=}$ (*see* **compound symbols**), and this method can also be used to produce new relations like $\xrightarrow{\alpha\beta}$, which was obtained by placing the $\alpha\beta$

automatic formatting, disabling]

over a \longrightarrow. But there's also a special mechanism for creating longer arrows when it is necessary to accommodate long labels.

If you type @>>> in math mode you will get a right arrow →, and @<<< will give you a left arrow ←. A triple '>>>' or '<<<' is used here, because formulas can be placed between the first and second symbol to produce a label that goes above the arrow, and between the second and third to produce a label that goes below the arrow:

$@> \alpha+\beta+\gamma >>$ $\xrightarrow{\alpha+\beta+\gamma}$

$@<< \alpha+\beta+\gamma <$ $\xleftarrow[\alpha+\beta+\gamma]{}$

$@> \alpha > \gamma^{-1} >$ $\xrightarrow[\gamma^{-1}]{\alpha}$

Of course, if for some reason you need an arrow like $\xrightarrow{x>y}$ with a > or < sign in the label of the arrow, then you'd better hide it in braces: $@>{x\,>\,y}>>$. (The thin spaces were added because TeX normally doesn't put space around binary relations that are in s-size.)

AUTHOR, TITLE, ETC.

If your \title is too long, you will get an Overfull box message, together with a black box after the title. You could eliminate the black box (*see* **boxes, black**), but the title will still stick out into the right margin. But if you type

    \title\overlong...\endtitle

then the title will be centered, and no Overfull box will be created. Journal editors will probably scream if you do this, and just introduce additional line breaks (\\), but this device might be useful if the title is just a tad too wide. You can also type \author\overlong, \affil\overlong and \heading\overlong, but no other combinations work.

AUTOMATIC FORMATTING, DISABLING

(*See also* $\mathcal{A}_{\mathcal{M}}S$-TeX logo, **page numbers** and **page size**.)

Whenever someone carefully constructs a system that provides lots of frills, someone else always comes along and wants to get rid of some of them. For example, \proclaim selects the \smc font, and it adds the final punctuation for you, but occasionally you might want something different:

Main Theorem!

It's easy enough to get $\mathcal{A}_{\mathcal{M}}\mathcal{S}$-TEX to switch into boldface, simply by typing
\proclaim{\bf ...}. But the punctuation is an extra frill, and you must tell
$\mathcal{A}_{\mathcal{M}}\mathcal{S}$-TEX to delete this by typing \nofrills right after the \proclaim:

```
\proclaim\nofrills{\bf Main Theorem!}
```

Similarly, you might type

```
\demo\nofrills{Proof (?)}
```

to get

Proof (?)

But you have to be careful when you use \nofrills, because spacing is one
of the frills that you probably take for granted. Whether you type

```
\proclaim{Theorem} Here's a theorem.
```

or

```
\proclaim{Theorem}Here's a theorem.
```

the **amsppt** style will print 'THEOREM. ' before switching to slanted type and
printing '*Here's a theorem*'. The space after 'THEOREM.' is provided for free,
and $\mathcal{A}_{\mathcal{M}}\mathcal{S}$-TEX ignores any space after the }, so that you don't have worry about
starting the statement of the theorem immediately after that right brace. But
when you use \nofrills, this space doesn't appear, so what you really have to
type is something like

```
\proclaim\nofrills{Main Theorem! } Here's a theorem.
```

Better yet, you could type

```
\proclaim\nofrills{Main Theorem!\usualspace}
  Here's a theorem.
```

This will give the usual space that follows the punctuation in a \proclaim.

You can also type \nofrills after \subheading, to get rid of the punctuation that's automatically selected; after \abstract, to get rid of the word
"Abstract.", "Summary.", etc., that the style automatically selects (you'll undoubtedly appreciate this if you're using the **amsppt** style, but typing a paper in

boxed formulas]

some other language); and even after \keywords and \subjclass. In all these cases, you can also use \usualspace for the spacing after the punctuation.

See also \Refs in Appendix B.

BIG AND BIGG

We've learned about \bigl, \bigr and \biggl, \biggr to get variable size delimiters, but there's also \big and \bigg, which produce a delimiter that acts as an ordinary variable. It is used primarily with slashes and backslashes (*see* **delimiters**), as in the following example.

$$\dfrac{a+1}b\bigg/\dfrac{c+1}d$$ $\dfrac{a+1}{b} \Big/ \dfrac{c+1}{d}$

And there's also \bigm and \biggm, to be used in the middle of formulas, producing a delimiter that acts as a binary relation, like =, so that TeX puts some space around it.

$\bigl(x\in A(n)\bigm|x\in B(n)\bigr)$ $\big(x \in A(n) \mid x \in B(n) \big)$

$\bigcup_n X_n\bigm\|\bigcap_n Y_n$ $\bigcup_n X_n \, \big\| \, \bigcap_n Y_n$

In addition, there are actually two more sizes for all these things: \Big, which is 50% taller than \big, and \Bigg, 2.5 times as tall as \big. But these harder to type control sequences are seldom used, since formulas are usually one or two lines tall, not $1\frac{1}{2}$ or $2\frac{1}{2}$ lines tall.

BOXED FORMULAS

A formula can be boxed by using the control sequence \boxed. For example,

$$\boxed{1+1=2}$$

produces

$$\boxed{1 + 1 = 2}$$

Boxed formulas almost never appear in journal articles, but they sometimes occur in books. (Typographical ornateness varies in inverse proportion to the level of the material.)

A boxed formula is simply a new math symbol, so it can be used within other formulas, and can even be boxed. Thus,

$$\text{Fundamental result:}\qquad\boxed{\boxed{1+1=2.}}$$

gives

$$\text{Fundamental result:} \qquad \boxed{\boxed{1+1=2.}}$$

Similarly, a \boxed formula can be given a \tag. For example,

```
$$\boxed{1+1=2}\tag 3--1$$
```

gives

$$(3\text{--}1) \qquad\qquad \boxed{1+1=2}$$

But don't try to put the \tag within \boxed—you'll just get a weird error message.

BOXES, BLACK

You can get TₑX to stop printing black boxes after each Overfull \hbox by typing \NoBlackBoxes (that's how the author got the formula on page 58 to stick out past the margin). This can be useful when you have a displayed formula that's too wide by just a pt or two (*see* **dimensions**)—if there's lots of white space above and below the formula the extra width probably won't be noticeable, and this might allow you to avoid splitting the formula.

This command is "global"—it affect everything that follows, even if it is included in braces or $ signs. There's also \BlackBoxes to get the black boxes back again, but you really shouldn't use both in a file. Just make sure not to put \NoBlackBoxes in your file until the very final stage, when you're quite sure that any Overfull \hbox that appears is OK.

BOXES, OVERFULL AND UNDERFULL

Various examples of Overfull \hbox messages have already occurred, with an occasional Underfull \hbox message thrown in. We've sometimes referred to these simply as Overfull box messages, because TₑX also has Overfull and Underfull \vbox messages. You're most likely to get such a message when TₑX hasn't been able to find a good page break. For example, if you've specified an \aligned that's longer than a page, TₑX will have to place it on a page by itself, and then it will complain about an Overfull \vbox. The \vbox in this case is that whole page, which TₑX has made by stacking the various lines of the \aligned vertically. And, of course, the page before this one may not have had enough material on it, so you may get an Underfull \vbox message about that page right before the Overfull \vbox message. Even if an \aligned isn't a whole page long, it might have to go at the top of a new page before the current page has enough on it, so you can still get an Underfull \vbox message.

comments]

BRACES

See **set notation.**

BRACES UNDER AND OVER FORMULAS

See **horizontal braces**

BREAKING DISPLAYS

See **aligning formulas.**

BREAKING FORMULAS

TEX allows * in a formula to represent a "discretionary multiplication"—if the line is broken at that point a multiplication sign × will be placed at the end of the line.

See also **aligning formulas.**

BREAKING LINES AND PAGES

See **line breaks** and **page breaks.**

BREAKING WORDS

You can use a discretionary hyphen \- or \hyphenation to tell TEX how to break a word in text, but sometimes you want to *prohibit* hyphenation. One way you can do this is by typing \text{strangeword} because \text always produces an unbreakable unit, even in ordinary text. Or you can type a discretionary hyphen \- at the very end of the word; this works because TEX will never add a hyphen to a word that already has a hyphen or discretionary hyphen. Or you can put \hyphenation{strangeword} in the file.

COMMENTS

You can "comment out" a large amount of text by typing

```
\comment
  . . .
  . . .
\endcomment
```

You **must** put the \endcomment on a line all by itself.

The process of throwing the input away takes some time, since TEX throws it away line by line, so if you \comment out a really large region, TEX may sit silently for quite a while.

Be careful not to nest your \comment's—**don't** type things like things like

```
\comment
.  .  .
\comment
.  .  .
\endcomment
...
\endcomment
```

COMMUTATIVE DIAGRAMS

If mathematicians are turned on by the possibility of typesetting matrices, they will just swoon with ecstasy when they can typeset "commutative diagrams", like

$(*)$

$$
\begin{array}{ccc}
G & \xrightarrow{\alpha} & H \\
f\downarrow & & \uparrow g \\
G' & \xleftarrow{\beta} & H'
\end{array}
$$

Commutative diagrams come in all sorts of varieties, of which something like

$(**)$

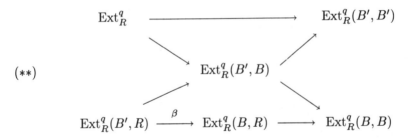

is but a simple example, but at present $\mathcal{A}_{\mathcal{M}}\mathcal{S}$-TEX can only handle "rectangular" commutative diagrams like $(*)$.

The commutative diagram $(*)$ was produced using \CD...\endCD, with \\ separating the various rows, as usual. The horizontal arrows are produced by the mechanism explained in the entry **arrows**, so the top row was typed as

```
\CD
G        @>\alpha>>      H  \\
```

commutative diagrams]

and the third row was typed as

```
G'      @<<\beta<    H'
\endCD
```

A vertical arrow pointing down is specified by @VVV—the upper-case V is supposed to suggest the head of the arrow. Now anything between the first and second V gives a label to the left of the arrow, while anything between the second and third gives a label to the right. (Of course, you have to be careful to use braces if the labels use a V). For vertical arrows pointing up we use @AAA, since A seems to be the closest thing to an upside down V.[2] Thus, the middle row of (∗) was typed as

```
@VfVV       @AAgA\\
```

so that the whole diagram was typed as

```
$$
\CD
G         @>\alpha>>     H  \\
@VfVV                    @AAgA \\
G'        @<<\beta<      H'
\endCD \tag {$*$}
$$
```

Notice that no &'s are used to keep the columns separated—the various arrow constructions keep track of this themselves. Notice also that in the middle row, where there are only vertical arrows, nothing should be typed in the "column" containing the horizontal arrows.

The constructions @VVV and @AAA can be used only within \CD, unlike @>>> and @<<<, which can be used anywhere in math mode (though they normally give shorter arrows than when they are used in a commutative diagram).

Sometimes you have only a piece of a commutative diagram:

$$
\begin{CD}
G @>\alpha>> H \\
@. @VVgV \\
@. H'
\end{CD}
$$

---

[2] You might think that it would be nice to type @^^^ for an up-arrow; alas, for TEXnical reasons that can't be done.

For the missing "corner" you can type {} or even nothing at all, but for a missing arrow you must type '@.' (analogous to '\left.' or '\right.' for a missing delimiter):

```
$$
\CD
G   @>\alpha>> H \\
@.             @VVgV \\
        @.     H'
\endCD
$$
```

Of course, this use of @. is completely different from the use in text, for the proper spacing after a period following an upper-case letter.

By the way, the diagram (∗∗) was typed as

```
$$\define\Ext{\operatorname{Ext}}
\CD
\Ext_R^q    @.                    @.      \Ext_R^q(B',B')\\ \\
        @.      \Ext_R^q(B', B)   @.                      \\ \\
\Ext_R^q(B',R)  @>\beta>>  \Ext_R^q(B,R)  @>>>  \Ext_R^q(B,B)
\endCD
$$
```

The \\ \\ combinations produced blank lines, for proper spacing, and the diagonal arrows and the long arrow at the top were drawn in afterwards.

Sometimes some of the arrows in a commutative diagram may be replaced by long horizontal or vertical = signs:

$$
\begin{CD}
G @= G' \\
@| @VVV \\
H @>>> K
\end{CD}
$$

Just use @= for a horizontal long = sign, and @| (or @\vert) for a vertical one.

Unfortunately, in the present version of \CD, arrows in the same column of a commutative diagram won't automatically be set to the same length. For

commutative diagrams]

example,

```
$$
\CD
G            @>\text{Clifford multiplication}>>      H  \\
@VfVV                                            @AAgA \\
G'                  @<<\beta<                      H'
\endCD
$$
```

gives

$$
\begin{CD}
G @>\text{Clifford multiplication}>> H \\
@VfVV @AAgA \\
G' @<\beta<< H'
\end{CD}
$$

To get $\mathcal{A}_{\mathcal{M}}\mathcal{S}$-TEX to extend the bottom arrow you have to pretend that the label β has the width of the label Clifford multiplication; you can do this by using \pretend...\haswidth.... If you type

```
$$
\define\bottomarrow{@<<\pretend\beta\haswidth
        {\text{Clifford multiplication}}<}
\CD
G            @>\text{Clifford multiplication}>>      H  \\
@VfVV                  @AAgA \\
G'            \bottomarrow        H'
\endCD
$$
```

you will get

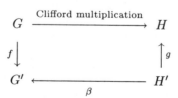

Sometimes you might want to shorten the arrows in a long commutative diagram, in order to get it to fit on a page. If you type

```
\minCDarrowwidth{⟨dimen⟩}
```

then the minimum width of the arrows will change to ⟨dimen⟩ (*see* **dimensions**), with longer arrows produced only when the length of the label demands it. You can only use `\minCDarrowwidth` within `$$` signs, and it applies only to that display.

COMPOUND SYMBOLS

(*See also* **fractions and related symbols.**)

   Mathematicians often like to make new symbols by setting things over or under a symbol, instead of as a superscript or subscript. $\mathcal{A}_{\mathcal{M}}\mathcal{S}$-TeX gives you `\overset` and `\underset` to accomplish this:

`$\underset X\to A$`	$\underset{X}{A}$
`$\underset\alpha\beta\to X$`	$\underset{\alpha\beta}{X}$
`$\overset\alpha\beta\to\longrightarrow$`	$\overset{\alpha\beta}{\longrightarrow}$
`$\overset\text{def}\to=$`	$\overset{\text{def}}{=}$
`$\overset s\to{\underset A\to X}$`	$\overset{s}{\underset{A}{X}}$

Notice that braces weren't needed around the double underscript `\alpha\beta` because the underscript is always neatly segregated between `\underset` and `\to`. Of course, in an `\underset...\to{...}` construction, the `\to` is just part of the "syntax"—it doesn't stand for the rightarrow → that has the alternate name `\to`.

● **Exercise 20.1:**
Typeset the following.

$$\overset{\frown}{BC} = \theta, \qquad \overline{AB} = \sqrt{2 + 2\cos\theta} \qquad \text{(by the law of cosines)}.$$

   `\underset` and `\overset` don't try to position things as cleverly as math accents (*see* **accents in math mode**). Fortunately, these constructions aren't used all that often, and you can adjust things yourself with a little experimentation:

   `$\overset \,\,,s\to{\underset A\to X}$` $\overset{s}{\underset{A}{X}}$

   When you `\overset` or `\underset` a binary operation or relation, the resulting symbol is a new binary operation or relation.[3] Thus, $\overset{\text{def}}{=}$ and $\overset{\alpha\beta}{\longrightarrow}$ will both be

---

[3]If for some reason you want the resulting formula to be treated as an ordinary symbol, just enclose it in braces.

compound symbols]

new binary relations. Of course, overscripts and underscripts ought to be rather short, but long overscripts and underscripts are possible on arrows, because TₑX can produce arbitrarily long arrows. However, such overscripted or underscripted arrows are produced in a completely different way. *See* **arrows**.

When you \overset or \underset an ordinary symbol, any sub or superscripts will end up at the right height:

$$\overset \,\alpha\to X_i^j$$ $\overset{\alpha}{X}_i^j$

The sub and superscripts appear at the appropriate height for the main character X, not as sub and superscripts to the entire construction $\overset{\alpha}{X}$. But if you use \overset and \underset to create a new binary operator or relation, things probably won't work out so well:

$$\overset+\to=^j$$ $\overset{+}{=}^j$

You can improve things by typing

$$\overset+\to={}^j$$ $\overset{+}{=}\, j$

but then there's extra space after the $\overset{+}{=}$ symbol. If you ever really need something like this, you'll have to enlist the aid of a TₑXnician.

It isn't necessary to use \underset or \overset for formulas like

$$\overbrace{x+\cdots+x}^{k\text{ times}} \qquad \text{and} \qquad \underbrace{x+y+z}_{>0}$$

since \overbrace and \underbrace have a special mechanism for this (*see* **horizontal braces**). But $\mathcal{A_M S}$-TₑX also provides you with \undersetbrace...\to and \oversetbrace...\to as an alternative:

$$\oversetbrace \text{k times} \to$$
$$\{x+\dots+x\}$$
$$\undersetbrace >\,0 \to\{x+y+z\}$$

$\overbrace{x+\cdots+x}^{k\text{ times}}$

$\underbrace{x+y+z}_{>0}$

Sometimes new symbols are constructed, in a rather different way, from large operators. For example, $\sum^*$ might be used as a special variant of $\sum$. Here the

* appears as a superscript even though we might want other formulas to appear as "limits":

$$\sum_{x \in A}^{*} f(x) = \sum_{0 \ne x \in A} f(x)$$

$\mathcal{A}_\mathcal{M}\mathcal{S}$-TeX gives you \sideset to provide for both a prescript and superscript:

```
\define\sumstar{\sideset \and^* \to\sum}
$$\sumstar_{x\in A}f(x)=\sum_{0\ne x\in A}f(x)$$
```

Typing \sideset^*\and \to\sum would put the * on the left.

CONTINUED FRACTIONS

Mathematicians sometimes like to set "continued fractions" like

$$a_0 + \cfrac{1}{a_1 + \cfrac{1}{a_2 + \cfrac{1}{a_3 + \cfrac{1}{a_4}}}}$$

which are hard to even think about, let alone typeset! But $\mathcal{A}_\mathcal{M}\mathcal{S}$-TeX gives you a simply way to describe them. The above display was typed as

```
$$a_0 + \cfrac1\\
  a_1 + \cfrac 1\\
  a_2 + \cfrac 1\\
  a_3 + \cfrac 1\\
  a_4\endcfrac
```

Get the idea? Each time that you start a new sub-fraction you type \cfrac, and you use \\ to separate lines, as usual. Then you finish off the whole thing with a single \endcfrac.[4]

Some mathematicians prefer something like

$$a_0 + \cfrac{1}{a_1 + \cfrac{1}{a_2 + \cfrac{1}{a_3 + \cfrac{1}{a_4}}}}$$

---

[4]If you typed \cfrac a+1 \\b+1 \endcfrac you'd get exactly the same thing as if you typed \dfrac{a+1}{b+1}. But using \cfrac for ordinary fractions isn't recommended!

delimiters]

with all the numerators, except the last, set flush left. This was typed as

```
$$a_0 + \lcfrac1\\
   a_1 + \lcfrac 1\\
   a_2 + \lcfrac 1\\
   a_3 + \cfrac 1\\
   a_4\endcfrac
```

with an `\lcfrac` substituted for a `\cfrac` whenever the fraction should have the numerator flush left. There's also `\rcfrac` to get a numerator flush right.

DELIMITERS

The delimiters | and \| are rather special, since the same symbols serve as both a left delimiter and a right delimiter. When | and \| appear without a preceding `\left` or `\right`, TeX has no way of knowing which way they are being used, so they are simply treated as ordinary symbols. This works out fine in a formula like $|x|$, but the spacing can go wrong when there are binary operators around, and `\left` and `\right` might be needed even for ordinary size symbols:

`$|-x|=|+x|$`	$\|-x\| = \|+x\|$
`$\left|-x\right|=\left|+x\right|$`	$\|-x\| = \|+x\|$

In the first case the spacing is wrong because TeX typesets the sum and difference of '|' and 'x'; the `\left` and `\right` in the second example give TeX necessary clues to typeset the formula correctly.

In addition to the delimiters mentioned in Chapter 14, there are also

reverse slash: \	`\backslash`
upward arrow: ↑	`\uparrow`
double upward arrow: ⇑	`\Uparrow`
downward arrow: ↓	`\downarrow`
double downward arrow: ⇓	`\Downarrow`
up-and-down arrow: ↕	`\updownarrow`
double up-and-down arrow: ⇕	`\Updownarrow`

See also **big** and **set notation**.

And there are few more, rather special, delimiters. `\arrowvert` and `\Arrowvert` produce delimiters made from the repeatable parts of the vertical arrows and double vertical arrows, but without the arrowheads. The results are similar to `\vert` or `\Vert`, but the lines have a slightly different thickness, and the space between them is slightly wider. And `\bracevert` produces a delimiter made from the repeatable part of the large braces, but without the curly part. You can also use `\lgroup` and `\rgroup`, which are constructed from braces without the middle parts; and `\lmoustache` and `\rmoustache`, which give you the top and bottom halves of large braces. Here are the `\bigg` versions of `\vert`, `\Vert`, `\arrowvert`, `\Arrowvert`, and the other five special delimiters:

$$\cdots \Big| \cdots \Big\| \cdots \Big| \cdots \Big\| \cdots \Big| \cdots \Big(\cdots \Big) \cdots \int \cdots \Big\{$$

`\lgroup` and `\rgroup` may be an attractive alternative to parentheses around large matrices; they are available only in sizes `\Big` or more.

DEMO

See **automatic formatting**.

DIMENSIONS

Occasionally you'll need to ask TEX to create some space of a particular dimension, like 3 inches, or 16 points, or 2 centimeters. So you might need to know about the way that TEX measures things.

"Points" and "picas" are printers' traditional basic units, so TEX understands points and picas. TEX also understands inches and certain metric units, as well as the continental European versions of points and picas. Each unit of measure is given a two-letter abbreviation:

pt	point (the lines of this manual are 12pt apart)
pc	pica ($1\text{pc} = 12\,\text{pt}$)
in	inch ($1\,\text{in} = 72.27\,\text{pt}$)
bp	big point ($72\,\text{bp} = 1\,\text{in}$)
cm	centimeter ($2.54\,\text{cm} = 1\,\text{in}$)
mm	millimeter ($10\,\text{mm} = 1\,\text{cm}$)
dd	didôt point ($1157\,\text{dd} = 1238\,\text{pt}$)
cc	cicero ($1\,\text{cc} = 12\,\text{dd}$)
sp	scaled point ($65536\,\text{sp} = 1\,\text{pt}$)

Typical "dimensions" are

```
.3 in
1pt
+ 29 pc
-0.01in
0cm
```

A space between the number and the unit is optional, as is the space between the number and a + or - sign. Moreover, a + sign is redundant, but allowed.

dots]

You don't have to remember all these units, of course. You will probably want to use inches or centimeters if you ever ask TEX to leave space for a figure (*see* **vertical spacing**). The one important to thing to remember is that a "dimension" is always specified by a number followed by a unit. You must say `1in` to specify an inch—`in` by itself is not enough. And if you want to specify something whose dimension is zero (for an example, *see* **multline**) you *must* specify `0pt` or `0cm` or `0something`—`0` alone is not a dimension. The notation ⟨dimen⟩ will be used whenever we want to indicate a place where a dimension should be specified.

For many typesetting purposes, the most important units are two that we haven't mentioned yet—the `em` and the `ex`. These units depend on the particular font being used. In the fonts used for this manual, an em-dash is one em wide, and the lowercase 'x' is one ex high; but a font designer is free to choose the sizes for the `em` and the `ex` at will. The advantage of usings `em`'s and `ex`'s is that any spacing you specify will automatically be adjusted to correspond to the type size eventually used for setting the paper. `em`'s are generally best for horizontal measurements, and `ex`'s for vertical measurements.

By the way, a `\quad` is simply a horizontal space of exactly `1em`. But be sure *not* to use `\quad` when you mean to specify a dimension; `\quad` isn't a dimension, but an instruction to TEX to insert a blank space of the dimension `1em`.

Examples of the use of various ⟨dimen⟩s will be found elsewhere in this chapter.

DOTS

$\mathcal{A}_{\mathcal{M}}\mathcal{S}$-TEX has `\ldots` and `\cdots` to produce low dots ($\ldots$) and centered dots ($\cdots$), but usually you just have to type `\dots`, and the proper dots are magically selected. Occasionally, however, you need to understand more about the workings of `\dots` in order to assist it with its sleight of hand.

`\dots` works like a control sequence with one argument—it decides what kind of dots to use on the basis of the next symbol in the formula. This is a little problematical, because the protocol for low dots and centered dots is not universally accepted—some printers like to typeset formulas like $a_1, \cdots, a_n$ and $a_1 + \ldots + a_n$ (shudder). So `\dots` actually does its work by selecting one of four other control sequences:

> `\dotsc` the dots that go before commas (or semicolons),
> `\dotsb` the dots that go between binary operators and relations,
> `\dotsi` the dots that go between integral signs,
> `\dotso` the dots that are used in all other cases

For example, when you type '`\dots,`' in math mode, $\mathcal{A}_{\mathcal{M}}\mathcal{S}$-TEX translates this into '`\dotsc,`' and then the style you are using determines what `\dotsc` should be—in this manual, and in the `amsppt` style, `\dotsc` gives low dots, but in some other style `\dotsc` might give centered dots.

Thus, when you use `\dots` in math mode, the particular kind of dots to be typeset is determined both by the style and by the next symbol in the formula. Unfortunately, there is one situation where this scheme fails, namely, when there *isn't* any next symbol. If you type

```
Consider the infinite sequence $a_1,  a_2,  a_3,\dots$.
Let $a_1 + a_2 + a_3 + \dots$ be its sum, and
let $a_1   a_2   a_3   \dots$ be its product.
```

then `\dots` can't be expected to know which sorts of dots you want—it can only look ahead, and has no way of knowing what symbol was typed before it—and `\dots` simply chooses `\dotso` in all these cases. So when a formula ends with dots, the proper thing is to tell $\mathcal{A}_{\!\mathcal{M}}\mathcal{S}$-TEX which sort of dots it should be using:

```
Consider the infinite sequence $a_1, a_2, a_3, \dotsc$.
Let $a_1 + a_2 + a_3 + \dotsb$ be its sum, and
let $a_1 a_2 a_3 \dotso$ be its product.
```

If you remember to specify the kinds of dots you need at the ends of formulas, you will get the right sort of dots 99% of the time.

There's one situation where even right-thinking people may disagree on the proper use of dots. Consider the sentence

The quadrilateral $A_1 A_2 A_3 A_4$ clearly has area $x_1 x_2 x_3 x_4$, and in general the n-gon $A_1 A_2 A_3 \ldots A_n$ has area $x_1 x_2 x_3 \ldots x_n$.

In the formula $A_1 A_2 A_3 A_4$, the juxtaposition of the letters A_1, A_2, A_3, and A_4 has no special significance—they are simply being listed one after the other. But in the formula $x_1 x_2 x_3 x_4$ the juxtaposition of symbols indicates multiplication—this formula is really an abbreviation for $x_1 \times x_2 \times x_3 \times x_4$ or $x_1 \cdot x_2 \cdot x_3 \cdot x_4$. Similarly, in the last formula of the sentence, the juxtaposition of the symbols x_1, x_2, ... implies the binary operation of multiplication, so some authors[5] like to type '`$x_1x_2x_3\dotsb x_n$`.' in order to get $x_1 x_2 x_3 \cdots x_n$.

Ideally, the style ought to determine whether or not `\dotsb` should be used instead of `\dotso` in such cases, but there's no way that $\mathcal{A}_{\!\mathcal{M}}\mathcal{S}$-TEX can decide when a juxtaposition indicates multiplication, so `\dots` can't be expected to take care of situations like this on its own. However, $\mathcal{A}_{\!\mathcal{M}}\mathcal{S}$-TEX does give you one other gadget to help out—`\dotsm` for the dots that go between multiplied symbols. If you type

```
$x_1x_2x_3\dotsm x_n$
```

---

[5]Including the author of this manual, but not the author of TEX itself.

dots]

then the style will determine whether \dotsm will become \dotsb or \dotso.

By the way, you can stick to \dots if you are typing something like

$x_1\times x_2\times\dots\times x_n$ $x_1 \times x_2 \times \cdots \times x_n$

because \dots automatically gives \dotsb before the binary operator \times. And $\mathcal{A}_{\mathcal{M}}\mathcal{S}$-TEX purposely makes one tiny exception to the rule that \dots followed by a binary operator gives \dotsb:

$x_1\cdot x_2\cdot\dots\cdot x_n$ $x_1 \cdot x_2 \cdot \ldots \cdot x_n$

If you really want centered dots here, you can type

$x_1\cdot x_2\cdot\;\cdots\;\cdot x_n$ $x_1 \cdot x_2 \cdot \cdots \cdot x_n$

(for the "thick space" \; *see* **horizontal spacing**).

- **Exercise 20.2:**

Typeset the following equation.

$$G(z) = e^{\ln G(z)} = \exp\left(\sum_{k\geq 1}\frac{S_k z^k}{k}\right) = \prod_{k\geq 1} e^{S_k z^k/k}$$

$$= \left(1 + S_1 z + \frac{S_1^2 z^2}{2!} + \cdots\right)\left(1 + \frac{S_2 z^2}{2} + \frac{S_2^2 z^4}{2^2\cdot 2!} + \cdots\right)\cdots$$

$$= \sum_{m\geq 0}\left(\sum_{\substack{k_1,k_2,\ldots,k_m\geq 0 \\ k_1+2k_2+\cdots+mk_m=m}} \frac{S_1^{k_1}}{1^{k_1}k_1!}\frac{S_2^{k_2}}{2^{k_2}k_2!}\cdots\frac{S_m^{k_m}}{m^{k_m}k_m!}\right) z^m$$

\dots knows how to deal with the math symbols that already come with $\mathcal{A}_{\mathcal{M}}\mathcal{S}$-TEX, like \alpha, \iint, \cap, < and \leq (\dots also chooses \dotsb when it is followed by \not, since you are presumably using \not to "negate" a binary relation that comes next). But \dots probably won't know what to do with a new symbol that you \define. For example, in a paper where the symbol $\int_{-\infty}^{\infty}$ occurs frequently, it might be very convenient to

\define\Int{\int_{-\infty}^\infty}

But if you type

\Int\dots\Int

you won't get \dotsi between the \Int's, you'll just get \dotso. To get around this problem, $\mathcal{A}_{\mathcal{M}}\mathcal{S}$-TEX gives you two other control sequences \DOTSI and \DOTSB; these

[double accents

control sequences don't produce any printed symbols, but when they appear at the beginning of a definition, they alert \dots to the fact that \dotsi or \dotsb should be used. Thus, you could type

```
\define\Int{\DOTSI\int_{-\infty}^\infty}
```

and then `$$\Int\dots\Int$$` would come out just right.

And there's one other subtlety about \dots that you might want to know about (the last, we promise). When \dots, or any of the particular dots, \dotsc, ... occurs at the end of a formula, $\mathcal{A}_{\mathcal{M}}S$-TEX automatically inserts an extra thin space, since this looks better. And an extra thin space is also automatically inserted when any of these control sequences is followed by a right delimiter, like) or \biggr], etc. Once again, however, \dots needs to be clued in when you \define some new right delimiter of your own. For example, the previous chapter said that the author likes to

```
\define\({\left(}
\define\){\right)}
```

But \) should actually be defined by

```
\define\){\DOTSX\right)}
```

The control sequence \DOTSX doesn't produce a printed symbol, but it will tell \dots or \dotsc or ... to leave the extra thin space.

DOUBLE ACCENTS

See **accents in math mode.**

ERROR MESSAGES

(*See also* **syntax checking.**)

In the answer to Exercise 4.5 we saw the possible options after an error message:

```
Type <return> to proceed, S to scroll future error messages,
R to run without stopping, Q to run quietly,
I to insert something, E to edit your file,
1 or ... or 9 to ignore the next 1 to 9 tokens of input,
H for help, X to quit.
```

Typing S in reply to an error message is like typing ⟨carriage-return⟩ after this error message and all subsequent ones. These error messages will flash by on your terminal, possibly too fast to be read, but they will also appear in the transcript file. You can also put \scrollmode in your file; this is like typing S

files]

after the first error message that comes up, except that a later \errorstopmode puts you back into the normal situation.

Typing R and Q are even more drastic; you probably don't have to worry about these unless you are running TEX in batch mode, and then your system's experts will give you the details.

It's also possible to type 1, ..., 9 to get TEX to delete the next 1, ..., 9 tokens of input (a "token" is either a character, like A or + or $, or a control sequence, which counts as just one token, no matter how long its name). This feature of error recovery requires more experience and finesse, but it can be quite useful. For example, suppose that we have a file with the sentence

```
You have to type 8=2^3 in math mode.
```

When you try to run this through TEX, you will get an error message like:

```
! Missing $ inserted.
<inserted text>
                    $
<to be read again>

                  ^
    You have to type 8=2^
                         3 in math mode.
?
```

Now TEX has inserted a $ right before the ^ (and is ready to read the ^ again). The characters '8=2' have already been typeset outside of math mode, so there won't be the right amount of space around the = sign. There's no way to correct that at the moment, but we still don't want to hit ⟨carriage-return⟩ right now, because TEX would start to typeset the remaining text as a math formula, and the error probably wouldn't be detected until the paragraph ended without a closing $ sign appearing. On the other hand, if we type 2, followed by ⟨carriage-return⟩, then TEX will delete two characters, namely the $ that it has inserted, and the ^ from the file that it's ready to read again, so it'll be safely out of math mode again.

FILES

TEX has the control sequence \input, which we've mentioned in only one connection: unless you are using a special amstex program, your file must begin with the line \input amstex, to tell TEX to read in the file amstex.tex. Actually, you can use \input at other times also. For example, if you have a file `defs.tex` with commonly used `\define`'s, it's not really necessary to have your text editor dump this file into the beginning of another file `paper.tex` that you're working on. Instead you can just type `\input defs` at the beginning of `paper.tex`, and then TEX will read in the file `defs.tex` when it starts to process `paper.tex`. This usually makes file management a lot simpler: Each text file will be unencumbered by a mass of `\define`'s at the beginning, and if you decide to make any permanent modifications of your `\define`'s, the changes only have to be made in `defs.tex`, not in each file that uses your `\define`'s. On the other hand, with this arrangement, you can't run your file through TEX unless the file `defs.tex` is also around. So if you send your files over to another computer, you have to be sure to send the file `defs.tex` over too.

You can also have files like `defs.1`, `defs.2`, ..., with some extension other than 'tex', but then be sure to type `\input defs.1`, `\input defs.2`, ...

`\input` can also be useful when you are dealing with a large manuscript. For example, this manual consists of numerous files, `jot1.tex`, `jot2.tex`, ..., each of which was first run separately (with page numbering beginning anew in each chapter). The file `jot.tex` that produced the finished book contains little more than `\input jot1`, `\input jot2`, ...

FONTS IN MATH MODE

Mathematicians often use bold letters in math formulas, like $a\mathbf{x} + b\mathbf{y}^n$. In $\mathcal{A}_{\mathcal{M}}\mathcal{S}$-TEX this is typed as

```
$a\bold x + b\bold y^n$
```

Notice that `\bold` in math mode works **completely differently** than `\bf` in text: it is a control sequence with an argument, *not* a directive to change fonts. This usually works out best in math formulas, because bold letters are so often intermingled with the usual italic ones. `\bold` letters automatically change size correctly, so `$x^{\bold y}$` produces $x^{\mathbf{y}}$.

If you have a paper with lots of $\mathbf{x}$'s, $\mathbf{y}$'s and $\mathbf{z}$'s, you might want to do something like

```
\define\x{\bold x}
\define\y{\bold y}
\define\z{\bold z}
```

and then you can type $a\mathbf{x} + b\mathbf{xy} + c\mathbf{xyz}$ as

```
$a\x+b\x\y+c\x\y\z$
```

fonts in math mode]

You might also be tempted to try

```
$a\bold x+b\bold{xy}+c\bold{xyz}$
```

but this can occasionally produce mysterious results. For example, `$\bold{ff}$` would actually give ﬀ with a ligature! In any case, it's bad style to type things like `\bold{xy}`. If you have only a few bold letters in a paper, it won't hurt to type `\bold x\bold y` when you need it, and if you have lots of bold letters, then you will have made new control sequences like `\x`, `\y` and `\z` that will make things even easier.

In addition to `\bold`, there's `\roman`, which can occasionally be useful, `\slanted`, which probably won't ever be needed, and even `\italic` (to get the usual italic font used in text, as opposed to the font used in math formulas). But the `\slanted` and `\italic` letters usually won't change size in superscripts, since most style files won't have any fonts of the appropriate size for them.[6]

`\bold` should be applied only to letters. If you type `\bold +` and `\bold <` you'll just get the ordinary $+$ and $<$ signs, which are usually appropriate in formulas involving bold letters, like $x < y + z$. Eventually $A_{\!M\!}S$-TeX will probably have a bold $<$ sign for special situations, but it will have a single control sequence to name it, like `\boldless`.

Another special font is `\Cal`, to produce "calligraphic" letters: `$\Cal A, \dots \Cal Z$` produces $A, \ldots, Z$. The capital C in `\Cal` is supposed to remind you that only *upper-case* letters can be obtained in the `\Cal` font (though there's also `\ell` to produce ℓ).

Bold face **uppercase** Greek letters are treated as another family of variants: `\boldGamma` gives Γ, etc. But right now bold lowercase Greek letters like α don't even exist.[7] If and when such symbols are installed, they will constitute a new font,[8] `\boldgreek`. Similarly, bold italic letters like i would constitute a new font, `\bolditalic`. $A_{\!M\!}S$-TeX will probably also have a `\script` font that will be something like `\Cal`, but with both lower- and upper-case letters.

Someday $A_{\!M\!}S$-TeX will have an even more exotic font, `\frak`, the German Fraktur font: `$\frak g$` will give $\mathfrak{g}$, while `$\frak G$` and `$\frak S$` will give $\mathfrak{G}$ and $\mathfrak{S}$ (which only people like $\mathfrak{Goethe}$ and $\mathfrak{Schiller}$ can distinguish). Mathematicians often refer to this font as "gothic". Printers reserve this name for a

---

[6]Occasionally an entire book might have all the letters in formulas set in roman or boldface type, or something equally screwy. This is probably just a question of style—some one has decided that roman or bold letters should be used instead of the math italic letters. If this is the case, you shouldn't bother indicating `\roman` or `\bold` over and over again. The designer of the style can arrange things so that TeX automatically chooses the desired font in math mode.

[7]*See* **poor man's bold**.

[8]See Appendix F for information about forthcoming fonts.

sans-serif font, but the improper use is so widespread that $\mathcal{A}_{\mathcal{M}}\mathcal{S}$-T$_{\!E}$X will give you \goth as an alternative to \frak (useful if you don't want to worry about mistyping \frac when you mean \frak).

$\mathcal{A}_{\mathcal{M}}\mathcal{S}$-T$_{\!E}$X also plans to provide one further font as a concession to perverse notational usage. Mathematicians used to write things like R on the blackboard, or in their manuscripts, to indicate boldface. Now some of them use similar symbols in print, so $\mathcal{A}_{\mathcal{M}}\mathcal{S}$-T$_{\!E}$X will have a "blackboard bold" font \Bbb; like \Cal, it will work only when applied to upper-case letters.

Even when boldface letters are accented, it's customary to use ordinary accents:

$\hat{\bold x}$ $\hat{x}$

But you can also get $\hat{x}$ by typing $\bold{\hat x}$—this is the one case where \bold might profitably be applied to a group. Most special math fonts don't have their own special accents, and then you'll just get the usual one. For example, $\Cal{\hat A}$ just gives $\hat{A}$, since the \Cal font doesn't have its own \hat accent.

FOOTNOTES

In the amsppt style superscript numbers ^{1}, ^{2}, ..., are used as footnote markers, but occasionally you might need something different. For example, some journal styles use footnotes on the \title or \author to indicate affiliation or acknowledgement of support, etc., and they might use the footnote markers *, **, etc., even though other footnote markers are used within the text.[9] You can get \footnote to produce any marker you want by using its "literal argument" feature: simply enclose that marker inside a pair of double quote marks " right after \footnote. For example, for a footnote with the marker *, type

\footnote"*"{...}

A space after the first " or before the second is *not* ignored. (On the other hand, if you typed \foonote""{...} then you would get no marker at all, just a note at the bottom of the page.)

Although $\mathcal{A}_{\mathcal{M}}\mathcal{S}$-T$_{\!E}$X takes pains to allow footnotes inside \title, \author, and similar things, occasionally you may find that a \footnote simply disap-

---

[9]Ideally, a journal style would take care of such things by itself, but at present that isn't the case.

footnotes]

pears because you have buried it inside some other construction, like a displayed formula

$$y = x^2 \qquad \text{for some}^{10} x > 0$$

But you can handle even strange things like this, because \footnote can be broken down into a pair of control sequences. Typing \footnote{...} is equivalent to typing

    \footnotemark\footnotetext{...}

The control sequence \footnotemark produces the mark [1], [2], etc., that goes in the main text, whereas \footnotetext produces the footnote at the bottom of the page, having the same mark as the most recent \footnotemark or \footnote command. So you can type

    $$
    y=x^2 \qquad\text{for some\footnotemark\ $x>0$}
    $$
    \footnotetext{This is a really stupid place to have
      a footnote!}%
    But you can handle ...

with the \footnotetext following the \footnotemark as soon as possible, so that it will come out on the same page.[11] Notice that we needed \␣ after \footnotemark; a space isn't inserted automatically, since you might not want one, if \foonotemark precedes a comma, for example. (On the other hand, a space *before* \footnotemark is always ignored.) And we also had to be careful not to introduce an extraneous space before the text that comes after \footnotetext.

Even with \footnotemark and \footnotetext you will have problems if you want two footnotes in the same displayed formula: presumably what you ought to do is type \footnotemark twice within the formula, and then immediately after type \footnotetext twice. But the very first \footnotetext is now primed to give the number of the *second* \footnotemark! So $\mathcal{A}_{\mathcal{M}}S$-TeX also gives you \adjustfootnotemark to change the current number for footnotes. You would have to type

    \adjustfootnotemark{-1}%
    \footnotetext{...}%
    \adjustfootnotemark{1}%
    \footnotetext{...}%

---

[10] This is a really stupid place to have a footnote!
[11] To be on the safe side, put \nopagebreak right before the \footnotetext, but if you're dealing with a displayed formula, remember to put the \nopagebreak *within* the displayed formula (*see* **page breaks**).

to reduce the current number by 1, to give the right number for the first
\footnotetext, and then increase it by 1 once again, to give the right number for the second \footnotetext.

Both \footnotemark and \footnotetext allow a "literal argument" "...".
So[12,13] you can even do things like this. You just have to type

```
So\footnotemark"$^{12,13}$" 'you can even do things like this.
\footnotetext"$^{12}$"{A footnote.}%
\footnotetext"$^{13}$"{And another.}%
You just have to type ...
```

(Of course, this only works if you know what numbers you want to use. If you were really typesetting a book with lots of footnotes, including lots of these double footnotes, then you would want a TEXnician to provide a style file that has some sort of \doublefootnote control sequence to do the whole thing automatically.)

In the previous parts of this book the numbering of footnotes began anew on each page. But in this chapter they are numbered consecutively. In the amsppt style footnotes are numbered consecutively within the whole paper. This is the sort of arrangement that printers traditionally prefer, because type is first set in large chunks called "galleys", and then broken up later into pages, so there is no way of knowing on what page a footnote will appear until the footnote number has already been set.

Some journal styles may call for footnote numbers to begin anew on each page, but this causes difficulties, because TEX has some of the same problems with footnotes as a traditional typesetter. Although TEX doesn't really produce "galleys", it has usually typeset quite a bit more than a page before deciding just where the best page break will occur. Consequently, TEX may have decided that a footnote should have number 3, say, before realizing that it will actually wind up on the next page and should therefore have the number 1.

If you are using such a style, then you can type

```
\adjustfootnotemark{-2}
```

to get the numbering correct. But journal styles that are serious about numbering footnotes in this way should really solve the problem by using a "two-pass" system: the first time you process the file TEX can write itself a file of notes about which footnotes got numbered incorrectly, and then it can use this file to get things right when it works on the file the next time.

---

[12] A footnote.
[13] And another.

greek letters]

In addition to the "literal argument" feature of \footnote, the **amsppt** style provides an "optional argument" feature, which can also be used to adjust footnote numbering. If you type

\footnote [2]{...}

you will get a footnote that is treated as if it were the second footnote. This means that the number will be ^{2} in the **amsppt** style, though in other styles it might be [**2**] or ‡, etc. This special numbering simply interrupts the standard one—if you use \footnote again, you will get the number you would get if the \footnote[...] hadn't intervened. \footnotemark and \footnotetext also have this "optional argument" feature.

FRACTIONS AND RELATED SYMBOLS

If you want to vary the thickness of the fraction line in \thickfrac, type

\thickfrac\thickness{⟨number⟩} . . .

\thickness2 makes the fraction line twice as thick, \thickness{1.5} makes it 1.5 times as thick, etc.

If you want delimiters around a \frac use

\fracwithdelims⟨left delimiter⟩⟨right delimiter⟩

For example, you can get the "Legendre symbol" with

$$\fracwithdelims()ab$$ $$\left(\frac{a}{b}\right)$$

You could also try using \left(and \right) around \frac ab, but it's preferable to use \fracwithdelims, because it causes TEX to adjust the spacing specially, in a way that isn't possible with a general \left...\right construction.

There's a \thickfracwithdelims for a thicker fraction line, and you can use \thickness{⟨number⟩} right after the two delimiters to vary the thickness. For example, you can type

$\thickfracwithdelims<>\thickness0nk$

to get the "Euler number" $\left\langle{n \atop k}\right\rangle$.

GREEK LETTERS

TEX has a few Greek letters that are never used in math, and are included only because they might be needed when you are using $...$ to imitate Greek type.

`\varsigma` (ς) shouldn't be confused with `\zeta` (ζ) and `\upsilon` (υ) is just a bit wider than **v** (υ). See also page 260.

HORIZONTAL BRACES

You can get horizontal braces over or under a formula with `\overbrace` and `\underbrace`.

$$\texttt{\$\$\textbackslash overbrace\{x+\textbackslash dots+x\}\$\$}$$

$$\texttt{\$\$\textbackslash underbrace\{x+y+z\}\$\$}$$

$$\overbrace{x + \cdots + x}$$

$$\underbrace{x + y + z}$$

You can get other formulas over an `\overbrace` or under an `\underbrace` simply by typing them as superscripts or subscripts, just as if you were dealing with a large operator:

```
$$\overbrace{x+\dots+x}^{\text
   {$k$ times}}
$$\underbrace{x+y+z}_{>\,0}$$
```

$$\overbrace{x + \cdots + x}^{k\ \text{times}}$$

$$\underbrace{x + y + z}_{>0}$$

(The thin space was inserted in the second example because TEX normally leaves no space around a binary operator in `\ssize`.)

See also **compound symbols.**

- **Exercise 20.3:**
Typeset the following.

$$\frac{b^{p+1} - a^{p+1}}{1 + \underbrace{1 + \cdots + 1}_{p\ \text{times}}} = \frac{b^{p+1} - a^{p+1}}{p+1}.$$

- **Exercise 20.4:**
How would you typeset the following display?

$$\underbrace{f\left(\frac{1}{n}\right) + \cdots + f\left(\frac{1}{n}\right)}_{n\ \text{times}} = f\left(\underbrace{\frac{1}{n} + \cdots + \frac{1}{n}}_{n\ \text{times}}\right) = f(1) = c.$$

HORIZONTAL SPACING

We've already mentioned that thin spaces `\,` should be used in formulas like $f(x)\,dx$. Thin spaces should also be inserted after exclamation points (which

horizontal spacing]

have a special meaning in mathematical formulas), when they are followed by a number or letter or by a left delimiter:

`$(2n)!/\bigl(n!\,(n+1)!\bigr)$`	$(2n)!/\bigl(n!\,(n+1)!\bigr)$
`$$\frac{52!}{13!\,13!\,26!}$$`	$\dfrac{52!}{13!\,13!\,26!}$

Thin spaces are also frequently useful after square roots that happen to come too close to the next symbol:

`$\sqrt2\,x$`	$\sqrt{2}\,x$
`$O\bigl(1/\sqrt n\,\bigr)$`	$O\bigl(1/\sqrt{n}\,\bigr)$

(The second sort of construction is so common that I find it convenient to

```
\define\ssqrt#1{\sqrt{#1}\,}
```

so that I can simply change \sqrt to \ssqrt whenever I decide it's needed.)

Other than this, you can usually rely on TEX's spacing until after you look at what comes out, and it shouldn't be necessary to insert optical spacing corrections except in rare circumstances. When you get to this fine tuning stage, you'll also want to have \! in your tool kit—this is a *negative* thin space that removes the same amount of space that \, adds. Here are some examples where \, and \! provide a little extra finesse:

`$\sqrt{\,\log x}$`	$\sqrt{\,\log x}$
`$[\,0,1)$`	$[\,0,1)$
`$\log n\,(\log\log n)^2$`	$\log n\,(\log\log n)^2$
`$x^2\!/2$`	$x^2\!/2$
`$n/\!\log n$`	$n/\!\log n$
`$\Gamma_{\!2}+\Delta^{\!2}$`	$\Gamma_{\!2}+\Delta^{\!2}$
`$R_i{}^j{}_{\!kl}$`	$R_i{}^j{}_{\!kl}$
`$$\int_1^b\!\int_a^b$$`	$\displaystyle\int_1^b\!\int_a^b$

Notice, by the way, that \! isn't necessary when you are using \iint and similar operators—these control sequences essentially insert their own \!'s.

The control sequence \thinspace is synonymous with \, and each can be used both in math mode and outside of it. Similarly, \negthinspace is synonymous with \! and they can be used either in math mode or out of it. There are also much less frequently used control sequences \medspace, \negmedspace, \thickspace and \negthickspace. A \medspace is the amount that T_EX normally inserts around binary operators, and a \thickspace is the amount it ordinarily inserts around binary relations. A \thickspace might be used now and then (*see* **dots**), and \; can be used as an abbreviation.

If you're extra fussy you may sometimes feel that even \, and \! aren't small enough for the fine adjustments that you would like to make. So A_MS-T_EX also gives you @, for a really small horizontal space ($\frac{1}{10}$ of \,), and @! for a negative horizontal space of this amount. Notice that these uses in math mode are completely different from their uses in text, for the proper spacing after punctuation following upper-case letters.

For larger horizontal spacing we have \quad and \qquad, but for more variety, *see* **phantoms**.

HYPHENATION

If you have some dubious words like databases and Treemunch, and you'd like to know how T_EX thinks they should be hyphenated, just type

```
\showhyphens{databases Treemunch}
```

(in your file, or after T_EX gives you a prompt). This will cause T_EX to type the following on your terminal:

```
Underfull \hbox (badness 10000) detected at line ...
[] \tenrm databases Treemu-nch
```

showing that T_EX doesn't find any place to put a hyphen in databases, and that it thinks Treemunch should be hyphenated after the u. Ignore the Underfull \hbox message—it's a side-effect of the way \showhyphens works.

See also **breaking lines**.

INPUT

See **files**.

LARGE OPERATORS

(*See also* **compound symbols**.)

Although the amsppt style normally uses "limits" on \sum and related large operators, you can change this convention by typing \NoLimitsOnSums. (If you type \LimitsOnSums you will get back the old conventions, but you really shouldn't switch back and forth between styles.) Similarly, there is \LimitsOnInts and \NoLimitsOnInts to control \int, \oint, \iint, etc. Style conventions can

large operators]

also affect operators like \max and \min that are produced by the control sequences \operatornamewithlimits: some styles might not use "limits" on *any* such operators. Typing \NoLimitsOnNames will invoke such conventions, and \LimitsOnNames will return to the old conventions. Of course, operators like \sin and others produced by \operatorname *never* have "limits".

These control sequences are "global"—they affect the rest of the paper, even if they are used in a group or between $ signs. When you use them in a journal style, they will simply be ignored.

The remainder of this entry deals with certain subtleties about large operators with limits that you can probably ignore, leaving journal editors to worry about them.

We've mentioned that when you enclose a \sum with limits in parentheses, or other delimiters, it's usually best to use the \bigg size, but Exercise 14.18 gives an example where you would really want to use \left and \right. Actually, if you type

$$\left(\sum_{i=1}^n p_ix_i \right)$$

you might get something surprising, like

$$\left(\sum_{i=1}^{n} p_i x_i \right)$$

That's because TeX adds extra "buffer" space above and below any limits, so that they won't interfere with surrounding formulas. The font used for this manual has a buffer of only 1pt, but in the above formula a buffer of 3pt was used. If you want to be totally safe in such situations, you can shave off the buffer space with \shave: the input

$$\left(\shave{\sum_{i=1}^n} p_ix_i \right)$$

will give

$$\left(\sum_{i=1}^{n} p_i x_i \right)$$

no matter what the buffer is.

It is also appropriate to use \shave for large operators enclosed in square roots:

$$\sqrt{\shave{\sum_{i=1}^n} a_i}$$

In addition to `\shave`, there's `\topshave` and `\botshave`, to shave off only the top or bottom buffer. For example, you might type

```
$$\sqrt{  \botshave{\sum_{0<i<n} }a_i }$$
```

to be sure to get

$$\sqrt{\sum_{0<i<n} a_i}$$

And if you've typed

```
$$\frac{\dsize 1+\sum_{i=1}^N a_i}
       {\dsize 1+\sum_{j=1}^M b_j}$$
```

to get

$$\frac{1+\sum_{i=1}^N a_i}{1+\sum_{j=1}^M b_j}$$

but now you want to put parentheses around the formula, the safest way is to type

```
$$\left( \frac{\dsize 1+\topshave{\sum_{i=1}^N } a_i}
        {\dsize 1+\botshave{\sum_{j=1}^M } b_j} \right) $$
```

—we want to shave off the space above the N in the numerator and below the $j=1$ in the denominator, but the buffer space below the $i=1$ and above the M shouldn't be diddled with.

$\mathcal{A}_{\mathcal{M}}S$-TEX also has the control sequence `\buffer` to specify the dimension of the buffer, which you might use to fine-tune certain output.

The style really ought to determine how big the buffer is, but you can type

```
\ChangeBuffer{⟨dimen⟩}
```

to change the buffer to some other ⟨dimen⟩ (*see* **dimensions**). Such a change is "global"—it affects everything, even if it is typed inside a group or inside $ signs. However, there's also `\ResetBuffer` to return the buffer to its old value. Generally, you should use `\ChangeBuffer` only to make a permanent change to the amsppt style, and most journal styles will probably ignore this control sequence.

line breaks]

LINE BREAKS

We've already learned about `\linebreak` to force a line break. $\mathcal{A}_{\mathcal{M}}\mathcal{S}$-TeX also has `\newline`. When you use `\newline` instead of `\linebreak` you force a line break, but the line isn't spread out to the right margin
so you can get things
printed like this when you type

```
... but the line isn't spread out to the right
margin\newline
so you can get things\newline
```

If you type `\newline\newline` you'll introduce a blank line. There's no point having `\newline` at the end of a paragraph, but you can do it. (If you do something sufficiently strange, like having `\newline\newline` at the end of a paragraph, you will get a spurious `Underfull \hbox` message, which you can just ignore.)

A tie ~ prohibits a line break, and also inserts an ordinary interword space. Occasionally you might want `\nolinebreak` to prohibit a line break, without this additional feature. For example, you might want to put `\nolinebreak` at the end of a sentence, if for some reason you didn't want the end of the sentence to occur at the end of a line. You should leave a space between the period at the end of that sentence and the `\nolinebreak` instruction that follows.

And finally, there's `\allowlinebreak` to allow a line break where TeX normally wouldn't do so. For example, line breaks are normally allowed only *after* hyphens and dashes; you can't start a line with a hyphen or en-dash or em-dash (except after something like a displayed formula). But occasionally you might want an em-dash to appear at the beginning of the next line, perhaps because it doesn't fit well at the end of the present line. Just type '`...\allowlinebreak---...`' and a line break will be allowed there.

Spaces before `\allowlinebreak` are not ignored, but using `\allowlinebreak` between words will have no effect at all, since line breaks are always allowed between words. In particular, `\allowlinebreak` won't help to eliminate an `Overfull \hbox`; these come about because TeX is unwilling to stretch spaces too much, and only `\linebreak` will force TeX to overcome it reluctance.

In addition to using `\allowlinebreak` before dashes, you might want to use it after slashes. TeX doesn't hyphenate a word like "input/output" that contains non-letters, and it won't break the word right after a / either. So you might resort to '`input/\allowlinebreak output`' if this word was causing problems.

TeX also has the control sequence `\slash` to indicate a / where TeX is allowed to break the line, so you could also type '`input\slash output`'. This is a little different from /allowlinebreak, because TEX considers a line break after \slash to be somewhat undesirable, namely, as bad as a line break after a hyphen (the style file decides just how bad this is). $\mathcal{A}_{\mathcal{M}}\mathcal{S}$-TEX will ignore any space before \slash.

MATRIX

A \matrix doesn't change size when you use it in text. So you can end up with things like $\begin{pmatrix} a & b \\ c & d \end{pmatrix}$, which is just what some authors want when a complicated matrix isn't displayed. But you can also get $\begin{pmatrix} a & b \\ c & d \end{pmatrix}$ in text by typing

```
$\left(\smallmatrix a&b\\
c&d\endsmallmatrix\right)$
```

There are no \smallpmatrix, etc.—you just have to put in the delimiters your-self. \format and \vspace are allowed with \smallmatrix, but the control sequence \spreadmatrixlines (*see* **vertical spacing**) isn't.

If you type something like

```
$$\pmatrix
0\\
0&1\\
0&1&2\\
0&1&2&3\\
0&1
\endpmatrix$$
```

you will get

$$\begin{pmatrix} 0 & & & \\ 0 & 1 & & \\ 0 & 1 & 2 & \\ 0 & 1 & 2 & 3 \\ 0 & 1 & & \end{pmatrix}$$

Rows with fewer than the maximum number of & signs simply get blank entries in the remaining columns.

\matrix and its relatives allow you to have as many columns as you like, but when you type a \format...\\ line after \matrix the number of &'s usually determines the maximum number of &'s that can be used per row. However, there is a special feature to deal with formats with a periodic structure. If you

matrix]

type && instead of &, then the part of the first "row" that follows will be repeated over and over. For example

```
\format \l&&\quad\l \\
```

specifies a matrix in which the first column is set flush left, and this column is followed by an arbitrary number of columns each set flush left and preceded by a \quad of space. Similarly a & at the very beginning implies a periodic structure:

```
\format &\quad\l\\
```

gives an arbitrary number of columns each set flush left and beginning with a quad of space (which probably isn't what you want). You can only have one && or initial & in the first "row".

Sometimes the matrix

$$\begin{pmatrix} a_{11} & a_{12} & \ldots & a_{1n} \\ a_{21} & a_{22} & \ldots & a_{2n} \\ \vdots & \vdots & \ddots & \vdots \\ a_{m1} & a_{m2} & \ldots & a_{mn} \end{pmatrix}$$

is set somewhat differently:

$$\begin{pmatrix} a_{11} & a_{12} & \ldots & a_{1n} \\ a_{21} & a_{22} & \ldots & a_{2n} \\ \multicolumn{4}{c}{\dotfill} \\ \multicolumn{4}{c}{\dotfill} \\ a_{m1} & a_{m2} & \ldots & a_{mn} \end{pmatrix}$$

You can get this by typing

```
$$
\pmatrix a_{11} & a_{12} &\hdots &a_{1n}\\
a_{21}&a_{22}&\hdots&a_{2n}\\
\hdotsfor 4\\
\hdotsfor4\\
a_{m1}&a_{m2}&\hdots&a_{mn}
\endpmatrix
$$
```

Here \hdotsfor4 tells TEX to print horizontal dots for 4 columns; the number of columns must be specified because TEX doesn't even know for sure how many columns there are going to be until it's finished with the matrix. Be sure to have the \\ after the \hdotsfor4, unless it is followed by '&...'.

Alas, \hdotsfor won't work quite right when you try to start the dots after the first column. If you typed

```
$$
\pmatrix a_{11} & a_{12} &\hdots &a_{1n}\\
a_{21}&a_{22}&\hdots&a_{2n}\\
a_{31}&\hdotsfor3\\
\hdotsfor 4\\
a_{m1}&a_{m2}&\hdots&a_{mn}
\endpmatrix
$$
```

you'd get

$$
\begin{pmatrix}
a_{11} & a_{12} & \dots & a_{1n} \\
a_{21} & a_{22} & \dots & a_{2n} \\
a_{31} & \dotfill & & \\
 & \dotfill & & \\
a_{m1} & a_{m2} & \dots & a_{mn}
\end{pmatrix}
$$

This looks bad because the \hdotsfor3 extend over the *entire* second column, and part of that column is the \quad of space that separates it from the previous column. If you really need the dots like that, in the inner columns, the right thing to type is

```
$$
\pmatrix a_{11} & a_{12} &\hdots &a_{1n}\\
a_{21}&a_{22}&\hdots&a_{2n}\\
a_{31}&\innerhdotsfor 3 \after \quad\\
\hdotsfor 4\\
a_{m1}&a_{m2}&\hdots&a_{mn}
\endpmatrix
$$
```

The construction \innerhdotsfor...\after{...} gives dots a specified number of columns, but beginning after the \quad (or whatever space you might specify if you use \format). Be sure to have the & before \innerhdotsfor.

By the way, if you don't like the spacing of the dots given by \hdotsfor, you can use the construction \spacehdots ⟨number⟩\for... for some ⟨number⟩ (in decimal form). The normal \hdotsfor uses ⟨number⟩ = 1.5; a smaller ⟨number⟩

matrix]

will make the dots closer, a larger ⟨number⟩ will make them further apart. And there's also

> \spaceinnerhdots⟨number⟩\for...\after...

You can get the input for a \matrix actually to look like a matrix with the TAB key. On most terminals this key moves the cursor over about 10 spaces, which is useful if you want your input

```
to      be      lined
up      in      columns
so      that    you
get     a       matrix
on      the     screen.
```

$\mathcal{A}_{M}\mathcal{S}$-TEX usually treats TAB exactly like a space, but inside a \matrix the TAB key has exactly the same meaning as the & sign. So you can type TAB instead of &:

```
$$\matrix\format
\c      (TAB) \quad\l (TAB) \quad\r\\
x       (TAB) .1       (TAB) 1\\
x+y     (TAB) .11      (TAB) 11\\
x+y+z   (TAB) .111     (TAB) 111
\endmatrix$$
```

Notice that you still put \\ between the rows. You probably won't want to use TAB this way unless the entries can be typed within the amount of space that TAB skips. But if you suddenly get stuck, remember that you can always use & in place of any TAB. (All this assumes, of course, that your text editor actually inserts a TAB character [ASCII Control-I] in your file when you hit the TAB key.)

Unfortunately, TAB won't work right if you try to use it in a definition, like

> \define\mymatrix{\matrix...(TAB)...\endmatrix}

If you really want to define certain matrices while using TAB, then you have to do the following:

```
\enabletabs
\define\mymatrix{\matrix...(TAB)...\endmatrix}
\disabletabs
```

A TAB appearing in your file anywhere between \enabletabs and \disabletabs is treated exactly the same as a &, even a TAB in ordinary text. This is pretty dangerous, because it's easy to have a stray TAB in your file without knowing about it, and a & is tolerated only in special situations. So you should remember to type \disabletabs as soon as possible. To encourage you in this practice, \enabletabs always expects to see \disabletabs before the end of the paragraph, and TEX will complain if it doesn't appear.

But if you like to live dangerously, there's \EnableTabs, which enables TAB permanently. There's also \DisableTabs, to disable them again, but the control sequence \EnableTabs doesn't have to be followed by \DisableTabs.

MOD

The word 'mod' often appears in formulas in roman type, but it functions rather differently than operators like sin and cos. Actually, 'mod' is used in two different ways; there is \bmod for situations where 'mod' occurs between two quantities, and is being used as a binary operator like +, and there is \pmod for the cases where 'mod' occurs parenthetically at the end of a formula:

```
$\gcd(m,n)=\gcd(n,m\bmod n)$        gcd(m, n) = gcd(n, m mod n)
$x\equiv y+1\pmod{m^2}$             x ≡ y + 1   (mod m²)
```

$$\gcd(m,n) = \gcd(n, m \bmod n)$$
$$x \equiv y + 1 \pmod{m^2}$$

Notice that \pmod inserts the parentheses automatically.

Some authors might prefer to set the second of the above formulas without the parentheses: mod m^2. So $\mathcal{A}_{\mathcal{M}}\mathcal{S}$-TEX also gives you \mod:

```
$x\equiv y+1\mod{m^2}$              x ≡ y + 1   mod m²
```

$$x \equiv y + 1 \mod m^2$$

And some folks prefer the formula

$$x \equiv y + 1 \quad (m^2)$$

without any mod at all, and just parentheses. They, of course, get \pod:

```
$x\equiv y+1\pod{m^2}$
```

MULTLINE

You can actually use \multline for a formula that takes several lines; simply put \\ between the lines, as usual. All the lines between the first and last will normally be centered. However, you can shove any of these lines to the left or right by typing

```
\shoveleft{...}\\
```

operators]

or

```
\shoveright{...}\\
```

Notice that `\shoveleft` and `\shoveright` are control sequences with an argument; the entire line that you want to shove over must follow it, enclosed in braces, and you still need the `\\` at the end.

You can use `\vspace` and `\spreadlines` to vary the spacing in a `\multline` (*see* **vertical spacing**).

You can also change the gap that `\multline` leaves at the left and right margins, by typing `\multlinegap{⟨dimen⟩}` (*see* **dimensions**). For example, if your `\multline` is a little too long to fit, you can eliminate the space at the left and right margins by typing

```
$$
\multlinegap{0pt}
\multline ...
    ...\endmultline
$$
```

The gap will revert to its original value at the end of the display. Notice that we must say `0pt` and not just `0`. But there's also `\nomultlinegap`, a synonym for `\multlinegap{0pt}`.

`\multlinegap` is allowed only within `$$` signs. But there's also `\MultlineGap`, to permanently change the gap, and thereby create a new style. Naturally, `\MultlineGap` will be ignored by most journal styles.

NEW SYMBOLS

See **compound symbols** and **fractions and related symbols** (and also **accents**, for `\accentedsymbol`).

NUMBERS, OLD STYLE

If you type `\oldnos{5,283.06}` you will get 5,283.06. You can also use `\oldnos` in math mode; the numbers will change size properly in superscripts, and, although a thin space is normally inserted after a comma in math mode, no spaces will be inserted after commas within `\oldnos`.

NUMBERS ON PAGES

See **page numbers**.

OPERATORS

We've already mentioned that when an operator consists of two parts, like lim inf, a thin space should usually be used between the two parts. Within

\operatorname or \operatornamewithlimits the symbols ', ', *, -, /, :, ; and , are all treated as ordinary text symbols, with ' ' and ' ' giving " and " and -- and --- giving – and — . Periods, commas and colons will be followed by a small amount of space.

OVERBRACING

See **horizontal braces**.

OVERSETTING

See **compound symbols**.

PAGE BREAKS

Corresponding to \linebreak, $\mathcal{A}_{\mathcal{M}}\mathcal{S}$-TEX has \pagebreak. When used between paragraphs, it forces a page break, spreading the page out to the bottom margin. When \pagebreak is used within a paragraph, it causes a page break *at the end of the line in which it appears*. \pagebreak isn't allowed in ordinary math mode, but it is allowed in *display* math mode. In fact, the proper way to cause a page break after a displayed formula is to use \pagebreak *within* the displayed formula (if you use \pagebreak right after the display, the page will end with the extra blank space that goes right after displayed formulas).

\nopagebreak is used to prevent a page break, in exactly analogous ways. In particular, if you want to prevent a page break after a displayed formula, you should type it *within* the display (if you type it right after the display it will have no effect).

$\mathcal{A}_{\mathcal{M}}\mathcal{S}$-TEX's \newpage can only be used between paragraphs; it causes a page break and fills up the rest of the page with blank space (analogous to \newline).

$\mathcal{A}_{\mathcal{M}}\mathcal{S}$-TEX doesn't have any \allowpagebreak to allow page breaks, since page breaks are normally allowed between any two lines of text. (For page breaks between lines of displayed formulas *see* **aligning formulas**.)

PAGE SIZE

You can change the size of the page in the amsppt style by typing

```
\pagewidth{⟨dimen⟩}
\pageheight{⟨dimen⟩}
```

paragraphs]

for suitable ⟨dimen⟩'s (*see* **dimensions**). The page height excludes the line for the page number. Other styles will probably ignore these commands.

When you change the dimensions of a page you will probably also want to changes its position on the $8\frac{1}{2}$ by 11 sheet of paper. Typing

   \hcorrection{⟨dimen⟩}

will move the entire page horizontally to the right by ⟨dimen⟩, and

   \vcorrection{⟨dimen⟩}

will move it down by ⟨dimen⟩.

PARAGRAPHS

You can get a paragraph to start flush left by preceding it with \flushpar. Of course, if you have several such paragraphs in a row, you'll probably want to put something like \smallpagebreak between them (*see* **vertical spacing**). But if you want your entire document processed in this way, you shouldn't have lots of \smallpagebreak\flushpar's in it; instead you should have someone create you a new document style that automatically produces such a format.

Paragraphs of text within displayed formulas are another matter. We've seen that \text gives text within formulas, but it's always a single, unbreakable, line of text. But sometimes you have more to say:

$$\sqrt{k+1} - \sqrt{k} = f(k+1) - f(k)$$
$$= f'(x) = \frac{1}{2\sqrt{x}} \quad \text{for some } x \text{ in } (k, k+1), \text{ by the Mean Value Theorem}$$
$$< \frac{1}{2\sqrt{k}}.$$

$\mathcal{A}_{\mathcal{M}}\mathcal{S}$-TᴇX gives you \foldedtext for situations like this. When you type

   \foldedtext{...}

the text '...' is folded into a paragraph (except that it starts with no indentation). The format determines the width of such \foldedtext, but you can specify any other ⟨dimen⟩ (*see* **dimensions**), by typing

   \foldedtext\foldedwidth{⟨dimen⟩}{...}

Thus, the above display was typed as

```
$$
\align
\sqrt{k+1}-\sqrt k &=f(k+1)-f(k)\\
    &= \frac1{2\sqrt x}\qquad
        \foldedtext\foldedwidth{2in}{for some $x$ in $(k, k+1)$,
            by the Mean Value Theorem}\\
    &<\frac1{2\sqrt k}.
\endalign
$$
```

Notice that the \foldedtext was treated as a new symbol, and the center line gets lined up with other symbols. There's also \topfoldedtext if you want the top line of the paragraph to line up with other symbols, and \botfoldedtext if you want the bottom line to line up.

As with \intertext (*see* **aligning formulas**) you can't use a \par or blank line in \foldedtext, but you can use \endgraf instead.

PHANTOMS

Sometimes you want a space that isn't a \quad or \smallvspace or ..., but simply a space "just the size of that thar formula". You can do wonders along this line with TEX's \phantom. If you type (in or out of math mode) you get a blank space that takes up exactly as much space as '...'. You might find useful if you want a new symbol that hasn't been defined yet, but which you want to be the size of an X. (But if you want something the size of a $\sum$, and which also acts like a large operator, then ask a TEXnician for help.)

If you type \hphantom{...} you get a "horizontal phantom", which has exactly the width of '...' but no height, so it acts effectively like a space of the desired width. For example, we can define the control sequence \dwidth, mentioned in the answer to Exercise 18.5, by

```
\define\dwidth{\hphantom0}
```

- **Exercise 20.5:**
Explain how to typeset the following display.

$$m' = m_1 + 2n_1 = 3m + 4n,$$
$$n' = m_1 + \ n_1 = 2m + 3n.$$

roots]

● **Exercise 20.6:**
Typeset the following display.

$$f(x) = \sum_{n=1}^{\infty} a_n x^{n-1} = 1 + x + 2x^2 + 3x^3 + \cdots ,$$

$$xf(x) = \sum_{n=1}^{\infty} a_n x^n = x + x^2 + 2x^3 + \cdots ,$$

$$x^2 f(x) = \sum_{n=1}^{\infty} a_n x^{n+1} = x^2 + x^3 + \cdots .$$

There's also \vphantom{...}, which gives a blank space that has no width, but which sticks up above the line (and down below the line) the same amount as '...' does. For example, a \mathstrut (*see* **struts**) is simply a \vphantom(. You can make TEX think that a formula has any size you want if you combine \phantom's with various kinds of \smash's (*see* **smash**).

POOR MAN'S BOLD

Eventually $\mathcal{A}_{\mathcal{M}}\mathcal{S}$-TEX may have boldface versions of various math symbols, but you can always get a poor man's version of bold with \pmb:

```
$\pmb\alpha^{\pmb\infty}$                    𝜶^∞
$\bold x\pmb<\bold y\pmb+\bold z$            x < y + z
```

The \pmb version of a binary operator or relation is another binary operator or relation. (But if you want to create another large operator $\sum$, by making $\sum$ bolder, then you'll have to consult a TEXnician.)

PROCLAIM

See **automatic formatting**.

QED

At the end of a proof you can type \qed. In the amsppt style this will give a black box '∎'; in other styles it might give 'Q.E.D.' or some other abbreviation, or perhaps nothing at all. If a proof ends with a displayed formula, the \qed should be included as the last line of that displayed formula.

ROOTS

It's easy to get something like $\sqrt[3]{x}$ or even such weird things as

$$\sqrt[\alpha+\beta]{1 + \frac{a}{b}}$$

You just type

```
$$
\root\alpha+\beta\of{1+\frac ab}
$$
```

$\mathcal{A}_{\mathcal{M}}S$-T$_{\!E}$X tries to place the root in the proper position, but if you want to adjust the position of the root somewhat you can type \uproot{⟨number⟩} after \root in order to move the root up ⟨number⟩ units, and you can move the root to the left ⟨number⟩ units by putting \leftroot{⟨number⟩} after it. You can use both \uproot{⟨number⟩} and \leftroot{⟨number⟩} together, in either order, as long as nothing else intervenes between them and \root:

```
$$\root \uproot 3 \leftroot{-2}
\alpha+\beta \of{1+\frac ab}$$
```

$$\sqrt[\alpha+\beta]{1+\dfrac{a}{b}}$$

The unit by which the \root is moved is quite small, so fine adjustments are easy to make.

ROSTER

\roster is often used within a paragraph, so the material following \endroster will not start a new paragraph unless you specifically leave a blank line or type a \par after it. Thus, \roster...\endroster interrupts a paragraph somewhat like a displayed formula. (On the other hand, \endproclaim and \enddemo always start a new paragraph.)

Although \roster numbers each \item automatically, \item can also have an "optional argument" (compare **footnote**). If you type

```
\item[5] ...
```

with the 5 in brackets, then that item will be given the number 5, regardless of its position in the list. Succeeding \item's will then be numbered starting from 6 (unlike the situation for \footnote, where an optional argument doesn't affect the numbering of succeeding \footnote's). This can be useful, for example, if you've made a \roster with four \item's, and now you want another \roster with the numbering continuing on from there. Just type the first \item of the second \roster as \item[5].

Of course, \item[5] will really give a label like (5), or possibly (v) or [e], etc. But you can also specify the label exactly as you want by using the "literal argument" feature of \roster (again compare with **footnote**.) If you type

```
\item"{\bf 3}"
```

set notation]

with {\bf 3} within a pair of double quote marks ", then the item will be labelled **3**, exactly as typed.

$\mathcal{A}_{\mathcal{M}}S$-T$_{\!E\!}$X also gives you \therosteritem to conveniently refer to a particular \item without knowing what style is being used. If you type \therosteritem7 you will get (7) or (vii) or [g] ..., depending on the particular style that is used.

Some authors like to run the first condition of a roster into the text, so that only the subsequent conditions start with a special indentation. Thus, they want (1) The first condition that we want to state when we use \roster to produce a list,

(2) The second, which doesn't have extra line spacing before it,

(3) The last.

which is followed by some extra line spacing. To get this, you type \runinitem instead of \item for the first item.

When the first item of a roster is treated like this, you might prefer to have the subsequent lines of the first item indented as much as all the remaining items. This turns out to be a little tricky; if you want this to happen, then you must type \Runinitem right before *the paragraph in which the* \roster\runinitem *appears*. \Runinitem will only affect the first \roster in the paragraph. If you want to have two such rosters within the same paragraph, type

```
\Runinitem ... \roster\runinitem
   ...
\endroster\Runinitem
... \roster\runinitem ...\endroster
```

SET NOTATION

For simple formulas like $\{a, b, c\}$ you just type the obvious things:

```
$\{a,b,c\}$                          {a, b, c}
$\{1,2,\dots,n\}$                    {1, 2, ..., n}
```

$\{a, b, c\}$

$\{1, 2, \ldots, n\}$

But when a vertical bar | or a colon : appears in the middle of such a formula, it looks better if there are thin spaces inside the braces, and instead of | (or \vert) you should use '\mid', which gives extra space around the | (the colon automatically gets extra space, so you don't have to worry about it):

```
$\{\,x\mid x>5\,\}$                  { x | x > 5 }
$\{\,x:x>5\,\}$                      { x : x > 5 }
```

$\{\, x \mid x > 5 \,\}$

$\{\, x : x > 5 \,\}$

When the delimiters get larger, as in

$$\big\{ \, \big(x, f(x)\big) \mid x \in d \, \big\}$$

the \bigl and \bigm for the delimiters should be accompanied by (*see* **big and bigg**) a \bigm| for the |:

$$\bigl\{\,\bigl(x,f(x)\bigr)\bigm|x\in d\,\bigr\}$$

SIZE OF TYPE

In the amsppt style everything is set in \tenpoint type, except that footnotes and references (*see* Appendix B) automatically get set in \eightpoint type. You can use \eightpoint yourself to reduce the point size. This might be useful for a displayed formula that doesn't quite fit.

SMASH

If you type \smash{...} you make TEX think that '...' doesn't stick up above the line or down below it. And there's \topsmash and \botsmash if you just want TEX to ignore that part above the line or the part below. By combining \smash's with \phantom's you can make TEX think that any symbol looks like any other, as far as spacing is concerned.

Here's a case where \smash's could be used for fine tuning the finished product. In Exercise 11.2 we typeset

Hölder's Inequality: Let $0 \le p, q \le \infty$ with $\dfrac{1}{p} + \dfrac{1}{q} = 1$. If $f \in L^p(\mu)$ and $g \in L^q(\mu)$, then $fg \in L^1(\mu)$ and

$$\|fg\|_1 \le \|f\|_p \|g\|_q.$$

Like any good typesetter, TEX left extra space after the first line, so that the fractions $\dfrac{1}{p}$ and $\dfrac{1}{q}$ wouldn't interfere with anything on the next line. But this is one of those cases where this stratagem misfired, because the next line doesn't extend that far over, so there really seems to be too much space. If we type

$\botsmash{\dfrac1p}+\botsmash{\dfrac1q}=1$

then TEX will ignore the amount that these fractions dip below the line, and we will get

Hölder's Inequality: Let $0 \le p, q \le \infty$ with $\dfrac{1}{p} + \dfrac{1}{q} = 1$. If $f \in L^p(\mu)$ and $g \in L^q(\mu)$, then $fg \in L^1(\mu)$ and

$$\|fg\|_1 \le \|f\|_p \|g\|_q.$$

syntax checking]

See Exercise 20.4 in the entry **horizontal braces** for another use of \smash.

SPACING

See **horizontal spacing** and **vertical spacing**.

SQUARE ROOTS

See **roots**.

STACKING SYMBOLS

See **compound symbols**.

STRUTS

When you take the \sqrt of a formula, the size of the $\sqrt{}$ depends on the formula: compare $\sqrt{a}$ and $\sqrt{d}$ and $\sqrt{y}$. When you have only one \sqrt in a formula this is fine, but instead of the formula $\sqrt{a} + \sqrt{d} + \sqrt{y}$ you might want the more uniform expression $\sqrt{a} + \sqrt{d} + \sqrt{y}$. You can obtain this by typing

```
$\sqrt{\mathstrut a}+\sqrt{\mathstrut d}
  +\sqrt{\mathstrut y}$
```

A \mathstrut is an invisible symbol that sticks above the line and below the line as much as any letter is going to. *See* **phantoms**.

SYNTAX CHECKING

The first time you run your file through TeX you're probably just hoping to catch all the syntax errors you've made, and don't expect to get output. If you type \syntax at the beginning of your file, after the \documentstyle line, then TeX won't produce any output, but it will process your file 2–4 times as fast, and still check any syntax errors.

The only slight problem with \syntax is that you also won't get any Overfull box messages. So after you've used \syntax you might want to change it to \galleys. This causes TeX to act like a printer that is typesetting galleys—so you'll be told when things don't fit—but the final pages are never assembled, so you don't get any output. You probably won't find \galleys that useful, because it only speeds TeX up a little, and frequently you can't deal with Overfull box'es intelligently until you actually see output.

$\mathcal{A}_{\mathcal{M}}\mathcal{S}$-TeX also allows one other possibility, in case you don't want to have to go back into the file to change or delete \syntax. If you type \printoptions, $\mathcal{A}_{\mathcal{M}}\mathcal{S}$-TeX will ask you

```
Do you want S(yntax check), G(alleys) or P(ages)
Type S, G or P, follow by <return>
```

You can type either S or s, etc., but if you type something inappropriate the question will just be repeated. You can also type ahead the reply before you even see the question, while TEX is taking its time reading in the amstex.tex file and the style file; TEX will take note of your reply, even though the reply won't appear on the screen until the appropriate time.

This is for TEX exegetes only. $\mathcal{A}_{\mathcal{M}}S$-TEX allocates quite a few boxes, dimensions, etc., but they normally don't appear in the transcript file, since they aren't of much interest to the casual user. If you type \showallocations at the beginning of the file, then the allocations will appear in the transcript file.

TAGS

In the amsppt style you can get tags set on the right instead of the left by typing \TagsOnRight. And \TagsOnLeft returns them to the left again. These commands are "global" they affect everything that follows even if used in a group {...} or between $ signs. Of course, journal styles will presumably ignore these instructions.

You ought to stick to either the \TagsOnLeft that comes automatically with the amsppt style or with \TagsOnRight. *Don't* try to use these control sequences to get all the formulas on even-numbered pages to have tags on the left and all the formulas on odd-numbered pages to have tags on the right! That's simply a totally different (inherently inconsistent) style.

If you have lots of tags like (A_1) and (A') or $(*)$ and $(**)$, but seldom use hyphens or en-dashes in your tags, you might prefer $\mathcal{A}_{\mathcal{M}}S$-TEX to treat your tags as math formulas instead of as text. You can get this by typing \TagsAsMath; and \TagsAsText returns to the other convention (these commands are also "global"). Journal styles will not ignore these instructions, since they don't affect the actual output, but only the input needed to produce it. It's definitely not a good idea to switch back and forth between \TagsAsMath and \TagsAsText, because if you get confused and type \tag A_2 when you should type \tag {A_2} things will get messy.

Some formats center the tags even on split formulas. You can get the amsppt style to do this by typing

        \CenteredTagsOnSplits

And you can revert to the usual tagging with

        \TopOrBottomTagsOnSplits

These are also "global" commands. If you just want to center the tag on a single split formula (to get it to fit better on the page, say), you shouldn't use these control sequences: simply type the split formula as an \aligned.

ties]

If you have to refer within the text to displayed formula (17), you have the slight problem that some style might set this some other way, say as [17] or **17** (the most common convention, by far, however, is to put the number in parentheses). So *AℳS*-TEX allows you to type \thetag{17}; then you will get whatever the style happens to use.

You might also want to override the style used for some special formula. Perhaps, for some reason, you want to be sure that one formula gets the tag **(3)**, with bold parentheses. You can do this by using \tag's "literal argument" feature: Type

```
$$...\tag"\bf(3)" $$
```

and the tag will come out exactly as you typed it between the pair of double quote marks " (compare **footnote** and **roster**).

TEXT IN MATH

See **paragraphs**.

TIES

We've already mentioned in Chapter 5 that it's usually a good idea to type the tie ~ after an abbreviation in the middle of a sentence. Here's a further list of places where ties belong. (Reprinted with permission from Donald E. Knuth, *The TEXbook*, © 1986 American Mathematical Society, published jointly by the American Mathematical Society and Addison-Wesley Publishing Company.)

(1) In references to named parts of a document:

```
Chapter~12          Theorem~1.2
Appendix~A          Table~B@-8
Figure~3            Lemmas 5 and ~6
```

(The use of @- was explained in the side-trip at the end of Chapter 5.)

(2) Between a person's forenames and between multiple surnames:

```
Donald~E. Knuth              Luis~I. Trabb~Pardo
Bartel~Leendert van~der~Waerden   Charles~XII
```

But if a name is too long we can't risk tying it all together:

```
Charles Louis Xavier~Joseph de~la Vall\'ee~Poussin.
```

(3) Between math symbols in apposition with nouns:

```
dimension~$d$        width~$w$          function~$f(x)$
string~$s$ of length~$l$
```

But the last example should be compared with

```
string~$s$ of length $1$~or more.
```

(4) Between symbols in series:

```
1,~2, or ~3
$a$,~$b$, and ~$c$.
1,~2, \dots,~$n$
```

(5) When a symbol is a tightly bound object of a preposition;

```
of~$x$
from 0 to~1
increase $z$ by ~1
in common with ~$m$.
```

This rule doesn't apply to compound objects, however:

```
of $u$~and~$v$.
```

(6) When mathematical phrases are rendered in words:

```
equals~$n$      less than~$\epsilon$      (given~$X$)
mod~2           modulo~$p^e$              for all large~$n$
```

Compare 'is~15' with 'is 15~times the height'.

(7) When cases are being enumerated within a paragraph:

```
(b)~Show that $f(x)$ is (1)~continuous; (2)~bounded.
```

Whew!

TITLE

See **author, title, etc.**

TOPMATTER

A paper in a journal might begin with some special material, like a dedication, or a note that the paper was presented as an invited address, etc. The amsppt style doesn't try to anticipate such things, but it does have

```
\pretitle{...}
\preauthor{...}
\preaffil{...}
\predate{...}
\preabstract{...}
\prepaper{...}
```

vertical spacing]

to specify extra material that goes before \title, \author, etc. But you can't use these unless you know something about TEX itself; all vertical spacing, change of fonts, etc., have to be specified directly to TEX within each of these control sequences.

UNDERBRACING

See **horizontal braces**.

UNDERSETTING

See **compound symbols**.

VERTICAL SPACING

Sometimes you want to leave some space between paragraphs for a figure, etc. If you type \midspace{⟨dimen⟩} between paragraphs, for some ⟨dimen⟩ (*see* **dimensions**), then TEX will try to leave ⟨dimen⟩ space between the paragraphs. Actually, TEX will leave this amount of space with a little extra space above and below, so that your ⟨dimen⟩ can be just the height of the figure itself. If there isn't enough room on the page for this space, then TEX will put it on the top of the next page.

If you type

\midspace{⟨dimen⟩} \caption{...}

then ... will be centered as a caption under the space. If the caption is long, it will be first be divided into lines of a certain length (3 inches less than the width of the page in the amsppt style). You can change that length by typing

\caption\captionwidth{⟨dimen⟩} {...}

You can also type \topspace{⟨dimen⟩} between paragraphs, and TEX will try to put the space at the top of the current page. If it doesn't fit, it will go on the top of the next page. \caption and \captionwidth can be used with \topspace also.

\midspace and \topspace cannot be used within a paragraph; they must be used *between* paragraphs.

Although \midspace and \topspace reserve a particular amount of space on a page, there are other situations where that's not quite what you want. For example, there is normally a certain amount of space before a \proclaim, but this space naturally disappears if the \proclaim happens to come at the top of a page. TEX provides a way of producing any amount of such disappearing vertical space, but this capability shouldn't be needed when you are using a particular style, which already determines the space before \proclaim's, etc. However, the amsppt style does provide \smallpagebreak, \medpagebreak and \bigpagebreak to produce vertical spaces this big:

\smallpagebreak ‗‗‗ \medpagebreak ‗‗‗‗ \bigpagebreak ‗‗‗‗‗

They should be used only between paragraphs (but the very beginning and very end of a paragraph will count as "between paragraphs"). You might use a \smallpagebreak or \medpagebreak before a \flushpar (*see* **paragraphs**).

The names \smallpagebreak, \medpagebreak and \bigpagebreak are used for these control sequences because they not only leave some space, they also tell TEX that a page break at this point would be not bad, fairly good, or rather good, respectively. Of course, if the page *is* broken at this point, the space will disappear. You can't add two or more of these spaces together by typing one after the other—the net effect will simply be that of the largest.

$\mathcal{A}_{\mathcal{M}}$S-TEX does allow much more leeway in specifying vertical spacing within displayed formulas. When you create a multi-line display with \align, etc., the lines are usually set just a jot further apart than normal lines of text. But when large symbols are involved, it's often useful to add some extra space yourself.

In any math construction that uses \\ to separate lines, like \align, \aligned, \gather, \Sb, \matrix, etc., you can type

\vspace{⟨dimen⟩}

right after any \\ to insert space of that ⟨dimen⟩ right after the line. Although any ⟨dimen⟩ can be specified, it's customary to express the amount as 1\jot or .5\jot, etc; then your adjustments will probably look good in any format.

Sometimes it's a good idea to add vertical space between *all* lines of a display. For example, the display in Exercise 19.11 would look better if 1\jot were added after each \\. But that's a lot of work, so $\mathcal{A}_{\mathcal{M}}$S-TEX also gives you \spreadlines. If you type

```
$$
\spreadlines{⟨dimen⟩}
 · · ·
 · · ·
$$
```

then all the lines of the displayed formula will be spread apart by ⟨dimen⟩. $\mathcal{A}_{\mathcal{M}}$S-TEX allows you to type \spreadlines only in a display (between $$ signs), and then it affects only this display.

vertical spacing]

\spreadlines will affect the spacing of an \align or \aligned or \gather, etc., but it *won't* affect the spacing in the lines of a \Sb or \Sp (which are rather special constructions), or in any sort of \matrix, since a \matrix is usually thought of as a separate subformula whose spacing shouldn't be diddled with. Of course, you can still vary the spacing between rows of a \matrix by putting \vspace{⟨dimen⟩} after any \\, and $\mathcal{A}_\mathcal{M}S$-TEX also gives you the control sequence \spreadmatrixlines to vary them all. If you type

> \spreadmatrixlines{⟨dimen⟩}

in a display, then the spacing after all rows of any \matrix in the display will be increased by ⟨dimen⟩ (you can type

> {\spreadmatrixlines{⟨dimen⟩}\matrix
> ...\endmatrix}

if you only want to affect one \matrix).

\cases is treated just like \matrix: \spreadlines doesn't affect it, but you can put \vspace{⟨dimen⟩} after any \\, and \spreadmatrixlines increases the spacing after rows of \cases just as it does with \matrix.

Appendices

Appendix A: Answers To All The Exercises

PPP.1. 1, 2, 4 or 8, depending.

1.1. In the first case the output would have been

> In addition to the upper- and lower- case letters, and the numerals:

There is still the desired space after "upper-", since the ⟨carriage-return⟩ after upper- has exactly the same effect as a space. But there is also an undesired space in "lower- case". A line of TEX input shouldn't end with a hyphen unless you really want a space after that hyphen.

In the second case the input might look perfectly respectable on a typewriter, but it would produce a much more serious error:

> In addition to the upper- and lower-case let- ters, and the numerals:

You should never add a hyphen to a word to hyphenate it on the screen, the way you might on a typewriter, since the linebreaks on the screen have nothing to do with the linebreaks that TEX will use, and TEX has no way of knowing that the hyphen wasn't meant literally.

1.2.

```
E said, ''I still type two spaces after
a period---I just can't break the habit---but
I'm always careful to use an en-dash rather than a
hyphen for number ranges like '480--491' in a
bibliography.''
```

Notice that there are no spaces, or ⟨carriage-return⟩s, around the em-dashes --- or around the en-dash --, which should be used in 480--491. Notice also that the " is not used anywhere in the answer. By the way, this exercise follows the standard grammarian's rule that punctuation is placed inside the quotation marks, but throughout this manual the author adheres to the 'logical' placement of punctuation and quotation marks, so that the sentence would end: ... in a bibliography". Of course, you would get this by typing

```
... in a bibliography''
```

1.3. -- - gives '– -', an en-dash followed by a space followed by a hyphen. ---- gives '—-', an em-dash followed by a hyphen, which looks quite horrible.

Incidentally, – and — are "ligatures", new symbols that TEX automatically inserts when it sees the combinations -- and ---, in exactly the same way that the combination fi is changed into the ligature 'fi'. Ligatures are not actually built into TEX, but are determined by the fonts being used. IF WE SET OFF THIS PHRASE—FOR ILLUSTRATIVE PURPOSES—IN THE "SMALL CAPS" FONT you can see that ff doesn't give a ligature in this font, although --- still gives an em-dash, and ` ` and ' ' still give double quote marks. A type designer might want Eir new typeface to have an extra long dash '——' and E might arrange for this dash to be a new ligature, which TEX could recognize by the input ----. (By the way, in the amsppt style you can get the "small caps" font with the control sequence \smc, but other styles might not recognize this control sequence.)

1.4. TEX distinguishes between upper- and lower-case letters in the name of a control word, so \Par would be an entirely different control word from \par. \Par isn't a control word that TEX recognizes, so it would cause TEX to stop and issue an error message, saying that \Par is undefined. We will learn a little more about error messages in Chapter 4.

1.5. It's just as if you had left two blank lines in a row; since TEX treats the two blank lines in a row as just one, the net effect is simply to end the paragraph. It might be useful to end paragraphs this way if you want to scan through a file a paragraph at a time, but your text editor doesn't have a convenient way of searching for blank lines. By searching for \par's you can use the text editor to find the ends of paragraphs, while the blank lines help you scan through the file visually.

1.6.

```
Most people can print '\$\$' passably, but it's
harder to print U.S. \$\$ that are passable.
```

Notice that a space was typed after the fourth \$ because the fourth $ is followed by a space in the output, but no spaces were typed after the other \$'s.

1.7.

```
\AmSTeX\ is just a specialized version of \TeX,
but once you have mastered it you will have joined
the \TeX nical revolution.
```

(We could also have put a space after \TeX at the end of the first line.)

1.8. \$\␣\␣ produces '\$ 1.00', with two spaces after the \$ sign. And the input \$␣\␣1.00 produces exactly the same output; the first space comes from the space after \$, which isn't ignored, since \$ is a control *symbol*, and the second space comes from the \␣ after it.

2.1. You can type

```
{\AmSTeX} is just a specialized version of {\TeX},
but once you have mastered it you will have joined
the {\TeX}nical revolution.
```

This looks a lot nicer in the input file, but it takes more typing strokes. Notice that now we *mustn't* have a space after either occurrence of {\TeX}.
    You could also type

```
\AmSTeX{} is just a specialized version of \TeX,
but once you have mastered it you will have joined
the \TeX{}nical revolution.
```

2.2. The spaces in the group {\P␣␣} would be ignored. Of the next two spaces, just one would count, in accordance with the rule that TeX ignores all but the first space in a sequence of spaces. But each of the next two groups {␣}{␣} would contribute one more space.

2.3. {-}{-} or -{-} or -{}-, etc.

2.4.

```
{\sl The Joy of \TeX\/} explains how to put things in the
file that will be ommitted [{\sl sic\/}] in print.
```

If you use \lbrack and \rbrack you must type

```
\lbrack{\sl sic\/}\rbrack\ in print.
```

2.5.

```
Italicizing just one {\it word\/} or even the
{\it pre\/}fix or {\it suf\/}fix of a word
is fine, but don't go {\it overboard}.
```

This example shows that it is important not to forget the space after the \/} combination; $\mathcal{A}_{\mathcal{M}}\mathcal{S}$-TeX won't put this space in automatically, since in certain cases you might not want it. On the other hand, there is no reason why you would want a space *before* the \/, so if you type {\it word \/}, $\mathcal{A}_{\mathcal{M}}\mathcal{S}$-TeX will simply ignore the space and assume that you meant to type {\it word\/}. By the way, without grouping, the sentence could be typed as

```
Italicizing just one \it word\/ \rm or even the
\it pre\/\rm fix or \it suf\/\rm fix of a word
is fine, but don't go \it overboard\rm.
```

This requires considerably more care with regard to spaces.

2.6.

```
Most grammarians say that punctuation after a word
should be in the {\it same font:\/} but many writers
prefer to {\it switch back\/}; this is especially
true when the punctuation is a semi-colon.
```

The italic correction after the colon wasn't very important; without it you would get ' ... in the *same font:* but many ... ', which might seem preferable to some.

2.7. If you typed ``{\it different}'' instead of ``{\it different\/}'' you would get "*different*", with the *t* bumping into the quotes.

2.8. We can type

```
W. Ambrose,
{\sl Higher order Grassmann bundles\/} {\bf3}
(1964), 199--238.
```

or we can include the \bf within the \sl group

```
W. Ambrose,
{\sl Higher order Grassmann bundles\/ \bf3}
(1964), 199--238.
```

In the second case, by the time TeX gets to the } the font has already been switched to \bf, which the } then turns off.

(The two answers aren't really equivalent, because in the first case the space before the **3** comes from the usual roman font, while in the second case it comes from the \sl font, but no one's going to notice the difference.)

2.9.

```
{\it Explain ... typeset a\/ {\rm roman} word
... sentence.}
```

2.10.

```
{\sl When a sentence is typeset in slanted
type, you might want to underline a\/ \underbar{\rm roman}
word for emphasis.}
```

2.11.

```
Everyone will be happy when \TeX\ finally arrives,
and Dr. Treemunch can start typing his own so-called
scholarly manuscripts. His last {\it opus\/}---%
which The Amer. Jour. Recr. Drugs recently published---%
created quite a sensation, particularly the material
that he has expounded on pages 22--23.
Including this material cost an extra
\$1,000, but it did make \P\P\ 1 and 2 quite popular.

The head of the department, our own I. M. Stable,
attributes Treemunch's recent aberrant behavior
to his ``research'' for this paper, but
others point out that Treemunch's name
isn't on many  computers' databases,
so  his name often gets hyphenated quite
strangely, which may account somewhat for his
feeling of being ill-used.
```

3.1. Now you get the message

```
Underfull \hbox (badness 1226) ...
```

The line has been spread out too much, resulting in an `Underfull` box, and the "**badness**" of this over-stretching is **1226**. By looking at the output you can decide for yourself how bad this actually is. The `amsppt` style normally prohibits linebreaks that result in a "**badness**" of more than 200, so it demands that the spacing between words be quite uniform.

3.3. It's worse than before! Adding \hyphenation{data-base} at the beginning of the file didn't help T_EX hyphenate "databases". If we're going to be using the word "database" frequently, we should add

```
\hyphenation{data-base}
\hyphenation{data-bases}
```

so that T_EX will know how to hyphenate all possible forms of the word— "database" and "databases" are simply two different words for T_EX, and it won't infer the hyphenation of one from the other. The unhyphenated word "databases" now sticks out even further into the margin because T_EX *did* know how to hyphenate "Treemunch's". That's because T_EX considers a "word" to be a sequence of *letters*, so "Treemunch's" is not really another word—it's just the old word "Treemunch" followed by an apostrophe. (As an interesting exercise, you might add

```
\hyphenation{Tree-munch's}
```

to your file and see what happens.)

4.1. The transcript file will begin:

```
This is TeX, Version 1.1 (preloaded format=plain 84.8.1)
**goof
(goof.tex (amstex.tex) (amsppt.sty)
! Undefined control sequence.
l.4 Here is a word in {\It
                           italics\/} and here is one
? i\it
```

Notice that your response i\it is included along with the error message. (Also notice that, even if you invoked T_EX with tex goof, the transcript file begins **goof, just as if you had simply typed tex and then typed goof in response to a ** prompt.)

The transcript file will also contain the help message you got, and finally end with

```
[1]
Output written on goof.dvi (1 page, 548 bytes).
```

4.3. You will get the error message

```
! Undefined control sequence.
l.4 Here is a word in {\ititalics
                                  \/} and here is one
?
```

Now T_EX is going to ignore \ititalics, so you should type i\it italics.

4.4. After the [1] that tells you page 1 has been typeset, there will be the message

```
(\end occurred inside a group at level 1)
```

When you look at the output, you will easily see where the unmatched brace occurs, because everything after "*italics*" will also be in italics.

In the case of a long paper, you might not want to take the time to print it, and hope instead to discover the error at the terminal. One procedure is to insert \enddocument about half of the way through the paper, and run it through TeX again. If you get the same message, then the unmatched brace must occur in the first half of the paper, otherwise it occurs in the second half. If it occurs in the second half, put a % before the \enddocument, so that it will be "commented out", but you will still be able to remember where it was, and try putting another \enddocument about three quarters of the way through the paper; similarly, if it occurs in the first half, comment out the first \enddocument and put a new one about a fourth of the way through. Continuing in this way, you'll eventually get the error trapped in a small region that you can examine carefully without too much strain.

4.5. '!' isn't a valid reply to an error message, so TeX lists your options:

```
Type <return> to proceed, S to scroll future error messages,
R to run without stopping, Q to run quietly,
I to insert something, E to edit your file,
1 or ... or 9 to ignore the next 1 to 9 tokens of input,
H for help, X to quit.
```

We've learned about typing <return>, I, H and X. Typing E in response to an error message should get you back to your editor, at the point where the error was discovered. The other options are mentioned in Part 3.

4.6. When TeX gets to the end of your file, it will give a * prompt. Unlike the ** prompt that asks for a file name when you first invoke TeX without naming a file, the * prompt is simply asking for more input. At this point you shouldn't type i, to tell TeX to insert something, because TeX is already expecting input. If you do type i, you won't get the \insert> prompt—TeX will simply assume that the i was more text to typeset, and it'll respond with the * prompt again. The right thing to type is simply \enddocument.

By the way, it's possible to get a * prompt even if you have the necessary \enddocument at the end of your file. Certain errors can put TeX into a weird state that causes it to gobble up your \enddocument, and then it may continue gobbling up anything else you type after a * prompt, simply handing you back another * prompt. At this point you might be tempted to resort to the operating system's interrupt, but this is a pretty desperate gambit, and you probably won't get a transcript file to allow you to study the situation further. Instead, you might try responding to such a * prompt with some undefined control sequence like \foo. TEX will probably give you an error message, saying that \foo is undefined, followed by the usual ? on the next line. Then you can type X or x and exit gracefully.

4.7. You will get the error message
```
! I can't find file 'goofy.tex'
<*> goofy
```

```
Please type another input file name:
```
At this point you can type the right name goof.

4.8. TEX will give the error message
```
! I can't find file 'mystyle.sty'.
1.2 \documentstyle{mystyle}
```

```
Please type another input file name:
```
Notice that the $\mathcal{A}_{\mathcal{M}}\mathcal{S}$-TEX directive \documentstyle{mystyle} tells TEX to read the file mystyle.sty, rather than mystyle.tex, since "style" files are given the extension sty. The proper thing to type at this point is amsppt.sty. If you simply type amsppt, TEX will try to find a file called amsppt.tex, and complain once again that it can't find it.

5.1. Zzzzzzzz

5.2. He changed the input '\P\P\ 1 and 2' to '\P\P\~1 and ~2', forgetting to delete the \ after \P\P. This introduced the control sequence \~, which, as we'll learn in the next chapter, causes a ~ accent to be placed over the next symbol.

5.3.
```
Weird fruit (mangos, papayas, etc\.) are
avoided by farmers, fastidious eaters, et al.
```
If 'etc.' were typed instead of 'etc\.' there would be a larger space after the right parenthesis—the extra space at the end of a sentence "transmits through" a right parenthesis, to take care of situations where an entire sentence is enclosed in parentheses. The '\.' *isn't* used after 'al', since this abbreviation happens to *be* the end of a sentence (and it isn't used after 'et', since this isn't an abbreviation at all!).

6.1. The rule fails when the % is part of the control symbol \%. (T_EX reads in a line from left to right and as soon as it sees the backslash character \ it immediately reads ahead until it has found the end of a control sequence; so \% gets removed from the line before there is a chance for T_EX to apply the rule to ignore things after a % sign.)

6.2.

```
My \#1 solace is  M~\&~M's, though any candy is dandy;
I agree 100\% with O.~ Nash\dag\ that liquor
is quicker, but a fifth of J~\&~B \@~\$13.95 \{price as of
this writing\} is beyond my means.
```

6.3. h\'a\vc ek is wrong because there is no space after the \v, so T_EX will think we are trying to use a control word called \vc. The input h\' a\v c ek has the required space after the \v (and a space after the \', which is allowed), but it has an incorrect space after the c; this input would give 'háč ek'.

6.4.

```
belov\'ed prot\'eg\'e; r\^ole co\"ordinator;
souffl\'es, cr\^epes, p\^at\'es, etc.
```

6.5. Type na\"\i ve (or na{\"\i}ve or na\"{\i}ve).

6.6. Ernesto Ces\'aro, P\'al Erd\H os, Serge\u i\ \t Iur\'ev, Eduard \v Cech, \b T\^abit ibn Qorra, Mu\d hammad ibn M\^us\^a al-Khw\^ariz% m\^\i. Notice the \␣ after the \i in Serge\u\i.

6.7. \AE sop's \OE uvres en fran\c cais. You could also type {\AE}sop's {\OE}uvres en fran\c{c}ais; this looks a little nicer in the file, but it's harder to type.

6.8. \O ystein Ore, Anders Jonas \AA ngstr\"om, Stanis\l aw \'Swie% rczkowski

6.9.

```
?`What did you say, Se\~nor?
I said, ``!`Ma\~nana is good enough for me!''
```

6.10.

```
{\sl Commentarii Academi\ae\  Scientiarum Imperialis
Petropolitan\ae\/} is now {\sl Akademi\t\i a
Nauk SSSR, Doklady.}
```

6.11. You'd get: Well ...,actually you do have to worry a little.

6.12.

> ```
> You can now use \TeX\ to print about 95\% of any ordinary
> text that you will ever encounter. But before you add
> \TeX pertise to your r\'esum\'e, we ought to resume our
> study of \TeX, since you still can't typeset things like
> \dots, well, like this paragraph.
> ```

7.1. Type

> ```
> \title Treemunch's Tribulations \\
> \rm Strange Names\\
> \rm And People
> \endtitle
> ```

The \rm is needed on both lines, because $\mathcal{A}_{\mathcal{M}}\mathcal{S}$-TEX treats the lines individually, and implicitly surrounds each with braces. Thus, if you wanted the third line to be in the same font as the first, you would only have to remove the second \rm (but you could also type {\rm Strange Names}\\ to be on the safe side).

8.1. You'd get "If the formula$y = x - 1$ is true … ", since the space within the $ signs is ignored. $\mathcal{A}_{\mathcal{M}}\mathcal{S}$-TEX doesn't automatically leave spaces before and after formulas, since you don't always want them, as the next exercise shows.

8.2.

> ```
> Deleting an element from an $n$-tuple leaves
>     an $(n-1)$-tuple.
> ```

Although $\mathcal{A}_{\mathcal{M}}\mathcal{S}$-TEX usually doesn't leave spaces before and after formulas, sometimes printers like to make the formulas stand out from the text more. They don't typeset $z = x + y$ but instead typeset $z = x + y$ by adding a little more space around the formula. If you happen to be using a document style that calls for such conventions, $\mathcal{A}_{\mathcal{M}}\mathcal{S}$-TEX will automatically add the desired extra space. Unfortunately, however, $\mathcal{A}_{\mathcal{M}}\mathcal{S}$-TEX has no way of knowing that the extra space *isn't* desired in special cases. So you'll have to tell $\mathcal{A}_{\mathcal{M}}\mathcal{S}$-TEX that you want a \snug fit:

> ```
> Deleting an element from an $n$\snug-tuple leaves
>     an $(n-1)$\snug-tuple.
> ```

8.3.

> ```
> Consider the graph of $f-g+h$ in the $x$--$y$ plane.
> ```

Notice that you mustn't type $x--y$ plane in this situation, since this would give '$x - -y$ plane'.

8.4. `$1+2\{3+4[5+6(7+x)]\}$`

8.5. You would get $1 + 23 + 4[5 + 6(7 + x)]$; the braces { and } would simply indicate a grouping, in which nothing of interest happens.

8.6. You would get the formula $x+y$, without the proper spacing around the + sign. In math mode, braces around a symbol cause it to be treated as an ordinary symbol, even if it would normally be a binary operator, or some other type of symbol requiring special spacing. So *don't* put in superfluous braces in situations like this unless you have some special reason.

8.7. Here's one of those special situations referred to in the answer to Exercise 8.6: If you type `$1{,}000z$` you will get $1,000z$, without any spacing around the comma.

8.8. First of all, you don't want to rashly replace *all* x's, since some of them exist in te<u>x</u>t. So your editor had better have a "query replace" feature that shows you each x and asks you whether you want to make the replacement. (Fortunately, x's outside of math formulas aren't all that common. If you had to replace all e's in formulas by `\epsilon`, then even this wouldn't work.) But now comes the tricky part: Be sure to replace the x's in formulas by `\kappa⌴`, not simply by `\kappa`, so that input like `xy` won't turn into `\kappay`!

8.9. Be sure to replace `\kappa` by ⌴k so that input like `\alpha\kappa` won't become `\alphak`.

8.10.

(1) `$X\setminus(A\cup B) = (X \setminus A)\cap(X \setminus B)$`

(2) `$x\notin A\not\subset B$`

(3) `$(X\times Y)\times Z\simeq X \times(Y \times Z)$`

(4) `$\omega\wedge(\eta\wedge\lambda)=`
    `(\omega\wedge\eta)\wedge\lambda$`

(5) `$V\oplus\Lambda(V)$`

(6) `$\|a(x+y)\|\le|a|\cdot(\|x\|+\|y\|)$`

(7) `$2\cdot\aleph=\aleph$`

(8) `$2\cdot\omega\ne\omega$`

(9) `$\nabla R(X,Y)$`

(10) `$(100\pm.001)\div5$`

(11) `$\forall x\gg A$`

(12) `$f*g\:A\to B$`

(13) `$x\mapsto\alpha+x$`

(14) `$f(x)\in o(x) \and g(x)\in O(x)`
     `\implies f\circ g(x)\in o(x)$`

In regard to (1) note that `\setminus` is to be distinguished from `\backslash`. In some fonts the same symbol may be used for both, but the spacing will still be different—`X\backslash Y` gives $X\backslash Y$, while `X\setminus Y` gives $X\setminus Y$. (Of course, you may have to consult with the author about which to use; `\setminus` is the more common.)

In (2) notice that $\not\subset$ is typed as `\not\subset`, to "negate" $\subset$, but $\notin$ is typed as `\notin`.

In (6) note that | gives |, while \| gives the double vertical line ‖. If you don't have | on your keyboard you can use `\vert` instead; in this case, you'll have to use `\Vert` for the double vertical line (you can't use `\\vert` because TEX will interpret this to mean the control sequence `\\` followed by the letters `vert`).

The `\nabla` in (9) is an "upside-down" `\Delta`, but the other Greek letters don't have similar versions.

In (10) note that `\pm` ($\pm$) is a single symbol—you can't get it with `$+-$`, which simply gives $+-$ and there's also `\mp` ($\mp$). Similarly $\gg$ in (11) is a special symbol, which you can't get with `$>>$`, which gives $>>$.

The formula $f: A \to B$ is often read "f takes A to B". For the formula $f * g: A \to B$ of (12), we used `\:` to get the right spacing around the colon (there are also situations where a bare `:` is what's needed). The right arrow $\to$ is called `\rightarrow` (there's also `\leftarrow` for $\leftarrow$) but `\to` is recognized as a synonym. Some authors are careful to distinguish between $\to$ and $\mapsto$ (`\mapsto`), which we used in (13).

The $\Longrightarrow$ in formula (14) could be obtained with `\Longrightarrow`, which is longer than `\rightarrow`; as you can see from Appendix E, the L at the beginning of the name distinguishes it from `\longrightarrow`, which is a single long right arrow. But in the present formula & and $\Longrightarrow$ stand for the logician's "and" and "implies"; `\and` gives even more space around the & than binary operators normally have, and `\implies` similarly gives extra space around the $\Longrightarrow$.

Actually, the most interesting point about formula (14) is the o and O that appear in the formulas o(x) and O(x). Notice that the letters o and O were typed here, not the numeral 0. As a general rule, o or O rather than 0 is meant when a left parenthesis (is the next symbol. The only exception would be a formula like 20(x+y), where the 0 is part of the longer number 20.

Other details of this sort will be found in Part 3.

8.11. First we get the error message

```
! Missing $ inserted.
```

. . .

```
\par
1.6
```

which is just like the error message we got previously, except that now the error is perceived when TEX gets to line 6, the blank line, which causes it to pretend that a \par had been typed.

The next error message

```
! Missing $ inserted.
```

. . .

```
1.7 This paragraph has the formula 3\alpha
                                      +\beta
```

is also similar to one obtained before. Notice, however, that TEX doesn't insert the $ before the 3, since it's perfectly possible for 3 to occur outside of math mode.

The next error message

```
! Missing $ inserted.
```

. . .

```
                         \par
1.8
```

comes when TEX gets to the end of the second paragraph: since TEX has inserted a $ sign before the \alpha it obviously has to insert another one before the paragraph ends!

A similar pair of error messages come next, with the first of the pair being

. . .

```
1.9 This is accurate within \pm
                            .0003 percent.
```

Once again, TEX knows to insert the $ before the \pm, since \pm is a math symbol that is allowed only in math mode.

(By the way, you might like to experiment with a file that ends

```
This is accurate within \pm.00003 percent.
\enddocument
```

You'll find that TEX gets extra confused, because it doesn't discover that it needs a closing $ until it's started to figure out what \enddocument means.)

8.12. ¡You get the following

The symbols ¡ and ¿ and — give < and > and | in math mode.

—you can use <, > and | outside of math mode, but you obviously don't get what you'd expect! TEX interprets things quite differently in math mode than it does it ordinary text.

9.1.

```
There exist such division algebras
only for $n=1$,~2, 4 or~8.
```

9.2.

```
We have $f(x)=A$, $B$ or~$C$ for~$x=0$,~1,\dots,~$n$.
```

9.3.

```
For all $a$ and $b$ we have $a<b$, $a=b$, or~$a>b$.
We say that $<$ is a {\it partial ordering}.
```

This example illustrates another point: Notice that the first period is typed *outside* of the $ signs. This is important. If we had typed $a>b.$ so that the period was part of the formula, then TEX's rules for spacing after periods in text wouldn't apply, and we would have only the ordinary interword space between the formula '$a > b.$' and 'We'.

9.4. If you type

```
If $a, b , c>0$, then $f(a,b,c)>0$.
```

you'll get

If $a, b, c > 0$, then $f(a, b, c) > 0$.

That's not really so bad, but if you type

```
If $a$,~$b$,~$c>0$, then $f(a,b,c)>0$.
```

the spacing will be slightly better. Admittedly, this is a rather special situation: the phrase "*a*, *b*, *c* > 0" is really an abbreviation for "*a* > 0, *b* > 0, *c* > 0", and it's hard to decide whether to treat it as one formula or as three. Notice, however, that in either case c>0 is kept within one math formula, so that the spacing around the > will be right.

9.5.

```
We have shown that $f(1,dots,n)\le f(0,\dots,0)+f(1,\dots,1)
  +\dots+f(n,\dots,n)$ for $n\ge1$.
```

9.6.

```
After the unspeakable exertions of the previous chapter,
we have finally succeeded in proving the fundamental
result that
$$1+1=2,$$
and now we are going to try to prove that
$$2+2=4.$$

As a first step in that direction, we will prove the
distributive law for multiplication.
```

Notice that TEX does not begin a new paragraph after a displayed formula unless you specifically request one, with a blank line or a \par.

9.7. How should I know, turkey?—multiline formulas aren't explained until Chapter 16. Right! We just wanted to emphasize the fact that TEX definitely won't break a formula for you. If you type

```
$$1+2+3+4+5+6+7+8+9+10+11+12+13+14+15+16+17+18+19+20=190$$
```

TEX will try to set this as a one-line formula, and you'll get an `Overfull box` message. This is a good experiment to try. And it is also instructive to see what happens when you type

```
$$a+b=c$$
$$A+B=C$$
```

Instead of getting

$$a + b = c$$
$$A + B = C$$

you'll get the two equations $a + b = C$ and $A + B = C$ displayed separately. There will be too much space between them (namely, the space after the first display *plus* the space before the second display), and each equation will be centered separately. Because of the difference in the width of the letters in these two equations the $=$ signs won't be lined up exactly.

10.1. Indeed there is! In the first case you get $x + {}_2F_3$, but in the second case you get $x +_2 F_3$, with the 2 set as a subscript to the $+$ sign (when a binary operator like $+$ gets a subscript, the subscripted combination is also treated as a binary operator, which accounts for the extra space after $+_2$ in this formula). That's handy to know, in case you ever need things like $+_1$, $+_2$, $\ldots$, but it probably isn't what was wanted in this case.

10.2.

```
If the $n-1$ numbers $x_1$,\dots , $x_{\alpha-1}$,
$x_{\alpha+1}$,\dots, $x_n$ are all $\ne x_\alpha\pm1$,
then $f(x_1,\dots,x_n)>0$.
```

(Notice the spaces between \dots , (or \dots,) and the next math formula.)

10.3. The first error message will be

```
! Missing $ inserted.

            . . . .

1.4 This paragraph has the formula x^
                                      2$.
?
```

In this case TeX has inserted a $ right before the ^, since ^ can only occur in math mode. The x doesn't trigger this response, since an x can certainly appear outside of math mode. Consequently, TeX will act as if you had typed x^2.

Pressing ⟨carriage-return⟩, we will now get the error message

```
! Extra }, or forgotten $.
1.6 This paragraph has the formula $x^10}
                                         $
?
```

This is similar to the ! Extra } message we have seen before. However, since TEX is presently in math mode it is only counting the braces within the $ signs; it allows for the fact that the extra } might have arisen simply because we forgot the closing $ sign—perhaps we really meant to type x^10} (if we had typed this, then TEX would have glided effortlessly through the formula x^10, producing x^10, but then given an error message when it hit the }.

Hitting ⟨carriage-return⟩ again, we come to the next error message:

```
! Missing } inserted.
```

```
                . . .
```

```
    1.7 and the formula $x^{10$
```

```
    ?
```

Now TEX has decided that a } is missing because it has reached the second $ sign that completes the math formula, but the braces inside this formula aren't balanced. Hitting ⟨carriage-return⟩ once again sends TEX to the end of the file.

10.4.
```
    In a non-commutative group we have
    $$(ab)^{-1}=b^{-1}a^{-1}$$
    and
    $$
    (ab)^{-2}=[(ab)^{-1}]^2=[b^{-1}a^{-1}]^2
      =b^{-1}a^{-1}b^{-1}a^{-1},
    $$
    but
    $$ (a^m)^2=a^{m+m}=a^{2m}.$$
```

10.5.
```
    $$
    2^{x_1+\dots+x_{n+1}}=2^{x_{n+1}}\cdot(2^{x_1+\dots+x_n})
    $$
```

10.6.
```
    Suppose that $x^{x^x}=
    (x^x)^x$. Prove that $x=1$ or~2.
```

10.7. The first gives x^{y^z} while the second gives x^{y^z}. In the first case the z is simply a superscript to the formula x^y so it appears in s-size, and at a different height. Mathematicians never want the first alternative, so you should never even think of it.

10.8. You will get an error message like

```
! Double superscript.
    $a^b^
          c$
?
```

If you press ⟨carriage-return⟩, TEX will continually merrily, and you will get a^{bc} in your output: TEX essentially inserts an empty group {} before the second superscript, so that it treats your formula as if it were $a^b{}^c$.

10.9.

```
Suppose that there is
no $\lambda$ with $x_i=\lambda y_i$, \ $i=1$,~
2. Then the equation $(\lambda y_1-x_1)(\lambda y_2-x_2)=0$,
i.e., the equation
$$
\lambda^2(y_1{}^2+y_2{}^2)-2\lambda(x_1y_1
   +x_2y_2)+(x_1{}^2+y_1{}^2)=0
$$
has {\it no\/} solution $\lambda$.
```

10.10. You'd get:

In the formula "$x + y''$ ...

The right thing to type is

```
In the formula ''$x+y$'' ...
```

so that the '' gives a double quote mark. (By the way, ' happens to give a left quote in math mode; in fact '' even gives the double left quote. But this is just an accident—some day some one will probably figure out some neat use for ' in math mode, analogous to the special use for '.)

10.11. TEX would translate such input into $g^\prime{}^2$, which is not acceptable.

10.12.

```
$$ f^{(n+2)} = [f^{(n+1)}]' = [f^{(n)}{}']'
   = [f^{(n)}]''$$
```

10.13. We might expect TEX to do something strange with $A_\notin$, since $A_\ne$ produced strange results. But now we actually obtain an error message

```
! Missing { inserted.

          .  .  .

          .  .  .

... This file contains only the formula $A_\notin
                                                  $.
?
```

more complex than any we have ever seen before. The last two lines show that TEX has gagged when it got to \notin and the top two lines show that it has tried to recover by putting a { before the \notin (which would have been just dandy in the case of $A_\ne$). The precise reasons for this are admittedly obscure—\notin is an abbreviation, like \ne, but obviously a more complex one—but once again the best bet is simply to try hitting ⟨carriage-return⟩ once again, and hope for the best! Indeed, if we do we get the next error message:

```
! Missing } inserted.

          .  .  .

... This file contains only the formula $A_\notin$

?
```

This time TEX has gotten a little further, all the way to the $ sign that ends the the math formula, and decided that a } needs to be inserted (pretty reasonable, since it inserted a { previously). If we hit ⟨carriage-return⟩ once again, we will find that we have managed to come to the end of the file.

Of course, you could have avoided this trouble if you had known to put braces around the subscript \notin yourself. Don't worry about it! The likelihood of your actually encountering $\notin$ (or any other symbol that produces similar problems) in a subscript is very small. But it's a contingency that has to be allowed for, and if it does occur, at least you'll know that a pair of braces will fix things up.

11.1. The safest thing to type would be

```
$$\frac x{1+{\dsize\frac x2}}$$
```

and

$$\frac{{\dsize\frac x2}+1}2$$

with the \dsize\frac x2 neatly enclosed in an extra pair of braces, in order to keep \dsize from affecting anything else. But in both cases we could actually have omitted these braces, typing simply

$$\frac x{1+\dsize\frac x2}$$

and

    \frac{\dsize\frac x2+1}2

In the first formula the effect of \dsize extends only until the next } (which is the end of the formula in any case); in the second formula the braces are unnecessary because \dsize\frac x2+1 looks exactly the same as {\dsize\frac x2}+1.

11.2.

    {\sl H\"older's Inequality\/}: Let $0\le p,q\le\infty$
    with $\dsize\frac1p+\frac1q=1$.
    If $f\in L^p(\mu)$ and $g\in L^q(\mu)$,
    then $fg\in L^1(\mu)$ and
    $$\|fg\|_1\le\|f\|_p\|g\|_q.$$

11.3.

    $$\frac x{1+\dfrac x2}$$

and

    $$\frac{\dfrac x2+1}2$$

11.4.

    $$
    fg={\tsize\frac12}[(f+g)^2-f^2-g^2]
    $$

As in Example 11.1, the braces aren't really necessary around \tsize\frac12, since \tsize wouldn't change the size of anything afterwards.

11.5.

$$fg=\tfrac12[(f+g)^2-f^2-g^2]$$

11.6.

$$\binom n{k/2}$$

or

$$\binom n{\frac12k}$$

and

$$\frac{\dsize\binom nk}2$$

11.7. $$\frac{\dbinom nk}2$$

11.8. The first error message is the most complicated yet to occur:

```
! Missing } inserted.

    .  .  .

    .  .  .

\frac #1#2->{#1\over #2
                       }
1.4 ... paragraph has $\frac1{a+b$ and $\frac 1a+b}
                                                   $.
```

Examining the last two lines, as usual, we observe that TEX *didn't* notice the missing } in the first formula; an error was noticed only when TEX got to the } in the second formula! The reason for this is that the { in the first formula caused TEX to start reading in the second argument for \frac, and when TEX is looking for an argument of a control sequence that begins with a {, it simply gobbles up characters until it hits the closing }; consequently, TEX thought that the whole string

```
a+b$ and $\frac 1a+b
```

was the second argument for \frac! Then TEX translated \frac into its own terms (that's what the cryptic message just above the last two lines means).

Finally, when TEX tried to substitute 'a+b\$ and \$\frac 1a+b' it discovered the first \$ and realized something had to be wrong. So it inserted } right before that \$ sign, which put it back in sync.

The second error message

```
! Extra }, or forgotten $.
\frac #1#2->{#1\over #2}

1.4 ...paragraph has $\frac1{a+b$ and $\frac 1a+b}
                                                  $.
```

is similar to ones we've seen before, except that, once again, TEX first translates \frac before discovering what's amiss. In this case, TEX simply omits the } so that it is setting $\frac{1}{a} + b$.

The final error message

```
Runaway argument?
{a+b$.
! Paragraph ended before \frac was complete.
<to be read again>
                   \par
1.7
```

occurs because, once again, TEX is looking for the second argument of \frac, which begins with {a+b. This time, however, TEX knows that something is wrong as soon as it gets to the blank line, denoting a \par, on line 7, since an argument for \frac mustn't contain a \par. If you ask for help, TEX will give you the message

```
I suspect you've forgotten a '}', causing me to apply this
control sequence to too much text. How can we recover?
My plan is to forget the whole thing and hope for the best.
```

TEX is serious about this! If you hit ⟨carriage-return⟩ TEX will simply ignore everything after the \frac, including even the closing '\$.' in that paragraph, so you'll then get the error message

```
! Missing $ inserted.
<inserted text>
                $
<to be read again>
                   \par
1.7
```

because TEX needs to balance the $ before the \frac. TEX will then proceed to complete the file, but if you print it you will see that the final formula simply comes out blank.

By the way, just as in the answer to Exercise 8.11, things get extra complicated if \enddocument occurs before the end of the paragraph containing the offending formula $\frac1{a=b$. You'll get the message

```
Runaway argument?
{a=b$
! Forbidden control sequence found while scanning use of \frac.
<inserted text>
                    \par
<to be read again>
                    \enddocument
        \enddocument

?
```

Again TEX is looking for the second argument of \frac, but now it's the control sequence \enddocument, rather than the end of the paragraph, which alerts TEX to the fact that something is wrong. \enddocument is a special type of control sequence that is forbidden to appear within the argument of another control sequence. The same is true of things like \proclaim and \demo (except that \proclaim can appear within \abstract{...}).

12.1.

(1) $$(f\cdot g)^{(n+1)}(a)=\sum_{k=0}^{n+1}\binom{n+1}k
        f^{(k)}(a)g^{(n+1-k)}(a)$$

(2) $$0=(1+-1)^n=\sum_{j=0}^n(-1)^j\binom nj$$

(3) $$\sum_{i=1}^nx_i{}^2\cdot\sum_{i=1}^n y_i{}^2=
        \sum_{i=1}^nx_i{}^2y_i{}^2+\sum_{i\ne j}x_i{}^2y_j{}^2$$

(4) $$\sum_{i=1}^p\sum_{j=1}^q\sum_{k=1}^ra_{ij}b_{jk}c_{ki}$$

(5) $$ \Sigma^2\:[X,S_0(\infty)]\to[\Sigma^2X,S_0(\infty)]$$

(6) $$\bigcup_{n=1}^m(A_n\cup B_n)$$

(7) $$X\setminus\bigcup_{i\in I}A_i=
        \bigcap_{i\in I}X\setminus A_i$$

Notice that in formula (5) we have the Greek Σ, *not* $\sum$. Note also that TEX handles the expression (1+-1) in equation (2) in just the right way.

12.2.

```
$$
\sum \Sb 1\le i\le p\\
       1\le j\le q\\
       1\le k\le r\endSb
     a_{ij}b_{jk}c_{ki}
$$
```

12.3. \Sb is complicated, and if you do this TEX gets completely bollixed up; if you keep hitting ⟨carriage-return⟩, you get a succession of error messages, culminating in a * prompt after TEX has already read the \enddocument, a situation already discussed in Exercise 4.6.

12.4. If you type

```
$$
\int\limits_{\partial(M-\bigcup_{i=1}^nU_i)} r^*\Pi=
  -\sum_{i=1}^n\int_{\partial U_i}r^*\Pi
$$
```

you get

$$\int\limits_{\partial(M-\bigcup_{i=1}^n U_i)} r^*\Pi = -\sum_{i=1}^n \int_{\partial U_i} r^*\Pi$$

I felt that the \bigcup was too big in this situation, even though it was in t-size (\bigcup doesn't have a smaller s-size). On the other hand, an ordinary \cup in s-size turned out to be too small! So I actually typed

```
$$
\int\limits_{\partial(M-{\tsize\cup}_{i=1}^nU_i)} r^*\Pi=
  -\sum_{i=1}^n\int_{\partial U_i}r^*\Pi
$$
```

Of course, you weren't supposed anticipate such after-the-fact corrections.

Notice also that Π here is the Greek letter \Pi. It should not be confused with \prod, another large operator that you can find in Appendix E.

12.5.

```
$$\iiint\limits_M d\omega=
\iint\limits_{\partial M}\omega$$
```

13.1.

(1)   `$$y\,dx-x\,dy$$`

(2)   `$$x\,dy/dx$$`

(3)   `$$\int_1^x\frac{dt}t$$`

(4)   `$$\int\,dy=\int\frac{dy}{dx}\,dx$$`

13.2. You can type

```
$$\frac{dz}{dx}=
\frac{\,\dfrac{dz}{dy}\,}{\,\dfrac{dy}{dx}\,}$$
```

using `\,` to make the numerator and denominator artificially larger.

13.3.

(1)   `1\,ml equals 1.00028\,cc`

(2)   `$g=9.8$\,m/sec${}^2$`

(3)   `O${}^\circ$\,C equals 32${}^\circ$\,F`

[In (2) and (3) the thin spaces could have been typed right before the $ signs instead of right after them.]

13.4.

```
$$
\int_0^\infty \frac{t-ib}{t^2+b^2}e^{iat}\,dt=
 e^{ab}E_1(ab),\qquad a,b>0.
$$
```

(By the way, in Exercise 9.4 we recommended that when a phrase like '$a, b > 0$' occurs in text, it might be better to type `$a$, $b>0$` to get a bigger space after the comma. But once the expression $a, b > 0$ has gotten itself embroiled in a displayed formula it's best not to worry about this any more.)

14.1.

(1)

```
The sum of the vectors
$\overarrow{OA}$ and $\overarrow{OB}$ is defined by
$$\overarrow{OA}+\overarrow{OB}=\overarrow{OP},$$
where $OAPB$ is a parallelogram.
```

(2)

> ```
> In any triangle $ABC$ we have
> $$\overline{AB}+\overline{BC}>\overline{AC}.$$
> ```

(3)

> ```
> {\sl The Pythagorean Theorem\/}:
> If $\angle C$ of $\triangle ABC$
> is a right angle, then
> $$\overline{AB}^2=\overline{AC}^2+\overline{BC}^2.$$
> ```

Here we used \angle to get the $\angle$ symbol that is common in elementary geometry; variant symbols are listed in Appendix F. And rather than using \Delta to get Δ, we used \triangle to get $\triangle$, which looks a little better in this context. (There are also \bigtriangleup and \bigtriangledown, which give symbols $\triangle$ and $\triangledown$ that act as binary operators. Don't worry if you missed some of these fine points—mathematicians are constantly appropriating old symbols to new uses, so you can never hope to keep up with them—let them make their intentions clear to you.)

14.2.

> ```
> $$B_{i,j}\longleftrightarrow A_{i+j,\overline{i+j}}$$
> ```

14.3.

> ```
> The solutions to $ax^2+bx+c=0$ are
> given by the {\sl quadratic formula\/}:
> $$
> x=\frac{-b\pm\sqrt{b^2-4ac}}{2a}.
> $$
> ```

By the way, in the Exercise, there isn't much space around the $+$ and $=$ signs because TeX had to squeeze things into the line size that is used for examples in this manual.

14.4. In each case TeX will first issue an error message saying that it is inserting a {; TeX knows this is necessary because \overline and \sqrt are instructions for processing symbols—they aren't symbols that could themselves appear as superscripts. The message for the second formula contains some additional lines, which as usual we wisely ignore, because \sqrt is actually constructed, in a mysterious way, from a more primitive control sequence called \radical. At the end of each formula TeX issues an error message saying that it is inserting a }.

14.5.

(1)

For $F=0$ we have the ``degenerate hyperbola''
```
$$
x+\frac B{2A}=\pm\sqrt{\frac{-C}A}\left(
    y+\frac D{2C}\right).
$$
```

(2)

The nth Fibonacci number F_n is given by
```
$$
F_n=\frac{\left(\dfrac{1+\sqrt5}2\right)^n-
      \left(\dfrac{1-\sqrt5}2\right)^n} {\sqrt 5}.
$$
```

14.6.

For $0<x\le1$ we have
```
$$f(x)=\frac1{\left[\dfrac1x\right]}.$$
```

14.7.

```
$$
\|f\|_p=\left\{\int_0^1|f|^p\right\}^{\frac1p}
$$
```

14.8.

```
$$\left\|\frac xa\right\|=\frac{\|x\|}{|a|}$$
```

14.9.

```
$\left]-\infty,T\right[\times\left]-\infty,t\right[$
```

14.10.

The connection ∇ is compatible with the metric
if and only if
```
$$\frac d{dt}\langle V,W\rangle
 =\left<\frac{DV}{dt},W\right> +
 \left<V,\frac{DW}{dt}\right>.$$
```

Notice that we had to use \langle and \rangle rather than < and > for the smaller $\langle$ and $\rangle$, but we could use \left< and \right> for the larger ones.

14.11.

```
We derive the quadratric formula by
''completing the square'':
$$ax^2+bx+c=a\left(x^2+\frac bax + \frac ca \right)
 =a\left[\left(x+\frac b{2a}\right)^2+\left(\frac ca
  -\frac{b^2}{4a}\right)\right].$$
```

14.12.

```
$$\left(\frac1{\sqrt A}+\tsize\sum\limits_{i=1}^na_i\right)
    \left(\frac1{\sqrt B}+\tsize\sum\limits_{i=1}^nb_i\right)$$
```

Notice that the first \tsize doesn't affect the \frac1{\sqrt B} that occurs after the first \right), so no braces are needed around it.

14.13. You get the error message

```
! Missing delimiter (. inserted).
<to be read again>
                      ,
... $$\left,
           \frac{dx^2}{dx}\right|_{x=a}=2a$$
```

Since , is not a valid delimiter, TeX inserts a delimiter for you; the empty delimiter . is the obvious choice, since TeX can't guess what delimiter you had in mind.

14.14. You'll get the error message

```
! Extra \right.
    $$\frac{dx^2}{dx}\right|
                          _{x=a}=2a$$
```

If you ask for help, you'll find that TeX will simply ignore the \right, since it has no matching \left.

14.15. If you type

```
$$\left[\left.\frac{dy}{dx}\right|_{x=a}\right]^2$$
```

you get

$$\left[\frac{dy}{dx}\bigg|_{x=a}\right]^2$$

This is one of those cases, discussed in Part 3, where you might want to adjust the spacing after seeing the output. The formula in the text was typed as

```
$$\left[\left.\frac{dy}{dx}\right|_{x=a}\,\right]^2$$
```

14.16.

```
$$x^2\left/\frac{c+1}d\right.$$
```

Notice that this formula doesn't look quite as good as the previous one, even though TEX follows the same spacing rules. This is another one of those situations where some tinkering is needed—a thin space really ought to be *deleted* after the x^2 so that the formula comes out

$$x^2 \left/ \frac{c+1}{d} \right.$$

Actually, a \left...\right construction wasn't really needed here, or in the formula on page 89, because \biggl and \biggr delimiters (see page 91) would be just the right size. In fact, TEX also has \bigg to give delimiters of this size that act as ordinary symbols (see Part 3), and they would be preferable in such cases.

14.17.

(1)
```
$$\biggl(\sum_{i=1}^nx_iy_i\biggr)^2=\sum_{i=1}^n(x_iy_i)^2
    +\sum_{i\ne j}x_iy_ix_jy_j$$
```
(2)
```
$$\pi(n)=\sum_{m=2}^n\left\lfloor\biggl(\,\sum_{k=1}^{m-1}
    \bigl\lfloor(m/k)/\lceil m/k\rceil\bigr\rfloor
        \biggr)^{-1}\right\rfloor$$
```
(3)
```
$$m^*\left(
    A\cap\biggl[\, \bigcup_{i=1}^n E_i \biggr]
    \right)=\sum_{i=1}^n m^*(A\cap  E_i)$$
```

Notice that there is a thin space after the \biggl(in (2) and the \biggl[in (3). Thin spaces are often useful when a \bigg delimiter is next to an operator whose limits stick out too far.

14.18.

(1)
```
$$\left(\sqrt{\frac AB}+\sum_{i=1}^Na_i\right)^2$$
```

(2) $$f\left(\sum_{i=1}^n p_ix_i\right)$$
           $$\le\sum_{i=1}^n p_if(x_i)$$

In the first formula \bigg delimiters wouldn't be large enough for the $\sqrt{\dfrac{A}{B}}$ part of the formula. The second formula is more a matter of taste: Since the parentheses play a special role in notation like $f(x)$, when we substitute $\sum\limits_{i=1}^{n} p_i x_i$ for x it seems appropriate to have the whole expression neatly enclosed in the parentheses.

15.1.

$$g(x)=f(x+\text{constant})+f(x-\text{constant})$$

15.2. You can change fonts within \text, but \text itself does *not* work like a font change!—it's simply a control sequence with an argument, as we said just a little while before. The input

$$y=f(x+{\text constant})$$

will produce

$$y = f(x + constant)$$

because TEX will think that the argument of \text is simply c, and the braces merely provide an irrelevant grouping.

15.3.

$$F_n=F_{n-1}+F_{n-2}\qquad$$
     \text{for {\sl every\/} $n>1$.}$$

(or you can type

$$\ldots \text{for {\sl every\/} $n>1$}.$$

with the period at the end of the whole sentence.)

You have to be methodical in cases like this, to get the final \$'s and }'s in the right order; it's probably helpful to leave some spaces:

$$\ldots \text{\for {\sl every\/} $n>1$.} $$

Of course, you're already in good shape if you habitually put the **$$** signs on a separate line:

```
$$
... \text{\for {\sl every\/} $n>1$.}
$$
```

15.4.

```
$1\,\text{ml}=1.000028\,\text{cc}$
$0^\circ\,\text{C}=32^\circ\,\text{F}$
```

Putting the formulas entirely inside **$** signs gets the right spacing around the = signs.

15.5. You first get the error message

```
! Missing } inserted.
<inserted text>
                    }
<to be read again>
                        $
1.6 \Gamma(n)=(n-1)! \qquad {\text when $
                                    n$ is an integer}
?
```

T_EX has already decided that the argument of **\text** is simply the next letter w, and that the remaining input is back in math mode. So when it sees the **$** sign of **$n$**, it thinks you are trying to *leave* math mode. But that { before the **\text** would be unbalanced, so T_EX is inserting what it assumes is the missing }. If you type h, T_EX will tell you this, though not in so many words.

If you hit ⟨carriage-return⟩ at this point, you'll find that once T_EX has gotten onto this track, it is trapped into further confusion. Since you've gotten into "display math mode", with **$$**, you should be getting out with **$$** also. But T_EX has seen only one **$** before the n, so it issues another error message:

```
! Display math should end with $$.
<to be read again>
                        n
1.6 \Gamma(n)=(n-1)! \qquad {\text when $n
                                    $ is an integer}
?
```

Again, you can hit h and have TEX tell you this in its own way. If you hit
⟨carriage-return⟩ again, TEX will now assume that you are starting a new math
formula $ is an integer, so it will complain when it hits the }:

```
! Extra }, or forgotten $.
1.6 ...n-1)! \qquad {\text when $n$ is an integer}

?
```

If you hit ⟨carriage-return⟩ again, TEX will either have to delete the } or else
insert a $ to finish off the math formula. If you hit h you will find that TEX is, in
fact, going to delete the }. This gets TEX through the formula, but it now thinks
that it is in math mode; if you have \enddocument right after this formula, TEX
will have to insert yet another $ sign before it can wrap things up.

15.6.

```
We have
$$\frac{(n+1)^{p+1}}{p+1}=\sum_{k=1}^n k^p
 +\text{terms involving $\sum_{k=1}^n k^r$ for $r<p$.}$$
It follows by induction that
$$\frac{\dsize\sum_{k=1}^n k^p}{n^{p+1}}=\frac1{p+1}+\text
  {terms involving negative powers of $n$}.$$
```

15.7. The first formula was typed as

```
$$
X_n=X_k\qquad\text{if and only if}\qquad
     Y_n=Y_k\quad\text{and}\quad Z_n=Z_k
$$
```

(Only a single \quad was used around the 'and', because the right hand phrase
'$Y_n = Y_k$ and $Z_n = Z_k$' was essentially one unit; \qquad separates this whole
unit from the left side of the formula.)

The second formula was typed as

```
$$
Y_n=X_n+1\quad\text{and}\quad Z_n=X_n-1
   \qquad\text{for all $n\ge 0$.}
$$
```

(In this case the side condition 'for all $n \ge 0$' applies to everything else, so
\qquad separates it from the left side, whose individual clauses are separated by
only a \quad.)

15.8.

> Everyone would like to know whether or not the set
> $\{\,p:p$~and $p+2$ are prime$\,\}$ is infinite or not!

This slippery approach requires some care with regard to spacing, and now undesirable line breaks have to be prohibited. Notice the tie ~ and observe that there is no space after prime.

15.9.

> the nth Fibonacci number F_n

15.10.

> $$
> \sum_{\text{1 odd}}\binom n1=2^{n-1}
> $$

15.11. $f^{\text{(iv)}}$, $f^{\text{(v)}}$, $f^{\text{(vi)}}$, etc.

15.12. As in Exercise 14.4, TeX first inserts a { and then inserts a }. The first error message also reveals that \text is a pretty complicated sort of gadget.

15.13.

> $$
> \frac{\dsize\max_{1<n<m}\log_2P_n}
>   {\dsize\lim_{x\to 0}\frac{\sin x}x}
> $$

15.14.

(1)

> $$
> \lim_{x\to0}\frac{\sin^2 ax}{\sin^2 bx}=
>   \left(\frac ab\right)^2
> $$

(2)

> $$
> \lim_{x\to\infty}x\sin\frac 1x=\lim_{x\to\infty}
>   \frac{\sin\dfrac1x}{\dfrac1x}=\lim_{x\to0^+}
>   \frac{\sin x}x
> $$

Notice that we typed x\to0^+ to get the superscript $^+$; some authors prefer $\lim_{x\to0+}$, which you get with x\to0+.

(3)

```
$$\frac12+\cos x+\cos2x+\dots+\cos nx=
    \frac{\sin(n+\frac12)x}{2\sin\dfrac x2}$$
```

(4)

```
$$(\log\circ f)'=f'/f$$
```

(5)

```
$$\lim_{x\to0^+}x(\log x)^n=0$$
```

(6)

```
$$
\lim_{h\to0^+}\int_{-1}^1\frac h{h^2+x^2}=
  \left.\lim_{h\to0^+}\arctan\frac xh
    \right|_{-1}^1=\pi
$$
```

(7)

```
$$
\arctan\tfrac12+\arctan\tfrac13
   =\arctan\left(\frac{\frac12+\frac13}{1-\frac16}
      \right)=\frac\pi4
$$
```

(8)

```
$$
1-m=\lim\Sb  n\to\infty\\ \text{$n$ even}\endSb
      \frac{2-a_n{}^2}{1+a_n}=\frac{2-m^2}{1+m}
$$
```

15.15. It was typed as

```
$$
\delta=\min\left(\sin^2\left(\frac
  {[\min(1,\varepsilon/10)]^2}9\right)+
    \min(1,\varepsilon/10),\,\,
[\min(1,\varepsilon/6)]^2\right)
$$
```

(A couple of extra thin spaces were inserted after the next to last comma, because it followed such a complicated expression.)

15.16.

```
$$\int\limits_{k\pi+\pi/2-\delta}
   ^{k\pi+\pi/2+\delta}\left|\frac{\sin x}x\right|
   \,dx\ge\frac\delta{k\pi+\pi/2}$$
```

and

```
$$\lim_{x\to\infty}
\frac{\dsize\int_x^{x+\frac{\log x}{2x}}e^{t^2}\,dt}
   {e^{x^2}}=\lim_{x\to\infty}
\frac{  e^{\left(x+\frac{\log x}{2x}\right)^2}-
               e^{x^2}}    {2xe^{x^2}}
=\frac12
$$
```

15.17.

```
$$
\frac{\max\limits_{1<n<m}\log_2P_n}
   {\lim\limits_{x\to 0}\dfrac{\sin x}x}
$$
```

15.18. `$\operatorname{arg\,sinh}$`

15.19. Type things like

`$\operatorname{\sl SO}(n)$`	$SO(n)$
`$\operatorname{\bf SO}(n)$`	$\mathbf{SO}(n)$

16.1. E typed

```
$$x=y\tag (3-2),$$
```

Now the tag has extra parentheses. Moreover, the comma is part of the tag, rather than part of the formula.

16.2. If you want A', with the A in italic math style, type

```
$$ ...\tag {$A'$}$$
```

The braces around `$A'$` help TeX keep straight which $ signs are part of the tag, and which indicate the end of the formula. (Actually, `...\tag $A'$ $$` would work also—the formula ends only when TEX encounters a **$$** combination, with no space between the two **$** signs—but there's no point looking for trouble.)

If you want A′, with a roman 'A', type

```
$$ ...\tag A{$'$} $$
```

with braces around the part of the tag that involves math. Another possibility is

```
$$ ...\tag{$\text{A}'$}
```

If you have lots of tags with primes or superscripts, and few with hyphens or en-dashes, you might prefer for $\mathcal{A}_{M}\mathcal{S}$-TEX to treat all your tags as math formulas, rather than as text. Part 3 explains how this can be arranged.

16.3. You should type

```
$$ ... \tag{$*$}$$
```

to get the tag (∗); if you simply type **\tag***, you'll get the tag (*), with the raised asterisk that comes from the ordinary text font. Since ∗ is a binary operator in math mode, you ought to put braces around it when you use more than one, to suppress any extra space that TEX might put in. (Actually, ...**\tag{$**$}$$** happens to work correctly, but ...**\tag{$***$}$$** would give the tag (∗ ∗ ∗); rather than worrying about why this happens, just type ...**\tag{${*}{*}$}$$** and ...**\tag{${*}{*}{*}$}$$** to be on the safe side.

16.4.

```
$$
\align
Q^l&=\biggl\{\sum_k(-1)^k(PQ_1-I)^k\biggr\}
    \tag 1{${}_l$}\\
Q^r&=\biggl\{\sum_k(-1)^k(Q_1P-I)^k\biggr\}
    Q_1\tag 1{${}_r$}\\
\endalign
$$
```

16.5. You get

$$(1_l) \qquad Q^l = Q_1\left\{\sum_k(-1)^k(PQ_1 - I)^k\right\}$$

$$(1_r) \qquad Q^r = \left\{\sum_k(-1)^k(Q_1P - I)^k\right\}Q_1$$

When you leave out the **&**, TEX simply inserts a blank formula for the second formula, so the whole second formula was treated as the left hand part, with the right hand part being blank.

16.6.

```
$$
\align \alpha_4&=\sqrt\dfrac12\\
\alpha_8&=\sqrt{\dfrac12+\dfrac12\sqrt{\dfrac12}}\\
\alpha_{16}&=\sqrt{\dfrac12+\dfrac12
  \sqrt{\dfrac12+\dfrac12\sqrt{\dfrac12}}}\\
\text{etc.}&
\endalign
$$
```

16.7.

```
$$
k_1,k_2=H\pm\sqrt{H^2-K}\qquad\text{where}\qquad
\left\{
\aligned K&=\frac{eg-f^2}{EG-F^2}\\
      H&=\frac{Eg-2Ff+Ge}{2(EG-F^2)}.\endaligned
\right.
$$
```

16.8.

```
$$
\aligned K&=\frac{eg-f^2}{EG-F^2}\\
      H&=\frac{Eg-2Ff+Ge}{2(EG-F^2)}
\endaligned \tag 23
$$
```

16.9. The situation is similar to that of Exercise 12.3.

16.10.

```
$$\gather
g=\det(g_{ij})\tag3-2\\
\text{$g^{kl}=(k,l)$ entry of the inverse matrix
    of $(g_{ij})$}\tag 3-3
\endgather
$$
```

16.11.

```
We have $(a+bi)^2=\alpha+\beta i$ if and only if
$$
\gathered a^2-b^2=\alpha\\ 2ab=\beta,
\endgathered\tag*$$
which can be solved to give
$$
\left. \aligned
a&=\sqrt{2\alpha+2\sqrt{\alpha^2+\beta^2}}\\
b&=\frac\beta{2\sqrt2\alpha+2\sqrt{\alpha^2+\beta^2}}
 \endaligned \right\}
\qquad\text{or}\qquad
\left\{ \aligned
a&=-\sqrt{2\alpha+2\sqrt{\alpha^2+\beta^2}}\\
b&=\frac{-\beta}{2\sqrt2\alpha+2\sqrt{\alpha^2+\beta^2}}.
\endaligned \right.
$$
```

17.1. You could think of this as three aligned formulas, where the left hand sides of the second and third formulas are blank. Thus, you could type

```
$$
\align
(a+b)^{n+1}&=(a+b)(a+b)^n=(a=b)\sum_{j=0}^n
   \binom nj a^{n-1}b^j\\
  &=\sum_{j=0}^n\binom nja^{n+1-j}b^j+\sum_{j=1}^n
   \binom n{j-1} a^{n-j}b^j\\
 &=\sum_{j=0}^n\binom{n+1}ja^{n+1-j}b^j.
\endalign
$$
```

with empty formulas before the second and third **&**'s (you could also type **{}&** if such emptiness leaves you feeling unsatisfied).

17.2. You can use

```
$$
\align (a+b)(a+b) & = a^2+2ab+b^2,\tag 1\\
\split  (a+b)(a-b) & = (a+b)a - (a+b)b\\
               & = a^2+ab-ab-b^2\\
               & = a^2-b^2.\endsplit \tag 2
\endalign
$$
```

`\split` is designed so that the $=$ signs of the `\split` will automatically line up with the ones from the `\align`.

17.3. In this formula, the second line is a continuation of the term $(a_{11}+b_{11}+c_{11}$, so instead of having the second line start two quads to the right of the $=$ sign, it's preferable for it to start two quads to the right of the *left parenthesis*. So it was actually set as

```
$$\split \Delta=[a+b+c]^n(&a_{11}+b_{11}+c_{11}\\
    &\qquad+a_{12}+b_{12}+c_{12}
    +a_{22}+b_{22}+c_{22}).\endsplit$$
```

17.4.

```
$$
\multline f^{(k)}(x)=e^{-1/x^2}\biggl[\,\sum_{i=1}^{3k}
  \frac {a_i}{x^i}\sin\frac1x+\sum_{i=1}^{3k}
  \frac{b_i}{x^i}\cos\frac1x\biggr]\\
\text{for some numbers $a_1$,\dots, $a_{3k}$, $b_1$,
      \dots, $b_{3k}$.}\endmultline
$$
```

(This display would look better if a little extra space were inserted between the lines; such details are discussed in Part 3.)

18.1.

```
$$
\split
\pmatrix a&b\\c&d\endpmatrix \cdot
  \pmatrix 0&1\\1&0\endpmatrix
  &= \pmatrix a\cdot0+b\cdot1&a\cdot1+b\cdot0\\
      a\cdot0+d\cdot1 & c\cdot1+d\cdot0\endpmatrix \\
  &= \pmatrix b&a\\d&c\endpmatrix
\endsplit\tag I.3
$$
```

(It would probably be better to insert a little extra space between the lines here; such refinements are discussed in Part 3.)

18.2. You can type

```
$$\matrix
\pmatrix 1&0\\0&0\endpmatrix
    & \quad\pmatrix 0&1\\0&0\endpmatrix\\
\\
\\
\pmatrix 0&0\\1&0\endpmatrix
    & \quad\pmatrix 0&0\\0&1\endpmatrix
\endmatrix
$$
```

making the elements of the second column have an extra quad of space on the left. (We'll soon learn other ways to vary the column spacing.)

18.3. The trick is to put the dots into rows and columns of their own:

```
$$
\pmatrix
a_{11}&a_{12}&\hdots&a_{1n}\\
a_{21}&a_{22}&\hdots&a_{2n}\\
\vdots&\vdots&\ddots&\vdots\\
a_{m1}&a_{m2}&\hdots&a_{mn}
\endpmatrix
$$
```

18.4.

```
$$
\pmatrix \format\r&\quad\r\\
\cos\theta&\sin\theta\\
{-\sin\theta}&\cos\theta
\endpmatrix
\pmatrix \format\r&\quad\r\\
\cos\phi&\sin\phi\\
{-\sin\phi}&\cos\phi
\endpmatrix
=\pmatrix \format\r&\quad\r\\
\cos\rho&\sin\rho\\
{-\sin\rho}&\cos\rho
\endpmatrix,
\qquad \rho=\theta+\phi.
$$
```

18.5. We can set this as a matrix with just *two* columns:

```
$$\matrix \format\r&\l\\
3&.14159\\
2&.71828\\
1&.61808\\
&.57701
\endmatrix
$$
```

But in a sense this is needlessly tricky. The only reason the individual columns of digits line up is because the digits in our font all have the same width (this is true for most fonts). If we had a control sequence \dwidth to specify a blank space of this width, then we could have used just *one* column:

```
$$\matrix \format\l\\
3.14159\\
2.71828\\
1.61808\\
\dwidth.5770
\endmatrix
$$
```

Part 3 explains how \dwidth could be defined.

18.6.

```
$$
\det\vmatrix \format\l\quad&\l\quad&\l\quad&\l\quad&\l\\
c_0&c_1&c_2&\hdots&c_n\\
c_1&c_2&c_3&\hdots&c_{n+1}\\
c_2&c_3&c_4&\hdots&c_{n+2}\\
\vdots&\vdots&\vdots&&\vdots\\
c_n&c_{n+1}&c_{n+2}&\hdots&c_{2n}
\endvmatrix >0.
$$
```

Notice that && simply leaves an empty formula at the corresponding position (you can also type &{}& if this makes you feel better).

18.7. A first guess would be

```
$$
\omega=\pmatrix
0&\omega_{12}&0&&&\hdots&0\\
-\omega_{12}&0&\omega_{23}&0&&\hdots&0\\
0&-\omega_{23}&0&\omega_{34}&0&\hdots&0\\
\vdots&&&&\ddots&&\vdots\\
0&&\hdots&&0&&\omega_{n-1,n}\\
0&&\hdots&0&-\omega_{n-1,n}&&0
\endpmatrix
$$
```

Actually, Exercise 18.7 was typed as

```
$$
\omega=\pmatrix
\format\c&\quad\c&\quad\c&\quad\c&\quad\c&\c&\,\c\\
...
$$
```

to make it look better.

18.8.

```
$$\multline
f^{(k)}(x)=ax^{m-k}\sin\frac1x\\
+\sum_{l=k+1}^{2k-1}\left(a_lx^{m-l}\sin\frac1x
 +b_lx^{m-l}\cos\frac1c\right)\pm
\cases x^{m-2k}\sin\dfrac1x,& \text{$k$ even}\\
   x^{m-2k}\cos\dfrac1x,&\text{$k$ odd}.\endcases
\endmultline
$$
```

(We needed \dfrac's because the lines of \cases are normally set in t-size.)

19.1.

```
$$\sqrt\ab+\sqrt{\gamma^2}\le x+\frac\ab\gamma$$
```

19.2. $2^{\ab}$ and $\Gamma_{\ab}$. Notice that we need the curly braces around \ab (compare page 70): if we simply typed $$2^\ab$$, then TEX would translate this into `$$2^\alpha^2+\beta^2$$` and complain about a double superscript, and `$$\Gamma_\ab$$` would be translated into

`$$\Gamma_\alpha^2+\beta^2$$` $\Gamma_\alpha^2 + \beta^2$

If we made the definition

`\define\ab{{\alpha^2+\beta^2}}`

with an extra pair of braces, then `$$2^\ab$$` would be translated into

`$$2^{\alpha^2+\beta^2}$$`

thereby avoiding this little problem. Extra braces of this sort are generally a good idea, but you have to be careful not to add them at inappropriate places. For example, you might try to

`\define\Ne{{\ne}}`

so that `$A_\Ne$` would work right (compare page 70). Unfortunately, `$x\Ne Y$` would then give the wrong spacing (compare Exercise 8.6).

19.3. Now TEX replaces `\ab` by `␣\alpha^␣2␣+\beta^␣2␣`, but that doesn't make any difference, since `\ab` will only be used in math mode, where the spaces won't matter.

19.4.

```
The \deRham\ cohomology ring $H^*(G)$
had, of course,  already essentially been
computed by ~\Cartan.
```

(Notice that you can't abandon thought entirely—you have to remember the `\␣` after `\deRham`.)

19.5. If you `\define\must{\bf must}` then TEX will replace an occurrence of `\must` by `\bf must`, so that 'must' *and all succeeding input* will be in boldface! The correct answer is

`\define\must{{\bf must}}`

with an extra pair of braces, so that `\must` gets replaced by `{\bf must}`. Then input like

`You \must\ remember braces!`

will be translated into

`You {\bf must}\ remember braces!`

and only 'must' becomes bold. You still need the `\␣` after `\must`, however—TEX ignores the space after `\must` as it reads it in, so the space has been ignored before TEX translates `\must` into `{\bf must}`.

19.6.

```
$$\a^\a+\a^{\a+\a}+\a^{\a^\a}+\sqrt{\a^2+\a^3}$$
```

19.7. Whenever TEX saw \ab it would replace it by \a^2+\beta^2, and then it would replace \a by \alpha. So \ab would ultimately be replaced by \alpha^2+ \beta^2. Thus, the net effect would be the same as

```
\define\ab{\alpha^2+\beta^2}
```

Abbreviations like \a for \alpha are so useful that you may end up using them consistently. Then it's nice to know that you can \define a new control sequence like \ab in terms of \a, without having to go back to the old name \alpha.

19.8. You would still have to type \a\␣ to get a space after α in text, but the main problem is that there wouldn't be a convenient way to type $\alpha + 1$. If you typed $\a+1$, the single $ sign would cause TEX to go into math mode, and the $ sign it found after expanding \a would then cause it to leave math mode. Then it would complain about the \alpha outside of math mode!

If you really must have a way of typing the same control sequence \a in text and in math, you can \define\a{{\text{α}}}, since \text can be used in both cases, and it produces the correct size changes in sub and superscripts. (The extra pair of braces insures that you can type $2^\a$.)

19.9. If you try

```
\define\c{\gamma}
```

you'll get an error message, because \c is already defined—it's the control sequence that produces a cedilla, as in the word 'façade'. So you have to put something like

```
\predefine\cedilla{\c}
\redefine\c{\gamma}
```

in your file. That way you can logically type $\c$ to get a γ, and you can type fa\cedilla cade when you need to present the right façade.

19.10. You get a vicious circle: \vicious gets replaced by \circle, which gets replaced by \vicious, which gets replaced by \circle, ... To get TEX out of this vicious circle you'll have to metaphorically pull the plug.

19.11. One possibility is

```
$$
\define\1{\(\dfrac{1+\sqrt5}2\)}
\define\2{\(\dfrac{1-\sqrt5}2\)}
\define\5{\sqrt5}
\align
a_n &=a_{n-1}+a_{n-2}\\
    &=\frac{\1^{n-2} - \2^{n-2} + \1^{n-1} - \2^{n-1}} \5\\
    &=\frac{\1^{n-2}\(1+\dfrac{1+\5}2\)
        - \2^{n-2}\(1+\dfrac{1-\5}2\)} \5\\
    &=\frac{\1^{n-2}\1^2 - \2 ^{n-2}\2^2} \5\\
    &=\frac{\1^n - \2^n} \5.\endalign
$$
```

The new control sequences \1 and \2 save most of the typing, and \5 helps a bit more. After the display is over, \1, \2 and \5 are undefined, ready to be \define'd again for some later emergency.

Actually, the author preferred typing

```
$$
\redefine\+{\(\dfrac{1+\sqrt5}2\)}
\redefine\-{\(\dfrac{1-\sqrt5}2\)}
\define\5{\sqrt5}
```

since \+ and \- were more suggestive names. \redefine was necessary because \+ and \- are both already defined (\- is the "discretionary hyphen" of Chapter 3, while \+ is a feature of TEX that we don't discuss in this manual, since it is seldom needed for mathematical text). Since the \redefine's are within $ signs, the old definitions will be reinstated once the display is finished.

19.12. $$\deriv{x^2}$$ and $$\deriv{(x^2+x^3)}$$. If we typed simply $$\deriv x^2$$ for the first formula, then we would get

$$\frac{dx^2}{dx}$$

and $$\deriv (x^2+x^3)$$ would produce something even weirder, as you should be able to figure out.

19.13. Type

```
\define\vec#1{(#1_1,\dots,#1_n)}
```

and then use $\vec x$ to get $(x_1,\dots,x_n)$ and $\vec y$ to get $(y_1,\dots,y_n)$, etc.

19.14. $\vec\alpha$ and $\vec{x'}$.

19.15. You can get $(x'_1, \ldots, x'_n)$ by typing `$\vec{{x'}}$`; now the argument is {x'} and {x'}_1 gives x'_1, etc. On the other hand, you can't get the formula $(x_1', \ldots, x_n')$ using \vec—you'd just have to type it out in full.

19.16. Forewarned by Exercise 19.2, we

```
\define\power#1{2^{#1}}
```

Then $\power x$ produces 2^x and $\power\alpha$ produces 2^α. Moreover, $\power{x+y}$ produces 2^{x+y}, as it should. Notice that this would *not* be true if we

```
\define\power#1{2^#1}
```

Even though we have braces around x+y in the input \power{x+y}, those braces simply tell TeX that the argument to \power is the whole formula x+y; so with the above incorrect \define, TeX would replace $\power{x+y}$ by 2^x+y.

19.17. Since the large \frac's have the same denominator, you might

```
$$
\redefine\+{\(\dfrac{1+\sqrt5}2\)}
\redefine\-{\(\dfrac{1-\sqrt5}2\)}
\define\fracc#1{\frac{#1}{\sqrt5}}
\align
a_n &=a_{n-1}+a_{n-2}\\
    &=\fracc{\+^{n-2} - \-^{n-2} + \+^{n-1} - \-^{n-1}} \\
    &=\fracc{\+^{n-2}\(1+\dfrac{1+\sqrt5}2\)
        - \-^{n-2}\(1+\dfrac{1-\sqrt5}2\)} \\
    &=\fracc{\+^{n-2}\+^2 - \- ^{n-2}\-^2} \\
    &=\fracc{\+^n - \-^n} .\endalign
$$
```

19.18. You can type `$\pd f{x_1}$`, `$\pd g{x_2}$`, etc., but if you

```
\define\pd#1#2{\dfrac{\partial#1}{\partial x_{#2}}}
```

then you can simply type `$$\pd f1$$`, `$$\pd g2$$`, etc. Notice (compare Exercise 19.16) that we need braces around that #2, for formulas like $\dfrac{\partial f}{\partial x_{n+1}}$.

19.19. If you `\define\sqrts` this way, then input like `$\sqrts ab$` will work OK, but if you wanted $\sqrt{a+b} + \sqrt{c+d}$ you couldn't type

> `$\sqrts{a+b}{c+d}$`

The braces would tell TEX that argument #1 is `a+b` and argument #2 is `c+d`, but TEX would then translate `$\sqrts{a+b}{c+d}$` into

> `$\sqrt a+b+\sqrt c+d$`

which gives the formula $\sqrt{a} + b + \sqrt{c} + d$. The proper definition is

> `\define\sqrts#1#2{\sqrt{#1}+\sqrt{#2}}`

As a general rule, within the definition itself your arguments #1, #2, ..., should be surrounded by braces to avoid such problems, unless you have a specific reason for not using them.

Actually, even if you define `\sqrts` this way, you won't get just what you want because `$\sqrts ab$` will give $\sqrt{a} + \sqrt{b}$ instead of $\sqrt{a} + \sqrt{b}$. See **struts** in Chapter 20.

19.20.

> `\define\vec#1#2((#1_1,\dots,#1_{#2}))`

19.21. Unless your text editor is quite nifty, there won't be any easy way to have it replace all occurrences of `R_i{}^{jk}{}_l` by `R^i{}_{jk}{}^l` and also all occurrences of `R_\alpha{}^{jk}{}_\beta` by `R^\alpha{}_{jk}^\beta`, etc., etc., etc. Fortunately, you've made the definition

> `\define\R#1#2#3#4{R^{#1}{}_{#2#3}{}^{#4}}`

and used `\R` throughout. So all you have to do is change this definition to

> `\define\R#1#2#3#4{R_{#1}{}^{#2#3}{}_{#4}}`

and TEX will take care of everything for you.

19.22. In Chapter 10 we recommended input like `x_i^2`, with the subscript before the superscript, because it's fairly easy to change this to `x_i{}^2` with a text editor. But that's still a lot of work, so if you know that lots of changes will be required, it might pay to

> `\define\sbsp#1#2{_{#1}^{#2}}`

and then type `x\sbsp i2`, `y\sbsp j3`, ... For an author who prefers $x_i{}^2$, $y_j{}^3$, ..., you just change this to

> `\define\sbsp#1#2{_{#1}{}^{#2}}`

Thus, by thinking ahead, you can use `\define`'s to make TEX act like a super text editor.

19.23. Just type

```
\define\vec#1#2{(#2_1,\dots,#2_{#1})}
```

Although #1 and #2 must appear in that order after the \define\vec, they can appear in any order within the definition itself.

19.24.

```
\define\vec#1,#2.{(#1_1,\dots,#1_{#2})}
```

with a comma after #1 and a period after #2.

19.25. You can type $\powers3,4.$ and $\powers 10.03, 1,034.$ for the first two (the space between the numbers isn't necessary in the second, but it makes things easier to read). But for the third you can't type $\powers 1,034, 10.03.$, because TeX would think that the first argument is 1 (everything up to the first comma), while the second argument is 034,10 (everything from there to the first period), and you'd get "$2^1 + 3^{034,10}03$.". What you have to type is "$\powers {1,034},{10.03}.$". Now the braces "hide" the comma and period—TeX won't assume that the first argument is {1, or that the second argument is 034},{10, since the braces in each argument must always be balanced properly.

19.26.

```
The \deRham/ cohomology ring $H^*(G)$
had, of course,  already essentially been computed
by \Cartan/.
```

Now the space after \deRham/ becomes a space in the output, and we *don't* want any space after \Cartan/. (You can also type \deRham / and \Cartan / since the spaces after the control words \deRham and \Cartan are still always ignored, but you probably wouldn't want to make things more confusing in this manner.)

19.27. This is a perfectly acceptible \define, but you are *not* defining a new control word '\AmS-TeX', since a control word can't have the non-letter - as part of its name. Instead, you are defining a new control word \AmS, and telling TeX that it must always be followed by the sequence -TeX. If you type \AmS-TeX then TeX will give you the $\mathcal{A}_{\mathcal{M}}S$-TeX logo, and you can also type \AmS -TeX, since the space after the control word \AmS is ignored, as usual. On the other hand, spaces after the -TeX aren't ignored, so this definition has the same advantage as \deRham/ and \Cartan/—you don't need to worry about using \␣ to get a space after \AmS-TeX.

19.28. The first definition is exactly equivalent to

```
\define\ab{\alpha^2+\beta^2}
```

—the spaces after the control words `\define` and `\ab` are *always* ignored.

But spaces aren't ignored after the control *symbol* `\1`, so the second definition tells TEX that `\1` must always be followed by a space. If you typed

```
\1+\gamma^2
```

you'd get the error message

```
! Use of \1 doesn't match its definition.
```

(There are actually two spaces after `\1` in its definition, but that's irrelevant, since TEX always treats a sequence of spaces as just one space.)

19.29. If some group eventually follows this input,

```
\define\a\alpha . . . { _ _ _ }
```

TEX will assume

(1) that you are trying to define the control sequence `\a`,

(2) that `\a` must always be followed by `\alpha . . .`,

(3) and that `\a\alpha . . .` is to be replaced by _ _ _.

If there is no such group, TEX will complain that it reached the end of the file without being able to complete the definition.

20.1.

```
$$
\overset\frown\to{BC}=\theta,\qquad
    \overline{AB}=\sqrt{2+2\cos\theta}\qquad
    \text{(by the law of cosines).}
$$
```

20.2.

```
$$
\align
G(z)&=e^{\ln G(z)}=\exp\left(\sum_{k\ge1}\frac{S_kz^k}k
        \right)=\prod_{k\ge1}e^{S_kz^k/k}\\
      &=\left(1+S_1z+\frac{S_1^2z^2}{2!}+\dotsb\right)\left(
          1+\frac{S_2z^2}2+\frac{S_2^2z^4}{2^2\cdot2!}+\dotsb
          \right)\dotsm\\
      &=\sum_{m\ge0}\left(\sum\Sb
          k_1,k_2,\dots,k_m\ge0\\k_1+2k_2+\dots+
          mk_m=m\endSb
        \frac{S_1^{k_1}}{1^{k_1}k_1!}
            \frac{S_2^{k_2}}{2^{k_2}k_2!}\dotsm
        \frac{S_m^{k_m}}{m^{k_m}k_m!}\right)z^m
\endalign
$$
```

(This display, from *The Art of Computer Programming*, Vol. 1, by D. Knuth, is used as an example in a *User's Guide to mathematical typesetting with the computer program* TROFF, by Brian W. Kernighan and Lorinda L. Cherry.)

20.3.

```
$$
\frac {b^{p+1}-a^{p+1}} {1+
    \underbrace{1+\dots+1}_{\text{$p$ times}} } =
   \frac {b^{p+1}-a^{p+1}} {p+1}.
$$
```

20.4. One possibility is

```
$$
\underbrace{f\biggl(\frac1n\biggr)+\dots+
    f\biggl(\frac1n\biggr)}_{\text{$n$ times}}=
f\biggl(\,\underbrace{\frac1n+\dots+
    \frac1n}_{\text{$n$ times}}\,\biggr)
=f(1)=c.
$$
```

using the specific \bigg size parentheses. (The thin spaces were added after seeing the first output.)

If you have a similar formula where you can't be sure of the height, so that you have to use a `\left`...`\right` construction, then things are trickier, because you don't want the parentheses around the entire formula

$$\underbrace{\frac{1}{n} + \cdots + \frac{1}{n}}_{n \text{ times}}$$

The best bet would be to first `\botsmash` this formula, and then follow it by a `\vphantom{\frac1n}`, so that TeX would think that it is only as high as $\dfrac{1}{n}$.

```
f\left(\,
   \botsmash{  \underbrace{\frac1n+\dots+\frac1n}_
       {\text{$n$ times}}  }\vphantom{\frac1n}\,\right)
```

20.5. You can type

```
$$
\alignat 2
m'&=m_1+2n_1&&=3m+4n,\\
n'&=m_1+\hphantom2n_1&&=2m+3n.
\endalignat
$$
```

The third column was preceded by && so that it would be aligned flush left.

20.6.

```
$$
\alignat 2
f(x)&= \sum_{n=1}^\infty a_nx^{n-1}
       &&=1+x+2x^2+3x^3+\dotsb,\\
xf(x)&=\sum_{n=1}^\infty a_nx^n
       &&=\hphantom{1+{}}x+\hphantom2x^2
          +2x^3+\dotsb,\\
x^2f(x)&=\sum_{n=1}^\infty a_nx^{n+1}
       &&=\hphantom{1+x+2}x^2+\hphantom2x^3+\dotsb.
\endalignat
$$
```

Notice that we typed `\hphantom{1+{}}`, with {} at the end, to provide the extra space after the + sign. Notice also that $\mathcal{A}_{\mathcal{M}}\mathcal{S}$-TeX automatically inserts thin spaces between the `\dots` and the commas and period, since it figures that you have included them as part of the formula only because you are typing displayed formulas.

Appendix Å: Atypical Accents

Although TEX comes equipped with most of the accents that you will need for foreign words, it doesn't handle all the special constructions that may be used in various exotic languages. The American Mathematical Society has designed many additional special accents, mainly for use by *Mathematical Reviews*. At the moment, however, these are not available on widely distributed fonts, nor have the control sequences for specifying them been finally determined. In later editions of this book, Appendix Å may be more informative.

Appendix B: Bibliographies

When you are ready to type the bibliography for a paper, you first type \Refs. This produces the heading REFERENCES, or whatever heading the particular style uses, and then sets things up for typing individual references. Actually, the particular words used in the heading are considered to be a "frill" (compare the entry **automatic formatting, disabling** in Chapter 20), and you can substitute your own heading by typing,

```
\Refs\nofrills{⟨Your heading⟩}
```

A typical individual reference would be

```
\ref \no 9 \by S. S. Chern \pages 947--955
\paper Integral formulas for hypersurfaces in Euclidean
space  and their applications to uniqueness theorems
\yr1959 \vol 8
\jour J. Math. Mech.\endref
```

which in the `amsppt` style will produce

> 9. S. S. Chern, *Integral formulas for hypersurfaces in Euclidean space and their applications to uniqueness theorems*, J. Math. Mech. **8** (1959), 947–955.

Notice that there is no need to specify the various parts of the reference in the order that they will be printed, nor do you have to worry about the proper fonts or punctuation, or details like parentheses enclosing the date; all this is taken care of by the style file.

Notice also that we don't need to use '\.' in 'Math.' and 'Mech.'; after \Refs all spaces will count as usual interword spaces, even those after periods. (If you do need the proper space for the end of a sentence, for example if a title consists of two sentences, you can always resort to the '@.' construction that is normally used to provide an end of period sentence even after an upper-case letter.)

Instead of \no for a number you can use \key for some other sort of "key", like \key[{\bf C1}] to get '[C1]' in front of the reference. Both \key and \no can be omitted.

If the paper is just one page long, you might use \page instead of \pages; in the `amsppt` style, that single page will get 'p. ' printed in front of it, so that a single number appearing alone won't be confusing.

There is no specific amount of information that you have to include in each \ref...\endref—the style file will do the reasonable thing with the information you give. For example, if you leave out the \vol, then it just won't get printed, but if you leave out \jour, then \vol and \yr will be ignored, even if you put them in.

Other things you can have within \ref...\endref are \toappear, which typesets '(to appear)' and \issue, which might be needed for some sort of special issue. If there is more than one reference by the same author, some formats will supply special constructions when the \by... in the first reference is typed as \manyby... and the other occurrences are simply replaced with \bysame. In the amsppt style, the succeeding references will have the author's name replaced by a horizontal line of the same length (or a line one inch long if the name is longer than that).

For book references there are \book, \publ and \publaddr. For example, in the amsppt style the input

```
\ref\no7\by H. Bass\book Algebraic $K$-theory\publ
W. A. Benjamin \publaddr New York\yr1968
\pages 15--19\endref
```

gives

    7. H. Bass, "Algebraic *K*-theory," W. A. Benjamin, New York, 1968, pp. 15–19.

Notice that in this case \pages gave 'pp. ' before the pages.

Sometimes a paper appears in a book, rather than in a journal. In this case, use \paper to name the paper, and use \inbook ⟨The Book⟩ to name the book. In the amsppt style, this prints 'in "⟨The Book⟩"'.

The special construction \moreref can be used when two references are combined in one. For example, in the amsppt style the input

```
\ref\no4 \by L. Auslander \paper On the
Euler characteristic of
compact locally affine spaces \jour Comment.
Math. Helv. \vol 35 \yr 1961
\pages 25--27 \moreref \paper II\jour Bull. Amer. Math. Soc.
\vol 67\yr 1961\pages 405--406 \endref
```

will give

    4. L. Auslander, *On the Euler characteristic of compact locally affine spaces*, Comment. Math. Helv. **35** (1961), 25–27; *II*, Bull. Amer. Math. Soc. **67** (1961), 405–406.

In addition to all these control sequences, `\paperinfo` may be used for extra material to be printed right after the title of the `\paper` (to indicate, for example, that this is a mimeographed preprint). Similarly, `\bookinfo` may be used for additional information after the `\book`. And `\finalinfo` puts in extra information at the very end. Punctuation is automatically generated after `\paperinfo` and `\bookinfo`, but explicit punctuation after `\finalinfo` needs to be supplied.

Appendix C: Comparison With 'plain' TEX

TEX normally comes equipped with numerous control sequences provided by the 'plain' style, and $\mathcal{A}_{\mathcal{M}}\mathcal{S}$-TEX builds upon these constructions. On the whole, $\mathcal{A}_{\mathcal{M}}\mathcal{S}$-TEX consists of plain, together with a lot of additional control sequences, and you can use most of the constructions from plain, if you are familiar with them, right along with $\mathcal{A}_{\mathcal{M}}\mathcal{S}$-TEX. For example, in $\mathcal{A}_{\mathcal{M}}\mathcal{S}$-TEX you can also use the \settabs and \+ commands, which are explained in *The TEXbook*, even though \settabs isn't mentioned anywhere in this manual. Similarly, you can use the \narrower and \item constructions explained in *The TEXbook* (just remember that \item functions quite differently when it is used within $\mathcal{A}_{\mathcal{M}}\mathcal{S}$-TEX's own \roster construction).

Certain features of plain *can't* be used with $\mathcal{A}_{\mathcal{M}}\mathcal{S}$-TEX, however, and, conversely, many control sequences of $\mathcal{A}_{\mathcal{M}}\mathcal{S}$-TEX extend, or even conflict with, the control sequences of the same name in plain. If you intend to use plain and $\mathcal{A}_{\mathcal{M}}\mathcal{S}$-TEX together, or to switch between them, the following information might be useful.

First of all, plain uses '\.' for the dot-over accent, but $\mathcal{A}_{\mathcal{M}}\mathcal{S}$-TEX uses '\.' for a period after an abbreviation—one that isn't the end of a sentence—and substitutes \D for the dot-over accent, to go along with plain's control sequence \d for the dot-under accent. Despite the outright conflict with plain, this use of '\.' seems too good to forego (and, besides, '\.' for the dot-*over* accent doesn't seem that logical anyway!) Since plain uses \b for the bar-under accent, it also seems natural to use \B analogously for the bar-over accent. In plain the bar-over accent is indicated by \=. In $\mathcal{A}_{\mathcal{M}}\mathcal{S}$-TEX this control sequence is *undefined*, so that it will be available when someone figures out a neat use for it. (If you already have a good use for \=, then you can \define it yourself; a \redefine won't be necessary.)

Such open conflicts with plain are rare, but there are numerous cases where $\mathcal{A}_{\mathcal{M}}\mathcal{S}$-TEX uses plain constructions in extended ways. For example, in plain you have to be careful not to have spaces on either side of the ~ tie, but any such spaces are simply ignored by $\mathcal{A}_{\mathcal{M}}\mathcal{S}$-TEX. And plain allows the control sequences \{ and \} and \, and \! to be used only in math mode, and provides \thinspace and \negthinspace instead of \, and \! for text. But $\mathcal{A}_{\mathcal{M}}\mathcal{S}$-TEX allows all six of these control sequences to be used both in math and in ordinary text.

Similarly, $\mathcal{A}_{\mathcal{M}}\mathcal{S}$-TEX provides \medspace, \negmedspace, \thickspace and \negthickspace, all of which can be used in or out of math mode, and \;

is supplied as a synonym for `\medspace`. In `plain`, the thick space `\;` can be used only in math mode. On the other hand, `plain` has the short name '`\>`' for $\mathcal{A}_{\mathcal{M}}S$-T_EX's `\medspace` (though '`\>`' can be used only in math mode), while $\mathcal{A}_{\mathcal{M}}S$-T_EX actually makes `\>` *undefined*, leaving it available for some future development, or for your personal use. Losing a short name for this medium space, which goes around binary operators, shouldn't bother you very much, since T_EX normally inserts the space on its own—explicit medium spaces are inserted very rarely (not once anywhere in the whole of *The T_EXbook*).

A minor point, which you might never notice, is that the tie accent `\t` works a little differently in $\mathcal{A}_{\mathcal{M}}S$-T_EX than in `plain`. In $\mathcal{A}_{\mathcal{M}}S$-T_EX the control sequence `\t` has two arguments, and you can even leave a space before the second, since T_EX always ignores spaces when looking for arguments of a control sequence. Thus `\t I ur\'ev` is a perfectly good way to get the name 'Iurév' in $\mathcal{A}_{\mathcal{M}}S$-T_EX; but in `plain` there mustn't be any space after the 'I'.

$\mathcal{A}_{\mathcal{M}}S$-T_EX and `plain` both insist that you use different names for accents in math mode (this helps T_EX detect missing `$` signs). But `plain` allows you to use the font change instructions `\bf`, etc., within math, while $\mathcal{A}_{\mathcal{M}}S$-T_EX is rather sternly consistent at this point, and also insists that you use different names `\bold` etc., in math mode; moreover, `\bold`, etc., are control sequences with an argument, rather than font changes. Font changes in a math formula can be used only in constructions like

```
$$  \text{\bf...}  $$
```

Now, of course, any spaces that you type within . . . will show up in the output, a feature that you *don't* get when you change fonts in the `plain` manner.

In the same vein, $\mathcal{A}_{\mathcal{M}}S$-T_EX has `\Cal`, a control sequence with an argument, to produce "calligraphic" letters, while `plain` does this with a font change construction `\cal`. In $\mathcal{A}_{\mathcal{M}}S$-T_EX, the control sequence `\cal` has become *undefined*. The same fate has befallen the "math italic" font change `\mit` from `plain`, which is used there to obtain the variant forms of the upper-case Greek letters; in $\mathcal{A}_{\mathcal{M}}S$-T_EX these simply have variant names `\varGamma`, etc. Finally, `\oldstyle`, which `plain` uses to change to old style numbers 1, 2, 3, . . . , has likewise become *undefined*, its role having been usurped by $\mathcal{A}_{\mathcal{M}}S$-T_EX's `\oldnos` construction.

We've already mentioned (see pages 70 and 119) that you have to be careful when `^` or `_` are followed by a control sequence, rather than a group of characters; braces may be necessary around these control sequences, unless the definitions of the control sequences already add an extra set of braces. In `plain` T_EX there are similar dangers with control sequences after `\sqrt`, `\underline` and `\overline`, but $\mathcal{A}_{\mathcal{M}}S$-T_EX warily steers clear of them. Consequently, constructions involving

\sqrt, \underline and \overline that work just fine with $\mathcal{A}_{\mathcal{M}}S$-TEX might provide puzzling output or error messages when used with plain TEX.

There's one other discrepancy between plain TEX and $\mathcal{A}_{\mathcal{M}}S$-TEX when it comes to superscripts. In addition to the special way that '' in math mode translates into ^{\prime\prime}, in plain TEX you can even type

f''^2

to get f''^2, instead of having to type

$f^{\prime\prime2}$ or $f''{}^2$

But $\mathcal{A}_{\mathcal{M}}S$-TEX hasn't implemented this feature, since there isn't any such neat trick for producing the output $f^{2''}$ (which also occurs, though more rarely).

There are numerous other slight differences between some of the mathematical constructions in plain and in $\mathcal{A}_{\mathcal{M}}S$-TEX. For example, $\mathcal{A}_{\mathcal{M}}S$-TEX's \ldots and \cdots automatically leave an extra thin space when they occur at the end of a formula or are followed by a right delimiter, just like the general \dots construction from $\mathcal{A}_{\mathcal{M}}S$-TEX. But such adjustments aren't automatically made in plain. Similarly, \pmod in $\mathcal{A}_{\mathcal{M}}S$-TEX actually uses different spacing in text and in displays. In addition, large operators like \sum, operator names like \max, and numerous other constructions, are actually defined quite differently in $\mathcal{A}_{\mathcal{M}}S$-TEX than in plain, so that they can do different things in different formats; but those differences shouldn't produce any conflicts.

\matrix and \cases are the two control sequences where the discrepancy between $\mathcal{A}_{\mathcal{M}}S$-TEX and plain is most pronounced. The proper "syntax" for these control sequences is completely different in the two situations. Other $\mathcal{A}_{\mathcal{M}}S$-TEX control sequences, like \align, naturally conform to the same syntax as $\mathcal{A}_{\mathcal{M}}S$-TEX's \matrix and \cases, while plain's control sequences, like \eqalign and \displaylines, conform to plain's basic syntax. But no further conflicts arise, because none of these other control sequences have the same name in plain and in $\mathcal{A}_{\mathcal{M}}S$-TEX.

Finally, there is one other discrepancy between plain and $\mathcal{A}_{\mathcal{M}}S$-TEX of a somewhat different nature. The control sequences \proclaim and \footnote are used in both plain and $\mathcal{A}_{\mathcal{M}}S$-TEX, and the appropriate syntax differs in both cases. For example, in plain the \footnote control sequence has *two* arguments, the first being the footnote mark, and the second being the footnote text, while in $\mathcal{A}_{\mathcal{M}}S$-TEX the footnote mark is chosen by the style. Actually, \footnote and \proclaim are not defined by $\mathcal{A}_{\mathcal{M}}S$-TEX itself, but by the particular style file that is used, and it is expected that all style files written for $\mathcal{A}_{\mathcal{M}}S$-TEX will use the proper syntax for them. If you use $\mathcal{A}_{\mathcal{M}}\mathcal{S}$-TeX without specifying any \documentstyle{...} at all, then you will essentially have the style that normally comes with plain. In that case, however, $\mathcal{A}_{\mathcal{M}}\mathcal{S}$-TeX will arrange for \proclaim and \footnote to be *undefined* and you will be provided instead with \plainproclaim and \plainfootnote for the versions of \proclaim and \footnote that plain normally uses, with their very different syntax.

Appendix D: Deficient Keyboards

The following control sequences may be used if your keyboard lacks certain keys, or if they are inconvenient to type:

Use	For
\lbrack	[
\lq	'
\rbrack	]
\rq	'
\sp	^
\sb	_
\tie	~
\vert	|

If you need to use a control sequence for a particular key like ', then you will also need another control sequence to stand for the combination \':

Use	For
\acuteaccent	\'
\graveaccent	\'
\hataccent	\^
\tildeaccent	\~
\underscore	_
\Vert	\\|

Notice that the shorter names \acute, ..., \tilde are already used for accents in math mode.

The control sequences

\lbrace	\{
\rbrace	\}

may be used for printed curly braces. On foreign keyboards, using the extended ASCII coding, the curly braces themselves may actually be replaced by accented letters. In such situations the < and > keys might be used for grouping instead, with special control sequences like \less and \greater supplied for these printed symbols.

Appendix E: Esoteric Symbols

The math symbols $+ \; - \; = \; < \; > \; | \; / \; (\;) \; [\;]$ and $*$ are available from the keyboard. \vert, \lbrack, \rbrack, \lbrace, \rbrace and \ast can be used instead of |, [,], \{, \} and *.

- **Lowercase Greek letters.**

α	\alpha	β	\beta	γ	\gamma	δ	\delta
ϵ	\epsilon	ε	\varepsilon	ζ	\zeta	η	\eta
θ	\theta	ϑ	\vartheta	ι	\iota	κ	\kappa
λ	\lambda	μ	\mu	ν	\nu	ξ	\xi
π	\pi	ϖ	\varpi	ρ	\rho	ϱ	\varrho
σ	\sigma	ς	\varsigma	τ	\tau	υ	\upsilon
ϕ	\phi	φ	\varphi	χ	\chi	ψ	\psi
ω	\omega						

- **Uppercase Greek letters.**

Uppercase Greek letters come in the ordinary style, in a slanted variant, and in boldface:

Γ	\Gamma	Δ	\Delta	Θ	\Theta	Λ	\Lambda
Ξ	\Xi	Π	\Pi	Σ	\Sigma	Υ	\Upsilon
Φ	\Phi	Ψ	\Psi	Ω	\Omega		

$\mathit{\Gamma}$	\varGamma	$\mathit{\Delta}$	\varDelta	$\mathit{\Theta}$	\varTheta	$\mathit{\Lambda}$	\varLambda
$\mathit{\Xi}$	\varXi	$\mathit{\Pi}$	\varPi	$\mathit{\Sigma}$	\varSigma	$\mathit{\Upsilon}$	\varUpsilon
$\mathit{\Phi}$	\varPhi	$\mathit{\Psi}$	\varPsi	$\mathit{\Omega}$	\varOmega		

$\boldsymbol{\Gamma}$	\boldGamma	$\boldsymbol{\Delta}$	\boldDelta	$\boldsymbol{\Theta}$	\boldTheta	$\boldsymbol{\Lambda}$	\boldLambda
$\boldsymbol{\Xi}$	\boldXi	$\boldsymbol{\Pi}$	\boldPi	$\boldsymbol{\Sigma}$	\boldSigma	$\boldsymbol{\Upsilon}$	\boldUpsilon
$\boldsymbol{\Phi}$	\boldPhi	$\boldsymbol{\Psi}$	\boldPsi	$\boldsymbol{\Omega}$	\boldOmega		

- **"Calligraphic" uppercase letters.**

The uppercase letters $\mathcal{A}, \ldots, \mathcal{Z}$ are obtained as \Cal A, ..., \Cal Z.

- **Binary operators.**

$\pm$	\pm	$\cap$	\cap	$\vee$	\vee, \lor
$\mp$	\mp	$\cup$	\cup	$\wedge$	\wedge, \land
$\setminus$	\setminus	$\uplus$	\uplus	$\oplus$	\oplus
$\cdot$	\cdot	$\sqcap$	\sqcap	$\ominus$	\ominus
$\times$	\times	$\sqcup$	\sqcup	$\otimes$	\otimes
$*$	\ast	$\triangleleft$	\triangleleft	$\oslash$	\oslash
$\star$	\star	$\triangleright$	\triangleright	$\odot$	\odot
$\diamond$	\diamond	$\wr$	\wr	$\dagger$	\dagger
$\circ$	\circ	$\bigcirc$	\bigcirc	$\ddagger$	\ddagger
$\bullet$	\bullet	$\bigtriangleup$	\bigtriangleup	$\amalg$	\amalg
$\div$	\div	$\bigtriangledown$	\bigtriangledown	$\&$	\and

Some mathematicians use the operator &, produced by \and, instead of $\wedge$. Notice that \dagger and \ddagger are used when † and ‡ function as binary operators.

- **Binary relations.**

$\leq$	\leq, \le	$\geq$	\geq, \ge	$\equiv$	\equiv
$\prec$	\prec	$\succ$	\succ	$\sim$	\šim
$\preceq$	\preceq	$\succeq$	\succeq	$\simeq$	\simeq
$\ll$	\ll	$\gg$	\gg	$\asymp$	\asymp
$\subset$	\subset	$\supset$	\supset	$\approx$	\approx
$\subseteq$	\subseteq	$\supseteq$	\supseteq	$\cong$	\cong
$\sqsubseteq$	\sqsubseteq	$\sqsupseteq$	\sqsupseteq	$\bowtie$	\bowtie
$\in$	\in	$\ni$	\ni, \owns	$\propto$	\propto
$\vdash$	\vdash	$\dashv$	\dashv	$\models$	\models
$\smile$	\smile	$\mid$	\mid	$\doteq$	\doteq
$\frown$	\frown	$\parallel$	\parallel	$\perp$	\perp
$\neq$	\neq, \ne	$\notin$	\notin		

\mid and \parallel are the same characters that you get with | and \|, but treated as binary relations, so that they get extra space around them.

Many of these relations can be negated by putting \not before them. For example, \not\subset gives $\not\subset$. And \ne and \neq are simply abbreviations for \not=. But the positioning isn't always ideal, and, in particular, you should always use \notin for $\notin$, rather than \not\in.

- **Miscellaneous ordinary symbols.**

ℵ	\aleph	′	\prime	∀	\forall
ℏ	\hbar	∅	\emptyset	∃	\exists
ι	\imath	∇	\nabla	¬	\neg, \lnot
ȷ	\jmath	√	\surd	♭	\flat
ℓ	\ell	⊤	\top	♮	\natural
℘	\wp	⊥	\bot	♯	\sharp
ℜ	\Re	‖	|, \Vert	♣	\clubsuit
ℑ	\Im	∠	\angle	◇	\diamondsuit
∂	\partial	△	\triangle	♡	\heartsuit
∞	\infty	\	\backslash	♠	\spadesuit
∫	\smallint	†	\dag	‡	\ddag
¶	\P	§	\S		

\imath and \jmath are for accenting: $\hat\imath$ yields $\hat\imath$. \backslash
(rather than \setminus) should be used for double cosets ($G\backslash H$), and to indicate
that p divides n ($p\backslash n$). \prime is mainly used for superscripts and subscripts.
The \angle symbol is built up from other pieces, and does not get smaller in
subscripts and superscripts (see page 262). \smallint and \surd are seldom
used. \dag, \ddag, \P and \S might be used for special effects; they change size
correctly in subscripts and superscripts.

- **Arrows.**

←	\leftarrow, \gets	⟵	\longleftarrow
⇐	\Leftarrow	⟸	\Longleftarrow
→	\rightarrow, \to	⟶	\longrightarrow
⇒	\Rightarrow	⟹	\Longrightarrow
↔	\leftrightarrow	⟷	\longleftrightarrow
⇔	\Leftrightarrow	⟺	\Longleftrightarrow
↑	\uparrow	⇑	\Uparrow
↓	\downarrow	⇓	\Downarrow
↕	\updownarrow	⇕	\Updownarrow
↗	\nearrow	↘	\searrow
↙	\swarrow	↖	\nwarrow
↦	\mapsto	⟼	\longmapsto
↩	\hookleftarrow	↪	\hookrightarrow
↼	\leftharpoonup	⇁	\leftharpoondown
⇀	\rightharpoonup	⇁	\rightharpoondown
⇌	\rightleftharpoons		

The vertical arrows are "delimiters", like the others listed below, and change size when used after \left and \right. The control sequence \iff produces an arrow just like \Longleftrightarrow, except that there is more space around it. $\mathcal{A}_{\mathcal{M}}\mathcal{S}$-TEX also provides \implies and \impliedby, which are just like \Longrightarrow and \Longleftarrow, respectively, but again with more space around them.

- **Large operators like $\sum$.**

All large operators come in two sizes, with the larger used for \dsize.

$\sum \sum$ \sum $\bigcap \bigcap$ \bigcap $\odot \bigodot$ \bigodot

$\prod \prod$ \prod $\bigcup \bigcup$ \bigcup $\otimes \bigotimes$ \bigotimes

$\coprod \coprod$ \coprod $\bigsqcup \bigsqcup$ \bigsqcup $\oplus \bigoplus$ \bigoplus

$\bigvee \bigvee$ \bigvee $\biguplus \biguplus$ \biguplus $\bigwedge \bigwedge$ \bigwedge

- **Large operators like $\int$.**

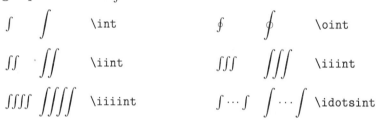

$\int \quad \int$ \int $\oint \quad \oint$ \oint

$\iint \quad \iint$ \iint $\iiint \quad \iiint$ \iiint

$\iiiint \quad \iiiint$ \iiiint $\int\cdots\int \quad \int\cdots\int$ \idotsint

- **Delimiters.**

The following symbols are recognized as "delimiters".

((	[[, \lbrack	{ \{, \lbrace
))	]], \rbrack	} \}, \rbrace
⌊ \lfloor	⌈ \lceil	⟨ \langle
⌋ \rfloor	⌉ \rceil	⟩ \rangle
	|, \vert	‖ |, \Vert	/ /
\ \backslash		

All the up and down arrows can also be used as delimiters. Moreover, < and > can be used instead of \langle and \rangle after \left and \right. And, of course, there is also '.' for an "empty" delimiter after \left and \right.

Appendix F: Future Fonts

Over the years mathematicians have inveigled printers into designing a tremendous assortment of special symbols, far more than those given in Appendix E. The American Mathematical Society is creating new fonts, to go along with the standard Computer Modern fonts, where these strange symbols can reside.

At present, two new fonts have been introduced, an `msxm` series (containing 5, 7 and 10 point sizes `msxm5`, `msxm7` and `msxm10`) and an `msym` series (containing `msym5`, `msym7` and `msym10`). $\mathcal{A}_{\mathcal{M}}\mathcal{S}$-TₑX accesses these fonts by a series of 6 instructions in the file `amstex.tex` beginning

```
\font\tenmsx=msxm10
...
```

and instructs TₑX how to use them by a series of 6 instructions beginning

```
\textfont\msxfam=\tenmsx
...
```

In some copies of `amstex.tex` these lines are "commented out" by % signs before them, because not all installations will have these new fonts. In addition, three other lines may be commented out,

```
%\mathchardef\angle="0\msx@5C
%\mathchardef\rightleftharpoons="3\msx@0A
%\mathchardef\hbar="0\msy@7E
```

If you remove any of these % signs without having the necessary fonts, you will get error messages when you try to use $\mathcal{A}_{\mathcal{M}}\mathcal{S}$-TₑX.

But if you do have the necessary fonts, then you can use a host of new symbols that these fonts contain, simply by deleting these 15 different % signs. The new symbols that become available are listed below, together with the control sequences that you can use to name them. (If you try to use these control sequences without having the fonts, or without removing the % signs, you will get a strange error message about missing fonts.)

• Non-math symbols.

First of all, we have four cute little symbols that are normally used outside of math mode:

✓	\checkmark	®	\circledR
✠	\maltese	¥	\yen

These symbols, like ¶, §, † and ‡, can also be used in math mode, and will change sizes correctly in subscripts and superscripts.

All the remaining symbols must be used only in math mode.

- **Lowercase Greek letters.**

  ϝ \digamma   ϰ \varkappa

- **Uppercase blackboard bold letters.**

  The uppercase letters $\mathbb{A}, \ldots, \mathbb{Z}$ are obtained as \Bbb A, ..., \Bbb Z.

- **Hebrew letters.**

  ℶ \beth   ℷ \gimel   ℸ \daleth

- **Binary operators.**

∔	\dotplus	⋒	\Cap, \doublecap	⊚	\circledcirc
╲	\smallsetminus	⋓	\Cup, \doublecup	⊛	\circledast
⋉	\ltimes	⋏	\curlywedge	⊝	\circleddash
⋊	\rtimes	⋎	\curlyvee	⊞	\boxplus
⋋	\leftthreetimes	⊼	\barwedge	⊟	\boxminus
⋌	\rightthreetimes	⊻	\veebar	⊠	\boxtimes
⋇	\divideontimes	⩞	\doublebarwedge	⊡	\boxdot
⊺	\intercal	⋅	\centerdot		

- **Binary relations.**

≦	\leqq	≧	\geqq	≑	\doteqdot, \Doteq
⩽	\leqslant	⩾	\geqslant	≗	\circeq
⪇	\eqslantless	⪈	\eqslantgtr	≖	\eqcirc
≲	\lesssim	≳	\gtrsim	≜	\triangleq
⪅	\lessapprox	⪆	\gtrapprox	≓	\risingdotseq
⋖	\lessdot	⋗	\gtrdot	≒	\fallingdotseq
⋘	\lll, \llless	⋙	\ggg, \gggtr	∽	\backsim
≶	\lessgtr	≷	\gtrless	⋍	\backsimeq
⪋	\lesseqgtr	⪌	\gtreqless	∼	\thicksim
⪟	\lesseqqgtr	⪞	\gtreqqless	≈	\thickapprox

⊆ \subseteqq	⊇ \supseteqq	≊ \approxeq
⋐ \Subset	⋑ \Supset	≏ \bumpeq
⊏ \sqsubset	⊐ \sqsupset	≎ \Bumpeq
≼ \preccurlyeq	≽ \succcurlyeq	⟈ \between
⋞ \curlyeqprec	⋟ \curlyeqsucc	⋔ \pitchfork
≾ \precsim	≿ \succsim	∝ \varpropto
⪷ \precapprox	⪸ \succapprox	϶ \backepsilon
◁ \vartriangleleft	▷ \vartriangleright	◀ \blacktriangleleft
⊴ \trianglelefteq	⊵ \trianglerighteq	▶ \blacktriangleright
⊨ \vDash	⊩ \Vdash	⊪ \Vvdash
⌣ \smallsmile	∣ \shortmid	∴ \therefore
⌢ \smallfrown	∥ \shortparallel	∵ \because

• Negated relations.

≮ \nless	≯ \ngtr	≁ \nsim
≰ \nleq	≱ \ngeq	≉ \napprox
\nleqslant	\ngeqslant	\nshortmid
\nleqq	\ngeqq	\nshortparallel
⪇ \lneq	⪈ \gneq	∤ \nmid
≨ \lneqq	≩ \gneqq	∦ \nparallel
\lvertneqq	\gvertneqq	⊬ \nvdash
⋦ \lnsim	⋧ \gnsim	⊭ \nvDash
⪉ \lnapprox	⪊ \gnapprox	⊮ \nVdash
⊀ \nprec	⊁ \nsucc	⊯ \nVDash
⋠ \npreceq	⋡ \nsucceq	⋪ \ntriangleleft
⪵ \precneqq	⪶ \succneqq	⋫ \ntriangleright
⋨ \precnsim	⋩ \succnsim	⋬ \ntrianglelefteq
⪹ \precnapprox	⪺ \succnapprox	⋭ \ntrianglerighteq

(continued)

- **Negated relations** (*continued*).

⊄	\nsubseteq	⊅	\nsupseteq
⊊	\nsubseteqq	⊋	\nsupseteqq
⊊	\subsetneq	⊋	\supsetneq
⊊	\varsubsetneq	⊋	\varsupsetneq
⊊	\subsetneqq	⊋	\supsetneqq
⊊	\varsubsetneqq	⊋	\varsupsetneqq

- **Miscellaneous symbols.**

ℏ	\hbar	∖	\backprime	★	\bigstar
ℏ	\hslash	□	\square	■	\blacksquare
∅	\varnothing	△	\vartriangle	▲	\blacktriangle
Ⓢ	\circledS	▽	\triangledown	▼	\blacktriangledown
∄	\nexists	◊	\lozenge	◆	\blacklozenge
∁	\complement	∠	\angle	⦞	\measuredangle
℧	\mho	ð	\eth	⊲	\sphericalangle

The $\angle$ and $\hbar$ symbols from these new fonts replace the symbols shown on page 257 (provided that you have the lines

```
\mathchardef\angle="0\msx@5C
\mathchardef\hbar="0\msy@7E
```

in your file). The new \angle symbol will change sizes correctly in subscripts and superscripts.

- **Arrows.**

⇇	\leftleftarrows	⇉	\rightrightarrows
⇆	\leftrightarrows	⇄	\rightleftarrows
⇚	\Lleftarrow	⇛	\Rrightarrow
↞	\twoheadleftarrow	↠	\twoheadrightarrow
↢	\leftarrowtail	↣	\rightarrowtail
↫	\looparrowleft	↬	\looparrowright
⇋	\leftrightharpoons	⇌	\rightleftharpoons
↶	\curvearrowleft	↷	\curvearrowright

↻ \circlearrowleft   ↻ \circlearrowright
↰ \Lsh   ↱ \Rsh
↑↑ \upuparrows   ↓↓ \downdownarrows
↿ \upharpoonleft   ↾ \upharpoonright, \restriction
⇃ \downharpoonleft   ⇂ \downharpoonright
⊸ \multimap   ⇝ \rightsquigarrow
↭ \leftrightsquigarrow

The ⇌ symbol from these new fonts replaces the symbol shown on page 257 (provided that you have the line

    \mathchardef\rightleftharpoons="3\msx@0A

in your file). This new \rightleftharpoons works correctly in subscripts and superscripts (though you're not likely to need it in such a position); the old one doesn't.

• **Negated arrows.**

↚ \nleftarrow   ↛ \nrightarrow   ↮ \nleftrightarrow
⇍ \nLeftarrow   ⇏ \nRightarrow   ⇎ \nLeftrightarrow

• **Delimiters.**

⌜ \ulcorner   ⌝ \urcorner
⌞ \llcorner   ⌟ \lrcorner

As we mentioned in Chapter 20, a Fraktur (German) font is in the works. Other possibilities are a "script font", with both upper and lower case script letters, and fonts with bold italic and bold lower case Greek letters.

The AMS has also produced a cyrillic font, for use by *Mathematical Reviews*, but these symbols are not meant for use in math formulas.

Appendix G: {TEX Users}

The TEX Users Group (TUG) was formed for the interchange of information about problems and solutions related to TEX. Since 1980 this organization has been publishing a newsletter, *TUGboat*, which appears three times a year. A network of TUG "site coordinators" helps bring up TEX on different computers; short courses in the use of TEX are offered at various times; and general TUG meetings are held at least once a year.

Information about membership in TUG and about subscriptions to *TUGboat* is available from

TEX Users Group
P. O. Box 9506
Providence, RI 02940 USA.

Appendix H: Help!

This manual points out all sorts of pitfalls and errors that you should avoid, but despite all the information given here, an error message might leave you mystified, or you might be stymied in your efforts to use $\mathcal{A}_{\mathcal{M}}\mathcal{S}$-TEX to produce some special effect. After floundering ineffectually for protracted periods of time, you might want to look back at Appendix G. Perhaps someone in TUG has encountered a similar problem, or can explain your mistake.

Of course, some mysteries might be due to a bug in $\mathcal{A}_{\mathcal{M}}\mathcal{S}$-TEX, rather than a misunderstanding on your part. If you're *sure* that you've found a bug in $\mathcal{A}_{\mathcal{M}}\mathcal{S}$-TEX, you might want to contact someone at the American Mathematical Society.

But whatever you do, gentle reader, please do not try to contact the author of this manual. Eir lack of erudition is amply illuminated by the style so blatantly displayed throughout this work, and attempts at meaningful dialogue with Em are fruitless, as E is merely a pseudonym for a group of intemperate expatriate mathematicians working on the lunatic fringe of typesetting technology.

Appendix I: Index

Some of the control words listed here bear the annotation [do not `\redefine`], because they are used internally by $\mathcal{A}_{\mathcal{M}}\mathcal{S}$-TₑX, and giving them new meanings could cause havoc. In addition, most control *symbols* should not be redefined either. You are free to play with \. and \<, \>, \+ and \= as well as \[, \], \(, \), \? and \0, ..., \9—that should be enough!

BCDEFGHIJ-89876